Jewish Stories
One Generation
Tells Another

Jewish Stories One Generation Tells Another

Retold by
Peninnah Schram

Jason Aronson Inc.
Northvale, New Jersey
London

The author gratefully acknowledges permission to reprint "The Storyteller's Prayer," by Elie Wiesel, originally a lecture presented at Washington University, St. Louis, Missouri, February 18, 1970. Reprinted from AGAINST SILENCE: THE VOICE AND VISION OF ELIE WIESEL, selected and edited by Irving Abrahamson. New York: Holocaust Library. Copyright © 1985 by Irving Abrahamson, with permission of Elie Wiesel.

Library of Congress Cataloging-in-Publication Data
Schram, Peninnah.
  Jewish stories one generation tells another.
  Bibliography: p. 491
  Includes index.
  1. Legends, Jewish.   2. Jewish folk literature.   I. Title.
BM530.S45 1989   296.1'9   88-34271
ISBN 0-87668-967-5

Manufactured in the United States of America. Jason Aronson Inc. offers books and cassettes. For information and catalog write to Jason Aronson Inc., 230 Livingston Street, Northvale, New Jersey 07647.

To my parents,
Cantor Samuel and Dora Manchester,
whose voices resonate in my *neshome*.
They taught me what stories to tell.

To my children,
Rebecca and Michael—
may they continue the oral tradition.

Contents

Foreword

THE STORYTELLER'S PRAYER

Rebbe Avraham Yehoshua Heschel of Apt was a great eighteenth-century Hasidic master. He was the great-grandfather of the philosopher Abraham Joshua Heschel. He was known for his saintliness as well as for his storytelling. The Apter Rebbe was the rebbe of rebbes. He settled their disputes. He presided over their gatherings. He was the old man of Hasidism then. It was he who consecrated the Rizhiner, he who had to decide whether the Pshiskher system was in harmony with the Baal Shem Tov's doctrine or not. Like most Hasidic masters he was generous, humble, and a believer in simplicity.

He preferred tales to complex discussions. But unlike other masters, he played the center role in all his stories. "Each man," he said, "must view himself as still standing at Sinai, ready to receive the Torah. Why? Because for God there is no past, present, future. He is still giving the Torah. So it is up to man, each man, to receive it." The Apter Rebbe saw himself standing there at Sinai every day of his life. He also saw himself in the Temple in Jerusalem. He claimed to have been a high priest. On *Yom Kippur* he used to say not "*Ve kah hayyah omer*," quoting the high priest in the third person, but "*Ve kah hayyiti omer*," recalling that he himself used to say the sentences in the first person.

All this is contained in his prayer, a prayer which fits storytellers of all times, of all places, whether Jewish or not:

"Master of the Universe, I do not understand what is happening to me. So many men and women, young and old, have to get up early in the morning, run to work or to school, and work hard and earn little for their sustenance, while I, Avraham Yehoshua Heschel of Apt, stay at home, having nowhere to go, nothing to do. Men and women come and give me money. So I ask You, God, what did I do wrong? No doubt people think I am able to help them in their distress. If so, please, God, let me help them. Let them say that I am one of the Just, a miracle-maker, one who can revoke misfortune. Why should You mind? Are You jealous of the honors given to Yehoshua Heschel? Do You really think it is he they are honoring? Who is he anyway? What is he? A broken vessel. But since they come to me, since they consider me their messenger to You, please, God, do not shame them. Let me be the stick on which they can lean, a stick and not a useless branch.

"Now, look here, since I, Yehoshua Heschel of Apt, am provided for, and people call me Rebbe, even *Tzaddik*, I ask You: What am I to do with my long days and nights? Do You want me to sit at the table and study Torah and Talmud? You have better scholars than I could ever be. The Koznitzer Maggid, for instance, or the Holy Seer of Lublin—each of their *hiddushim*, each of their discoveries, provokes enthusiasm among the angels. Do You want me to spend life in prayer? You have cantors so fervent that I could never even follow their footsteps. For instance, when Levi Yitzhak of Berditchev opens the prayer book and begins to pray, one hears the angels in heaven shout, 'Shhhhhhh—silence! Levi Yitzhak is saying his prayers.' But I, who am poor and miserable, who remain always on the same spot, what can I do to spread Your glory? And what can I do to reward all those men and women who give me so much of themselves? I am neither laborer nor merchant. Do You want me to walk around as an idle shadow among the living?

"Well, You know I have discovered the knack of telling stories. So I tell stories. And believe me, Master of the Universe, I swear to You, I want You to believe me, I invent nothing. Whatever I tell is true. Whatever I tell did really occur to me—yes, to me. All the incidents and episodes in my stories—I remember perfectly when and where they took place. I take them from my own memory, my own soul. But the people—You know them. What do they say? They say that the Apter Rebbe is exaggerating again. Could I exaggerate even if I wanted to? What wonders could I invent in a world which is full of wonders?

"Listen. I tell them, for instance, that I have already lived here in previous centuries. Well, that is the absolute truth. Have I not heard the thunder and seen the lightning at Sinai? Have I not joined my voice to those saying, '*Naaseh v'nishma*,' shouting their fidelity to You and Your Covenant and Your Torah? Then why should it be surprising that I also remember my years in Jerusalem? Indeed, I was high priest. I can still see the Jew who brought his cow as an offering. The cow escaped, and the Jew ran after her. It was so funny a sight that I burst out laughing. And even now, in retelling it, I cannot help but laugh. But the people who listen also laugh. I laugh with joy because I remember the Temple and its splendor. They laugh because I amuse them. I entertain them. They say, 'Here he goes again, the Apter Rebbe and his stories, his miracles, his fantasies.'

"The fools. Some think I make miracles, others think that I simply exaggerate. But I say to them,'You are the greatest miracle of all, you who are alive, you who listen to each of my words. Everything I say is true.' My only prayer, God, is that You give me good listeners—listeners like Reb Barukh of Medzebozh, the great-grandchild of the Baal Shem Tov."

I would like to take the Apter Rebbe's prayer and make it mine, because it contains all that a storyteller in the twentieth century, especially in the second half of the twentieth century, feels—the anguish, the bewilderment in facing the word, the tale itself.

Once I asked my own master, "I understand why the *mitzvot*, the laws, were so scrupulously transmitted from generation to generation, but why the *aggadot*? Why the legends?" And my master answered, "They are important because they stress the importance of the listener."

If I do a mitzvah, if I obey a commandment, it is my link to God. But, when I speak of legends, the listener must be here. God himself needs man to make His word heard. The tale affects the teller, and therefore certain tales were transmitted only in silence among the initiated. Tales have their own strange destiny because people sometimes read into them non-existent meanings.

If a teller tells you tales, listen to them. Laws can be forgotten. We know from the Talmud that Moses forgot some. His disciple Joshua forgot three hundred. Yet no mention is made in the Midrash or in the Talmud of forgotten legends. The Midrash says, "Do you want to know Him who created the entire universe by the power of His word? Learn legends." Like the Law they are God's link to man. They are the tools received by man from God to challenge God.

So, stressing the importance of the listener is part of the tale, what Buber called the I-and-Thou. When one tells a tale, one relives it. One does not talk to the listener. One talks with the listener. To listen is as important as to talk, sometimes more so. Some Hasidim used to boast that they went to the Pshiskher, the master of the Kotzker, "to listen to the rebbe's silence."

It is no accident that "*Shema Yisrael*—Listen, O Israel" has become imperative in Judaism. God needs an audience. Thus the quality of any exchange depends upon the listener. The storyteller is no more than a messenger whose role is to create links between word and being, man and himself, shadow and the memory of that shadow.

I would like to make the Apter Rebbe's prayer mine for another reason. Like him I believe man to be the sum total of his own experiences and those of his predecessors. We were all at Sinai, and in Egypt before that. We all saw the Temple in Jerusalem, both in its splendor and in its flames. We were all in Spain at the time of the Inquisition. We were all in Treblinka. "No heart is as good as a broken heart," said Rebbe Nahman of Bratzlav. No conscience is as genuine as the collective conscience. And the same applies to memory.

If I do not accept my heritage in its totality, with its burdens and calls for passion and commitment, I accept none of it. If in our prayers we invoke the God of Abraham *and* the God of Isaac *and* the God of Jacob, it is first to teach us the poetry inherent in repetition, but it is mainly to make us realize that we are the descendants of all three. Abraham's fear and trembling, Isaac's melancholy, and Jacob's taste for expatriation—we accept all or none. Each of us bears in his soul the remorse of Cain and the Psalms of David, the visions of Jeremiah, and the messianic hopes of the Ari Hakadosh and of the Baal Shem Tov.

All the characters of our history are linked to each other. And we are the link. The agony of Job, the absurd fate of Adam, the silent anguish of Abraham—to evoke them is to show their topicality as well as their timelessness. Tales linked specifically to one era—the destruction of the Temple, the march in the desert, the receiving of Torah at Sinai—are reformulated and rediscovered in every generation. Every period contains all periods. Every man was seen and comprehended by Adam. Rabbi Akiba and Moses were responsible for one another: Moses for Akiba's future; Akiba for Moses' past. Each man is thus responsible for all men, for each man resembles Adam in his solitude and Job in his suffering and Abraham in his defiance. Such is the unfathomable depth of Judaism.

The Apter Rebbe is right. Adam still wonders why he was expelled from Paradise. Job is still being punished without knowing why. And somewhere father and son descend Mount Moriah in total bewilderment, irrevocably changed by the unconsummated sacrifice.

As a storyteller I try to show how all these characters are our contemporaries. Their problems are our problems. Their anxiety contains ours. Their interrogation is to us a source of breathless dreaming. Adam, Job, and Abraham are my favorite characters. What do they have in common? They were not Jewish, not in the strict sense of the word. Yet their experience and their struggle are part of our conscience. Though we speak of Jews, we illustrate the human condi-

tion through them. We have never made a distinction between Jew and man. We say, and we repeat, that a Jew can
be a man only through his Jewishness. Our legends aim to
abolish the distance between one and the other. To be a Jew
is to put the accent on being, on the necessity of the Jew to
have faith in his fate. Adam, Job, and Abraham—no tale
could be more Jewish than theirs. Yet no mention is made
of their Jewishness. All Jewish legends and all Jewish figures try to help men live and survive in a stifling world
where good and evil wear the same mask, where fire devours
night and its shadows. Providing the food of friendship in a
universe without warmth—that is the essence of these
tales.

Our tales try to show that the road to God must go
through man, just as God's link to His Creation and himself
is assured by men. Our tales try to show that man is allowed
to say no to anything inhuman, to any system, even God's,
when he believes God to be inhuman. Man may rebel in
silence and in words provided his rebellion is for man, on
his behalf, and does not carry him outside of his community
and his people. One becomes a renegade not by saying no,
not by rebelling, but by turning away, by becoming *akher*,
another. A Jew is someone who does not turn away.

All legends in Judaism have a common desire: to asso-
ciate man with Creation and make him aware of the links
with what surrounds him and preceded him. Destroy these
links, destroy this consciousness, and man himself is destroyed, and so is his universe. For we are responsible for a
world we have not created. We are responsible for God's
exile, the *galut ha-Shekhinah*, for we are responsible for
our beginning, which is our link to the mystery of Creation.
In other words, legends of our times must be legends for all
times and for all men.

Of course, God also plays an important role in my tales,
because God plays an important role in Israel. The word *El*
is in Israel: God is there. So my problems with God go on. I
have written many things about my problems. But I have
written one prayer—my prayer—for today:

I no longer want You to grant me happiness or immortality.

All I want from You is to listen and make me aware that You are listening.

I no longer ask You to answer my questions but to receive them and become part of them.

I no longer plead for peace and wisdom.

All I ask is to remain open to gratitude, surprises, and friendship.

Love? You are not the one to give it to me.

My enemies? I no longer want You to punish them, not even to enlighten them.

All I ask is not to lend them Your mask and Your powers.

If You must give them one or the other, give them Your powers, not Your face.

My requests are not exaggerated.

They are humble.

I ask from You what I would ask from a stranger I might have met at twilight on hostile territory.

I ask You, God of Abraham and Isaac and Jacob, enable me to repeat these very words without betraying the child who handed them down to me.

God of Abraham and Isaac and Jacob, enable me to forgive You and make him forgive me.

I no longer plead for this child's life, not even for his faith.

I only beg You to listen to him and to allow me to listen together with You.

Jewish survival and tales of Jewish survival may seem absurd. Why survive in a world that denies us the right to survive? But—and this is what we must always remember—a tale of absurdity ultimately means a tale against absurdity.

Elie Wiesel

Preface and Acknowledgments

I love stories. From the time I first heard them, the love of story and storytelling took hold. I was taught through teaching tales, Bible stories, and proverbs. When I began to work on this book, I had several options as to the kind of book it would be: an anthology of Jewish stories, comprehensive and representative of different periods of Jewish literature and genres; a book of stories representing various motifs or themes; or a book of stories I love and feel most connected to and could tell in my own way. I chose the last option.

I have chosen stories that I love. In looking over the ones I decided to use, I realized that many of them dealt with riddles, questions, *hokhme*, and love. Through these tales we meet various characters and understand certain customs. I have written these stories not as a folklorist who preserves the original texts as they were collected and transcribed or as they were found in the ancient sources, not as a scholar who might want to analyze and document every change found throughout the ages, but rather as a storyteller who continues in the folklore process to make changes that make sense to me and to bring my personal imagination, life experiences, religious values, and traditions to the telling of each tale.

While I have chosen narratives that may seem to some to be old-fashioned or somewhat removed from the concerns of the present day, these texts are a treasure house of intuitive wisdom about human nature and the world. There is truth in these stories that affects our daily lives. I have refrained from giving a literary analysis of the stories in the introductions because I believe the readers must discover the value of each story for themselves. Let me tell you a story I adapted from a tale told by the Hasidic rabbi, Hayyim of Zanz: It will, perhaps, explain my point better.

Once a student met his rebbe in the park.
"*Sholom aleikhem*, rebbe," said the student.
"*Aleikhem sholom*," answered the rebbe.
"I'm glad I met you just now, for I have many questions to ask you," continued the student. "To begin with, tell me what this parable means?" And the student showed the rabbi the first story in a large book. Sitting down on a park bench, the rebbe smiled as he took the book from the student. He noted that the book was new and had barely been opened, and he understood that his explanations would only begin with that first story. Discussion and clarification might continue into the second and third stories, and on and on without the young man having first read and studied the stories himself. The rabbi said, "Let me tell you a parable."

A long time ago, a young man went for a walk in the woods. He walked down a clear path, listened to the birds, marveled at the leaves as the sunlight filtered down through them. When the light began to fade, the young man decided to return home. However, as he turned down one path and then another, and yet another, he realized he had become lost in the maze of the forest.

For three days he wandered alone, hungry and scared. On the third day he saw, on another path, a bearded man. This man looked like a woodsman. He was wearing clothes made of leather, and he was carrying a long carved branch as a walking stick.

"At last!" cried the young man. "Oh, you look like a good guide to help me find my way out of the woods. I'm lost and have been in these woods for three days."

"Only three days," laughed the man of the woods. "I have been lost in these woods for three years."

"What are you saying?" asked the young man in desperation. "Three years? You have been lost all that time? Then there is no possible hope for me." And the young man began to weep.

"No, no, my young friend, don't despair," replied the man of the woods. "It is true that I cannot show you the paths that lead out of the woods, but I can point out to you the paths that do not."

And the rabbi and his student began to read the stories aloud.

Stories connect to our lives. They "talk" to us on different levels. Sometimes we have to hear a story many times in order to discover its meaning. We have to live with the story, think about it, dream about it. There is much wisdom in the requirement that the Jews read and listen each year to the same stories of the Bible, the Hanukka story, the Megilla, the Haggada. The same words, the same trope, yet the stories change as we grow wiser with each hearing and as we ourselves change.

I resisted the temptation to explain the stories and discuss their meanings. Instead, I have chosen to note the sources of each tale, the universal tale types and motifs for most of the stories, how I found the tale (or, in some cases, how it found me), the special fascination each story has for me, and occasionally how a non-Jewish story became transformed into a Jewish tale that Jews have continued to keep in their storytelling repertoire. In a way, the introduction to each story is the story of the story. It puts the story in a context, as storytellers are apt to do. By reading the introduction, you the reader will hopefully be ready to tell the story in your own way with your own interpretation.

If I have chosen well, the search for what each story means to you will continue throughout your life.

One often thinks of writing as a solitary experience. In my case, however, the actual writing of the stories from the oral tradition and from our written sources was not solitary at all: I sat in the same circle of women plucking goose feathers while listening to their stories; I davened in the *shul* with all the Jews throughout the ages; I listened and learned from the heroes Elijah and Solomon and the clever heroines; I was a child again—and I touched the child in me again and again. I was never alone.

While the telling of stories requires at least two people—a teller and a listener—the making of a book involves many more people. Numerous friends shared my efforts, enabling me to write down these stories. This was, in a real sense, a cooperative venture.

First of all, there was the person who encouraged me to retell my stories for the printed page, Arthur Kurzweil, my editor and friend. Arthur planted the idea of writing down these Jewish stories years ago. Because of his gentle persuasion and enthusiasm, I must credit this beautiful *mensh* as the one responsible for this book. I thank him from my heart!

I want to express my appreciation to Muriel Jorgensen for her skillful guidance and design of this book, and thanks also to Lori Bergman, production editor, and Sol Sverdlin, copy editor, for their excellent "ear," "eye," and use of the blue pencil.

My thanks to Jacqueline Kahane, a talented artist and friend, who has captured the essence of these stories through her line drawings.

I offer my sincerest thanks to Dr. Pack Carnes of the University of California for his valuable contribution of identifying the universal motifs and tale types for the stories in this book.

My thanks also to calligrapher Jay Greenspan for his exquisite writing of the talmudic story in Aramaic (see "The Wedding Blessings") and to music copyist David Sherman for his musical renderings.

I am honored and grateful that Elie Wiesel has added his words as a Foreword for my book.

A special thank you goes to Sylvia Wallach, whose insightful comments and typing of my handwritten manuscript helped me enormously throughout the years of writing.

My gratitude to Professor Dov Noy of Hebrew University as a source of inspiration, especially for his extraordinary work as founder of the Israel Folktale Archives, which has saved and preserved so many of our folk stories.

I owe a great debt to Professor Howard Schwartz, whose collections of folktales have contributed to the renaissance of storytelling. I am grateful for his valued and generous suggestions.

A special thanks to Dr. Ruth Rubin, ethnomusicologist specializing in Eastern European Yiddish folksongs, for helping me choose the *nigunim* and one of the lullabies included in my stories.

My heartfelt thanks to my husband, Jerry Thaler, for giving me the needed encouragement to write this book, for reading and listening to the stories, for questioning—and smiling.

Another special thanks goes to my daughter, Rebecca Schram, for her beautiful work with some of the Hebrew translations, which helped me greatly, and to Evelyn Abel for her expert translations of many stories from Hebrew and Yiddish.

For their cooperation whenever I had a question or needed a translation, an interpretation, or a source, I would like to thank head librarian Edith Lubetski and her staff at the Hedi Steinberg Library at Stern College, Yeshiva University; Philip E. Miller, librarian of Hebrew Union College; Dina Abramowicz, librarian at YIVO; Eleanor Gordon Mlotek, music archivist at YIVO; Roslyn Bresnick-Perry; Peretz Kaminsky; Dr. Meir Havazelet; Rabbi Stanley M. Urbas; Shelly Frier; Dr. Baruch H. S. Mazor, and many others.

For sharing stories with me, I am especially grateful to Rabbi Alter Metzger, Rachayl and Hillel Davis, Sheila Lassman, Maurice Stone; and to the collectors and tellers of the tales included in this book.

Thanks to all the people who through the years were open to my stories and generous with their encouraging words for me to continue telling stories.

This brings up a question that the editor and I had to resolve. How do you transfer an oral performance to the printed page? How do you capture in print the fleeting moments of vocal sound and images, not to mention the gestures, the facial expressions, and the physical presence of the storyteller and her audience? We have attempted to resolve this dilemma in certain ways.

1. Some Yiddish and Hebrew words are used in the narratives, just as I do in reciting them. Readers not familiar with these words can refer to the glossary for translation. We feel that the Jewish languages retain a certain flavor, even on the page.

2. Spacing between different parts of a story serves to indicate where major vocal transitions occur.

3. Sentences are short, words are short and familiar, paragraphs are brief. The oral tale needs to be comprehended, at least on a *peshat* (literal) level on first hearing. And so I have tried to write the stories as I would tell them in my own voice. The reader is free to change and retell each story another way, as no doubt I myself have, or will the next time I tell the tale.

Introduction

I am often asked: "How did you become a storyteller?" The first time someone asked me this question, I felt a rush of questions racing through my own mind as I groped for an answer: When *did* I begin? Where? Who was listening? How old was I then? When I opened my mouth, this was what emerged:

"I became a storyteller when I began listening to stories—that is, when I was a child. My father told me biblical, talmudic and midrashic tales; my mother taught me through folktales, teaching tales and proverbs. All these stories gave me the sense of belonging to a people—the Jewish People—and they taught me how to live and what values and traditions to cherish. My parents left me a rich legacy through their tales, and these, in turn, taught me what to transmit to my children."

That was my first answer, and it has not changed, even after years of hearing the oft-repeated question.

The Jews are a storytelling people. We cherish our memories and celebrate them through our stories. We are called the People of the Book, but we are also a People of the Spoken Word. Biblically, the world was created with the spoken word; the Torah was given at Mount Sinai along with the spoken word; and the stories of our people are told and retold orally, for we all carry within us ancient memories of our history, legends, songs, and movements that must be passed along.

There are all kinds of stories in our rich Jewish cultural heritage: biblical tales, narratives from rabbinic literature (*midrashim*), folktales and fairy tales, parables and myths, proverbs, legends, and anecdotes, as well as personal and family stories. But the telling itself, the joy of telling, comes from the very heart of the Jewish people and can be traced back to the very beginnings of the children of Israel.

When the Written Torah (the first five books of the Bible) were given to Moses at Mount Sinai, Moses also received *Torah Shebe'al Peh*, the Oral Law, whose explanations of the Torah and application of its laws were taught orally to generations of students. Eventually, the Oral Law was written down. By the second century c.e., Reb Yehuda Hanasi had edited and collected all the written and unwritten portions of the Oral Law and compiled them in the Mishna. The Talmud consists essentially of the Mishna with the addition of the Gemara (commentaries on and application of the Mishna), and Aggada (stories and maxims that deal with the spirit of the Oral Law rather than its letter). Aggada comprises two-thirds of the entire Talmud.

Together with the Oral Law, the oral tradition (lower case "o") is central to the reinforcement and transmission of Jewish values. The oral tradition is the accumulation of Jewish customs and folk wisdom that are passed along by word of mouth. It stresses the human connection between the teacher–storyteller and the student–listener in transmitting stories not found in the Talmud. In addition to the wealth of new interpretations added during every age, the oral tradition preserves various styles of telling, different versions of stories. In a sense, the oral tradition exists alongside the Oral Law; yet it remains separate.

Jews tell stories all the time. Every holiday—and there are many—offers an opportunity for storytelling, both in the home and in the synagogue. On the Sabbath especially, storytelling becomes a shared event that entertains, teaches, opens children and adults to a sense of wonder.

The magical "I'm going to tell you a story" around the Sabbath table creates a willingness to listen and a desire to know, to participate. In my own case, when my father prepared to tell us a story, something special happened within us. With each story, we took a journey to distant lands (especially the Land of Israel), met new characters, understood new ideas, discovered options and, most of all, absorbed the values of Judaism. Jewish values, such as learning Torah, peoplehood, the Sabbath, family, *tzedaka*, and freedom, are folk values in that they reflect collective, rather than individual, judgments. Within the diversity of Jewish stories, these values continue to evolve continually and remain meaningful to the Jew today.

My mother's specialty was Yiddish folk wisdom: "Don't spit in the river, there may come a time to drink." "A mountain and a mountain cannot come together, but a person and a person can." Often, in response to my questions, she told me parables and immigrant stories. When I lost my temper, she would tell me the following story, to teach me to restrain my anger:

> Once there was a couple who had a baby son. Soon after the birth of the child, the husband was forced to leave his home to fight in the Russian Army, and he was away for many many years.
>
> One night, he returned home. Just as he was about to knock on the door, he heard voices in the house: first a man's deep voice and then his wife's voice answering. He could not hear their words, only their voices.
>
> The soldier-husband was infuriated at the thought that his wife was unfaithful and had taken a lover during his absence. In his rage, he drew his revolver and prepared to rush in and kill the man in his house. As he forced the door open, he suddenly heard the word "Mama," and he realized that the man was his son, now grown up. Fortunately, he had stopped himself in time.
>
> The husband fell to his knees and begged his wife and son for forgiveness, shuddering over what he might have done.

The images from this story have stayed with me over the years. Only recently have I discovered that my grandmother told a similar story to a cousin who lived near her in New York City when he was a child. She told him this story to teach him patience. All this time I had thought it a story my mother had heard somewhere, or a tale based on something that had actually happened in Russia.

"How wonderful," I mused, "that this is a story my mother probably heard from her mother." What excitement I felt, then, when I discovered while I was doing my research for this book that a variant of this story is to be found in a thirteenth-century collection of ethical precepts and folktales called *Sefer Hasidim*, assembled by Reb Yehuda Hahasid. Now I know that it is a part of Jewish lore, having taught its lesson of restraint for generations. Through such narratives I learned to identify and act as a good person and a Jew, not for myself alone, but as part of a community.

Stories worked for me because my parents did not just lecture me on principles. Instead, they used the power of stories to work on my imagination and lead me to discern the values they upheld. Through the power of the spoken word, my parents transmitted concrete as well as moral meanings, emotions, attitudes, and interpretations of Jewish values.

Unlike writers, storytellers know to whom they are speaking and, above all, know that they are being listened to. Theirs are a dynamic, multilevel process that starts by creating a trust and bond between teller and listener, and ends (if it ever ends) by energizing and revitalizing our civilization. When listeners enter this event with their whole mind and imagination, they emerge with a rich treasure chest of ideas (e.g., responsibility for carrying on the tradition of ancestors), values (e.g., respect for parents), experiences (e.g., being a slave in Egypt and wandering in the desert), and definitions of himself as a Jew.

All that sounds like a powerful claim for what many think of as mere entertainment. But the importance of storytelling in the Jewish world should not be underestimated: In the *shtetls* of Eastern Europe, stories were exchanged by rabbis and traveling messengers, by *badhanim* (storytellers and improvising rhymesters who performed at weddings and other festivities), and by the common folk. A very popular figure was the *maggid*, a traveling preacher who told stories to teach Judaism. These *maggidim* (plural) helped spread the principles of the Hasidic movement through their sermons, and especially through their stories.

In the Middle East, Jews had the same rich and varied Jewish storytelling traditions, but they also drew upon Islamic tales for their repertoire. Many of those stories, translated into Hebrew or told in the Jewish languages of that region (e.g., Judeo-Arabic, Judeo-Persian, Ladino) eventually reached Europe. Jews can be credited as mediators between the folk literatures of East and West, especially throughout the Middle Ages. The medieval period produced a number of outstanding collections of Jewish tales, among them: *The Aleph Bet of Ben Sira* (eleventh century), *Sefer Hayashar* (eleventh century), *Mishlei Shualim* (thirteenth century), and *Hibbur Yafe Mehayeshua*, also called *Hibbur Yafeh Mehayeshuah* or *Sefer Hamaasiyot* (Book of Stories) by R. Nissim b. Jacob Ibn Shahin of Qairawan (eleventh century), edited by H. Z. Hirschberg in 1954. This last book was originally written in Judeo-Arabic, which was forgotten, and early Hebrew translations made the collection a part of Hebrew medieval literature. Ibn Shahin used mainly talmudic-midrashic stories and episodes, but added many folktales from Muslim and Arabic sources.

It should be noted that many of the narratives found in these and other volumes (and even some in the talmudic and hasidic anthologies) were not indigenous to the Jews. They were borrowed or adapted from the folktales of other peoples. The multilingual Jews were open to other national folk traditions, and foreign influences, interwoven with Jewish folk traditions, traveled with the Jews to many countries. Isaac Disraeli understood this when he wrote: "Tales have wings, whether they come from the East or from the North, and they soon become denizens wherever they alight." In the telling and retelling of the adapted stories, however, the tales began to mirror the cultural and religious contexts of the storytellers and soon became the carriers of Jewish values and traditions.

In Eastern Europe, storytelling reached a peak of creativity with the hasidic movement, founded in the eighteenth century by Rabbi Israel Baal Shem Tov (the Master of the Good Name). He stressed the joyousness of Judaism through song, dance, and stories. In Hasidism, the human voice is used as a powerful means of speaking directly to God and achieving salvation. Wordless tunes, ecstatic dancing, magical stories—these are the *hasid*'s tools of religious expression, in addition to prayer. The Baal Shem Tov made these elements more important to the Jewish common folk than great scholarly achievement in Torah study, until then the highest ideal of every Jew.

Through the years, in the Jewish world of Eastern Europe, parents and grandparents told stories to children and grandchildren. Women entertained themselves with stories while they plucked goose feathers or did needlework in the evenings. Men gathered in the synagogue and, between prayer services, told stories. Storytelling was integral to daily life, as natural as the morning milking. This was no doubt equally true in other regions where Jews lived.

In some communities, especially those with higher rates of illiteracy, the storytelling sessions served a wide variety of social functions and had important cultural value. Gathering around the storyteller before and after evening prayers, Jews not only listened to stories, but also exchanged information about recent political events, maintained social contacts between members of the community, and took care of such prosaic matters as reading mail from the Government.

Recently, Dr. Baruch H. S. Mazor shared with me his personal reminiscences of similar storytelling gatherings in Palestine. Born in Zikhron Yosef, the Kurdish quarter of Jerusalem, Dr. Mazor vividly recalls a storyteller who was active in the 1930s and 1940s. The man, who went by the name of Hakham Zekhariah, owned a building in which he used a room facing the front porch as a grocery store. Hakham Zekhariah, however, preferred telling stories to running a grocery. So he had his four wives (who by the way lived together peacefully, a story in itself) tend the store in his place while he, in typical Near Eastern style, would tell stories—heroic tales about King Solomon and Ashmedai, David and Goliath, or Hannah and her seven sons—interspersed with the chanting of relevant songs.

Much as Zekhariah loved to tell the stories, the men loved to hear them even more. And they gathered, after evening prayers, smoking and drinking tea or coffee, and listening even after nightfall, when only Zekhariah's voice could be heard in the darkness. Sitting cross-legged on the biggest of the worn wooden benches on his porch, Zekhariah would also tell political stories and describe what was happening in the Second World War. He was a kind of village *mukhtar*, a representative of his community; and he was entertainer, teacher, commentator, liaison between past and present—all in one.

Because of Zekhariah's position in the community, the mailman would often leave letters for neighborhood people with Zekhariah, knowing that they would be passing by or attending his storytelling session that evening. During the storytelling sessions, Hakham Zekhariah would interrupt a story by pointing to someone in the audience and saying, "Here's a letter for you." He would even open the letter and read it if asked to do so, for many of the people were illiterate. And so Hakham Zekhariah became the contact between the people and the postman. (Some of his stories and chants have been recorded by Dr. Yosef Rivlin in his *Shirat Yehudei Hatargum* (*Poetry of the Aramaic-Speaking Jews*).

The rich oral tradition has assured the continued existence of the Jewish people through the centuries. Today, especially in the hasidic world, the oral tradition remains a part of religious and social life. Storytelling is shared in synagogues, at the Sabbath and festival meals, on the anniversary of a beloved rabbi's death, and also on the *yahrzeit* (anniversary of a death) of the beloved writer Sholom Aleichem. (See the introduction to "The Clever Will.") Personal stories, family stories, traditional and sacred tales are all told and shared when Jews come together in sorrow and in joy, to pray and to celebrate, to grieve and to remember.

In his book, *The Gates of the Forest*, Elie Wiesel relates

a hasidic tale about tales and the importance of retelling them:

> When the great Rabbi Baal Shem Tov saw misfor-
> tune threatening the Jews, it was his custom to go into
> a certain part of the forest to meditate. There he would
> light a fire, say a special prayer, and the miracle would
> be accomplished and the misfortune averted.

The story tells us that, with each successive generation, the rabbis forgot how to light the fire, then how to say the prayer, and finally they no longer knew how to find the place in the forest:

> Then it fell to Rabbi Israel of Rizhyn to overcome
> misfortune. Sitting in his armchair, his head in his
> hands, he spoke to God: "I am unable to light the fire
> and I do not know the prayer; I cannot even find the
> place in the forest. All I can do is tell the story, and this
> must be sufficient." And it was sufficient.

Remembering to tell the tale is important, not only in and of itself, but because it brings redemption. The oral tradition is the ethical guide and inspiration, the link that ties together the cultural heritage and the values of the Jewish people. In Judaism, storytelling is a celebration of memory, a sharing of the values and concerns of the Jewish people, and a precious gift as one generation tells another stories about itself. Elie Wiesel wrote:

> My father, an enlightened spirit, believed in man.
> My grandfather, a fervent Hasid, believed in God.
> The one taught me to speak, the other to sing.
> Both loved stories.
> And when I tell mine, I hear their voices.
> Whispering from beyond the silenced storm.
> They are what links the survivor to their memory.
> God created man because He loves stories. [1972, p. 1]

Stories are what link Jews to their heritage, to the memory of those who came before them, to their past and to their future. Stories are the legacies of my parents and the treasures I transmit to my children. May our children continue to tell our stories!

My Storyteller's Prayer

Rebono shel olam, God of the Universe, listen to my heart
and my voice as I stand before You, wanting to tell our
story.

Help me to understand and find the right feelings and
words with which to transmit the tale.

Make my voice expressive and clear so that the collective
wisdom of our people can reach the hearts of those who
listen.

May I merit to hear well with my ears and heart.

Keep me from the jealousy of other tellers and from my
jealousy of them so that we may be able to share and
hear each other with open hearts.

Allow me to assume this responsibility as my forebears did
before me—to continue to retell our stories.

Help me to choose my stories wisely and let my words live.

Make me worthy to be a storyteller of our Jewish people.

Peninnah Schram

The Bull's Eye

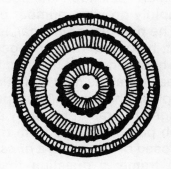

This Maggid of Dubno parable has become my theme story, my "signature." I usually open my performances with it because audiences respond to the humor and the surprise element, both of which gently lead them to change the direction of their thinking and to be more open to the story. It sets up the opening for whatever stories I have chosen to tell during my program; through it, the audience and I become partners in a shared experience. It's a story I especially love. And because I love it, it makes me feel comfortable with any audience—immediately.

What is a parable? A parable is a teaching tale, similar to a fable, usually short and to the point, often using animals as the main characters (e.g., Aesop's fables). In earlier Jewish fables (many of them probably translated and adapted from Indian, Roman, and Greek sources), the animals were not only endowed with human personalities; they spoke wisely about Torah.

The greatest collector and teller of fables was, without doubt, Rabbi Meir, the student of Rabbi Akiva, who lived in Hellenic Asia Minor during the second century C.E. According to the Talmud, Rabbi Meir collected three hundred fables, some of which are found in the Talmud and in *midrashim*. During the Middle Ages, Jewish scholars, namely Berechiah Hanakdan and Joseph ibn Zabara, contributed to the rapidly growing number of Jewish fables.

The parable, or *mashal*, is similar to the fable and does, in fact, belong to the same genre. However, the main difference between them is that fables are absolutely fiction, whereas parables may be fiction but could also be historical examples. The *mashal*'s purpose is to illuminate a verse or passage of Torah or to clarify a Jewish custom or tradition. A Jewish parable differs from the general parable in that it is composed of two parts: a *nimshal* and a *mashal*. The *nimshal* is the frame: a question that is set up at the beginning followed by a connection at the end that serves as a direct response to the question first posed. The *nimshal* teaches us what we can learn from the *mashal* and how to apply that lesson. The *mashal*, the story-example in the middle, is the tale inside the *nimshal*, a statement of the lesson or its application. Parables are fascinating and delightful, transmitting knowledge and inspiring understanding in a nonthreatening way and always in the language of the people.

Parables are considered a very Jewish genre. They were supposedly invented by King Solomon, but it was Rabbi Jacob Kranz, the Dubner Maggid (1741–1804), who developed the parable as a primary teaching tool. Called "the Jewish Aesop," he imitated the *aggada* and *midrash* by combining lessons from the Bible and its commentaries with the folktales of the people he met on his travels. He adapted these folktales with creativity and imagination in order to teach as he must have done with "The Bull's Eye." The central motif of drawing the bull's eye is well known in many cultures and is generally told as a joke or humorous anecdote. See the variant in Ausubel (1948)(4).

There is an *aggadic* statement that says: "With a penny candle one may often find a lost gold coin or a precious pearl. By means of a simple parable, one may sometimes penetrate the most profound ideas." I find this to be true of all stories, but it is my hope that with this simple parable we can become partners as storytellers in a shared experience of storytelling.

long time ago, the Dubner Maggid was walking with one of his students along the banks of a river. As they walked, the Maggid told a story to explain a certain Jewish tradition. Suddenly, the student stopped and asked, "Rabbi, tell me, how do you always know the right story to explain the subject being discussed?"

The rabbi smiled and said, "I'll answer you with a story."

Many years ago, a nobleman's son was a student at a military academy, and one of the sports in which he was an expert was shooting bull's eyes. In fact, he had won many gold medals for his marksmanship. After he was awarded his diploma, the young officer rode home on his horse. Passing through a tiny village, he saw a hundred circles drawn on the side of a barn—and in the center of each circle was a bullet hole.

The officer was so amazed, he stopped his horse and yelled out: "Who is this expert shot? A hundred perfect bull's eyes! That's incredible! Even I could not do that!"

Just then, a young boy walking by looked up at the officer on his tall horse and snickered, "Oh, that's Nar, our town fool!"

"I don't care what he is," interrupted the officer. "Whoever can shoot a hundred perfect bull's eyes must have won every gold medal in the world! I must meet him and shake his hand!"

"Oh no, no, no, you don't understand," laughed the boy. "Nar doesn't draw the circle first and then shoot. He shoots first, and then he draws the circle."

"And that's how it is with me," continued the Dubner Maggid, "I don't always know the right story for the subject being discussed. What I do is read many stories, and listen to many stories, and remember all of these stories. Then when I find a story I want to tell, I introduce the subject that leads me into telling that perfect story."

And the Maggid and his student continued their walk.

Elijah and
the Three Wishes

Elijah the Prophet is the most beloved character in Jewish folklore. How he became so popular is often a bit of a puzzle for those who know the Elijah of the Bible. How, they ask, was the stern biblical prophet transformed into a kindly folklore hero? Why is Elijah so well-loved a character in every age and in every land where Jews have lived?

Elijah the Tishbite was a prophet in the Kingdom of Israel during the ninth century B.C.E. A fiery, zealous preacher, he fought against cults and alien religious influences—and against social injustice. According to biblical accounts, Elijah did not die, but ascended to Heaven in a fiery chariot. The book of Malachi (3:24) describes Elijah as the one who will "turn the heart of the fathers to the children, and the heart of the children to their fathers. . . . Behold, I will send you Elijah the Prophet before the coming of the great and terrible day of the Lord."

So we see that it is Elijah who will not only reconcile parents and children, but will also be the messenger to announce the coming of the Messiah. As Jews, we include Elijah in our celebrations: We fill a cup for Elijah at the Passover seder and reserve a chair for him at every *brit milah*.

In Jewish folklore, however, Elijah is quite different. He excels in his domain, the domain of miracles. In the oral legends, Elijah comes to the rescue of the Jewish community and worthy individuals. He helps those in need, especially the poor and pious. He brings hope and reconciliation. He tests and heals. He sees who is unselfish, who offers hospitality, who gives charity, who learns humility, who deserves help. His chameleonlike disguises are marvelously clever. He becomes a poor man, a student, a matchmaker, a slave—always so as to heighten suspense and fantasy, always to bring about a happy resolution.

Elijah, like Solomon, also has the ability to understand the language of animals. He learns valuable information from them. After all, while a person may hide information from his business or marriage partner, animals see and hear all.

Most of all, Elijah cannot bear to see injustice and wants to set things right through his miracles.

Elijah's miracles make him a sort of *deus ex machina* of Greek drama, always bringing about a happy ending.

In our Jewish life, we conceive of Elijah as still wandering, testing, bringing miracles. Elijah stories continue to give us that hope and optimism for justice and peace in our world. May it all come soon!

Because Elijah stories have meant so much to me since early childhood, I am drawn to them. I like to hear them and to tell them. And I realize now that I have included in this book 12 stories in which Elijah appears.

My earliest recollection of any story is this Elijah tale that my father used to tell me, one I requested over and over, as I sat on his lap in his oversized, cushioned living-room chair. They say that a voice memory is lost faster than any other sense memory. But I still hear my father's voice saying, in Yiddish, "Elijah whistled." That must have captured my imagination, for this story has remained in my storehouse of memories as special and powerful. To my knowledge, it has never been published before.

This tale is a variant form of the type listed as 750A in Aarne and Thompson (1964). The tale is extremely popular, with versions known from Europe to China. There are at least six versions of this tale in the Israel Folklore Archives from Moroccan forms to Persian. Typically this tale contains motifs (as catalogued by Thompson (1966) [TMI]): K1811 God (or Saints) in disguise visit mortals; Q1.1 God (Saints) in disguise reward hospitality and punish inhospitality; D1761.0.2 Limited number of wishes granted.

hen Elijah the Prophet wanted to see how the people were behaving in a certain town, he would disguise himself as a beggar and walk around its streets. He would observe how the people were acting toward each other in the shops, in the parks, in the marketplace, in the synagogue. As he walked, he would blink his eyes, nod his head, shrug his shoulders, stroke his long white beard, or tap his walking stick as though he were recording what he saw, adding that message to the already bulging sack he carried over his shoulder. He often smiled to himself, too, while humming a melody as he walked from place to place.

One day, he noticed a small cottage. "This place needs a great many repairs," he observed. "A new roof, better window shutters, a gate. Yet here are some beautiful flowers growing in the tiny front yard. Hollyhocks, poppies, a mandrake plant. I like that!" Weary from traveling, and hungry too, Elijah decided to stop at this house to rest a while. He knocked on the door.

In this cottage, there lived a poor man and his wife. The man came to the door. When Elijah asked him for some water to drink, the man invited him in. Seeing how hungry and tired this traveler was, the couple asked him to stay and share their meal.

"Come and eat with us," said the good wife. "Eating

with a guest makes the meal feel like a banquet, even though we cannot offer you more than the little we have."

"Come," said her husband. "We will gladly share whatever we have." The couple offered him what they had prepared for their dinner. There was a small piece of herring and a thick slice of black bread, and some water to drink. The meal was hardly enough even for the two of them.

When the stranger had eaten and was refreshed, he turned to the couple and said, "Because of your kindness to me, I will grant you any three wishes."

At first not believing what he had heard, the poor man just stood there quietly. Then he began to think to himself, "Let me test him to see if what this bedraggled traveler says is true. There is some mystery about him. Maybe God has answered our prayers to help us out of our hard times."

After a few minutes, the poor man replied, "This house needs so much repair and it is so tiny that I don't have room enough for my books. I would like to have a large house, like a palace."

Elijah whistled, and instantly a mansion appeared where the cottage had stood.

At that moment, the woman, looking down at her clothes and quickly taking off her old apron, exclaimed, "Oh, we should have beautiful clothes, with shining, glittering jewels," gesturing wildly as she pointed to her hair, ears, neck, and wrists. "We look so plain in this wonderful house," she explained.

Again Elijah whistled, and the couple was instantly dressed in clothes of velvet and satin, with magnificent diamond, pearl, and emerald jewelry covering the wife's head, ears, neck, and wrists.

"Gold!" they both shouted together with great excitement for their third wish.

Elijah whistled for the third time, and sacks of gold appeared. A moment later, Elijah disappeared.

Several years went by, and Elijah wanted to see how the good couple had fared. When Elijah appeared at the gate of their mansion, again disguised as a beggar, he looked around first. He saw heavy shutters on the windows and high fences around the house. While there was a great deal of land around the house, nowhere were there any flowers. As he stood looking through the gate, the servants, seeing this stranger through the watchman's door near the gate of the yard, would not let him stand there.

"I would like to see the master of the house," demanded Elijah. The servants laughed and brought the dogs closer to the gate, signaling the beggar to leave. The master of the house himself came to the door to see what the commotion was. Since he did not recognize the beggar, he shouted orders for the beggar to leave or be chased away.

Disappointed and saddened by what he had seen, Elijah whistled once and the gold disappeared.

He gave another whistle, and the beautiful clothes and jewels vanished.

Then Elijah gave a third whistle, and the mansion instantly turned back into the small cottage that had once before stood in that place.

In the same moment, the couple realized how selfish they had become. They understood then how poor they had been, even when they had all the riches in the world.

The Three Brothers

The beloved figure of Elijah the Prophet appears throughout Jewish literature and song as a symbol of hope. We hope for him to come and take us out of trouble and lighten our hearts. That's what we sing in the song, *Eliahu Hanovi*, every week at the close of *Shabbat*, after *havdala*. But Elijah appears when we don't necessarily expect him, as in this story of three brothers who are allowed to choose their rewards for obeying their father's deathbed request. As in all stories, we enter into it by making our own choices along with the characters.

The specific idea of Elijah's giving a coin to someone who then becomes rich can be found in other stories. One of the most famous is Isaac Leib Peretz's "The Seven Good Years," which in turn was inspired by a folktale. As always in these stories, Elijah returns to test the now-rich person's generosity. The wisest choice brings other rewards and is certainly an honored and cherished Jewish choice.

This tale again forms part of a set of tales described by A-T 750D, "Three Brothers each Granted a Wish by Angel Visitor." There are at least ten versions of this tale recorded in the Israel Folktale Archives (IFA), some without Elijah: IFA 8747 from Morocco, IFA 8439 from Iraq, and at least four others. The tale also appears in European Jewish tradition as recorded by Bin Gorion (1916–1921)(V, 85 and VI, 22)and Gaster (1924) (355).

This story, "The Three Brothers," comes from *Sefer Hamusar*. Interestingly, the stories about Elijah, along with many other religious tales, have been borrowed, adapted, and retold by non-Jewish neighbors, which would explain the parallel variants of this tale in Russian and Serbian folktales.

nce there was a man who lived a life filled with good deeds (*mitzvot*), charity, and justice (*tzedaka*). When this man was about to die, he called his three sons to him and said, "My children, the time of my death is near. I have lived a long life. What I hope and pray for you is that you will live in peace with one another. Just as I have never taken an oath in anger, so you too must follow this path. Quarreling can lead to oath-taking, so try never to quarrel. Love God, as your beloved mother and I have taught you. Live in this cottage as your home, and take care of my beautiful spice garden. Guard it from thieves in the night. I bless you, my sons, as Jacob blessed his sons."

With tears in their eyes, the sons promised to follow their father's wishes. And the old father gave his blessing to each of his sons.

After the father died, the sons faithfully remembered his words and stood watch in the garden, each one taking his turn.

One night, as the eldest brother was guarding the place, a stranger mysteriously appeared. "I am Elijah the Prophet," said the newcomer, "and I have come to reward you for following your father's wishes. But you may choose only one of three wishes: to become wealthy, to have great knowledge, or to marry a good wife."

Without a moment's hesitation, the eldest brother cried out, "I want to be rich! I want to have the most money in the world."

Elijah took a gold coin from his pocket and placed it in the eldest brother's hand. "This coin will bring you great wealth," said Elijah. When the brother looked to see what was in his palm, Elijah disappeared.

The next night, as the second brother was standing in the garden, Elijah suddenly appeared again and offered him the same gifts. "I want to know everything. I want to be the wisest man in the world," replied the second brother. "Through this book, you will become a great scholar," said Elijah as he placed a book in the brother's open hands. As the second brother looked to see what was in his hands, Elijah disappeared.

Now, on the next night, the youngest brother was in the garden when Elijah appeared and gave him the same three choices. The youngest brother smiled and said, "A good wife is better than riches." He nodded to Elijah, indicating that this was his choice.

Elijah smiled, too, and answered, "Come! We must take a short journey together to find this good wife." And Elijah and the youngest brother started on their search.

By evening, they were tired and stopped at an inn. While the young man slept, Elijah, who could understand the language of all animals, listened to the barnyard animals talking to one another. And what did he hear? The chickens and geese said, "Oh, this young man must have committed a terrible sin if he is to marry the innkeeper's daughter. She is so vain, and her parents are wicked people." Elijah did not like what he heard, and in the morning the two of them left to continue on their way.

The next night, they stopped at another inn. Elijah listened to the animals talking. And again he heard how hard-hearted and dishonest the innkeepers were. Once more, Elijah was displeased by what he had heard, so in the morning he left with the youngest son and they continued walking.

Late in the afternoon, they were tired again, and when they came to a small inn, they decided to stay there for the night. That night, Elijah heard the animals talking with great excitement: "Have you heard? Have you heard? This young man who just arrived must be a righteous man if he is destined to marry our innkeeper's daughter, for she is not only beautiful, but so wise and kind, just like her parents."

Early the next morning, Elijah went to see the innkeeper in order to arrange the marriage between the youngest brother and the innkeeper's daughter. The innkeeper was pleased but said, "My daughter must give her consent as well. If she agrees, then they will marry." The daughter had seen the handsome young man when he had arrived the night before. She had noticed his manner as he spoke with Elijah, and she had fallen in love with him.

So the young woman readily gave her consent, and a marriage was arranged. Elijah performed the ceremony and then disappeared.

Soon after, the young couple returned to the young man's home. When they arrived at the cottage, they found that the two brothers had left; the eldest one had bought a mansion and moved there. The second brother was traveling around the world giving lectures, and wherever he went he was acclaimed a great scholar and *hokhem.* So the young couple planted the garden, sold the spices and herbs they raised in order to earn a living, had children, and lived together peacefully in their small home.

Several years passed. Elijah decided to find out what had happened to the three brothers since he had visited them in the garden. Master of disguises that he was, Elijah assumed the appearance of a beggar and went to the rich brother's mansion. The servants refused to allow him in.

When the beggar called out, "I am here to reclaim what I have given your master," the eldest brother recognized the voice of Elijah.

He came running to the door and pleaded with Elijah to allow him to keep the coin.

"No," said Elijah. "Give me back the coin that I gave you. You have not used the wealth to help people in need. Instead, you have become greedy and have used it for yourself alone. You are not worthy to keep the coin." And the eldest brother had to return the gold coin to Elijah.

Then, in the guise of a scholar, Elijah went to a discourse given by the second brother. He listened and then asked a question on a point of the law. The second brother ignored the question. But when Elijah asked it again, the brother rebuked him and said, "I have no time for such foolish questions."

"No time for answering even a *foolish* question?" asked Elijah. "What good, then, is your scholarship if you cannot take the time to teach and explain the complex ideas you are talking about. It might be better if you returned the book I gave you years ago, since all that you know comes from the book and not from your own questioning and learning."

The scholar-brother immediately understood that this was Elijah, and he pleaded with him for another chance. But Elijah asked for the book. "You are not worthy to keep it," he said. And the second brother had to return the book.

Finally, Elijah assumed the guise of a poor man and went to the home of the youngest brother. As he approached the house, the wife opened the door. Seeing a person who was tired and thirsty, she invited him in to rest and put food and drink on the table for him.

When he had rested, Elijah said to the couple, "I give you wealth and learning, because of your good wife's deeds." And as Elijah handed them the gold coin and the book, he added, "In your home, you will know how to use the wealth wisely and to help others, and you will know how to share your knowledge and learning only for good and not for evil."

Then Elijah blessed the couple and disappeared.

The couple lived a happy life for the rest of their days.

And when they grew old, they gave the coin and the book to their children.

Elijah's Mysterious
Ways

Life is puzzling. Sometimes good things seem to happen to undeserving people, while bad things happen to righteous people.

I remember that as a youngster I often asked my father why this was so. He would respond by saying, "We cannot know everything. All of life is like a circle, but a person can see only an arc and not the complete circle. We often do not know the reasons for what happens, but while a person must ask questions, he should not ask too many questions." My father was a religious man who believed in God's goodness. His reply was one that has often served me as an anchor on stormy days.

The beloved figure of Elijah brings with it eternal hope and a perspective on life that we need in order to keep our balance.

This story may be found in the Hebrew collection of folktales, *Hibbur Yafe Mehayeshua* (Ibn Shahin 1557) dating from the eleventh century. Reb Nissim composed this book of stories for "Dunash, his son-in-law, to speak to his heart and to console him." Many of the tales found in this anthology are entertaining and humorous, but they are all inspirational and deal with the theme of God as a righteous judge, no matter how mysterious his ways may seem. This genre of "tales of relief after adversity and stress" was widely known in Arabic folklore during the eleventh and twelfth centuries. No doubt the Arabic stories served as models for many Jewish writings and collections of tales.

This tale is also a complex form, including tale type 750B and motifs from other sources. Thompson Motif Index (TMI) Q141, "Hospitality granted by poor man to Saint," the central feature, is a very common motif. There are versions of this tale in Gaster (1924) (350) and in Bin Gorion (1916–1921) (II, 131 and 134).

n a certain town, there lived a God-fearing and good man, Reb Shmuel ben Yosef. He trusted God and accepted whatever happened to him and to his family—most of the time. Sometimes, though, he was puzzled by the things that happened to his people.

"Why should such a good woman as our neighbor Sarah is—why should she suffer the death of her only child while others who do not practice *tzedaka*, or fulfill *mitzvot*—why do they enjoy large families?" he would ask of God, not to speak ill of people, Heaven forbid, but only out of a sense of confusion.

Once, he saw a wealthy family become poor. "How cruel that this family will be without all the things they are accustomed to," he thought. "Why did God do this?"

Other things troubled Reb Shmuel as well. Day after day, as he looked around, he would ask again and again "Why?" and "How?" And he began to ask more and more often.

"*Ribono shel Olam*, Lord of the Universe," he would call out, "help me understand your ways. I know your miracles are everywhere. But I am beginning to see only the despair, and I am perplexed by what I see. If only I could meet Elijah the Prophet. Maybe then I could begin to understand and see once again your daily miracles."

Reb Shmuel fasted and prayed that he might see Elijah.

One day, as he was walking in an open field, a stranger approached him and said, "I am Elijah. What would you ask of me?"

Reb Shmuel answered, "I need to see the wonders that you perform in the world, for my world is dark, and I do not understand much of what goes on around me."

And Elijah said, "When you see what I do, you will certainly not understand my actions. Then I will have to explain them to you, which will take time. . . ."

"No, no, I promise I will not take up your time or ask you to trouble yourself with me," Reb Shmuel assured him. "I will just come along with you to observe—to witness your miracles. That is all."

"Very well," said Elijah, "but remember—if you ask for any explanations, I shall leave at once."

Reb Shmuel had no choice but to agree to this condition.

He began to walk with Elijah until they came to a small cottage where there lived a poor man and his wife. They had very little and owned only one cow, but the couple received the strangers with a warm welcome. Placing whatever food they had on the table, they invited the two men to sit and eat. All evening, they discussed some points of law, and the poor man was delighted to have such learned men in his home.

In the morning, as they were about to leave, the cow, this couple's *only* cow, suddenly died.

As Reb Shmuel and Elijah continued on their way, Reb Shmuel muttered to himself in anger, "This is some repayment for kindness! That these kind people, who welcomed us so graciously to their home, should be so repaid!" Unable to hold back his deepening confusion, he turned to Elijah and pleaded, "Why? *Why* did you cause their cow to die?"

Elijah kept walking as he replied, "Have you forgotten what I asked of you? You must not ask for an explanation, no matter what I do—or else I will leave."

Reb Shmuel wanted to argue and ask, "But where are your miracles that save lives or help the poor?" Instead, he said nothing more and continued to walk behind Elijah.

That evening, they came to the mansion of a wealthy man. They knocked on the door. The master of the house sent his servant to bring the two men to the place where the servants slept. But since they were offered no food, not even a piece of bread, they went to bed hungry. In the morning, as they were leaving, Elijah noticed a tree near the house that had been uprooted by a storm. Elijah passed by the tree, and the tree was returned to its former position, with its roots deeper in the ground than before.

When Reb Shmuel saw this, he was even more puzzled. He thought to himself, "To restore his tree! Why should a stingy man receive such a reward from Elijah?" But he said nothing to Elijah. He hoped he would understand in some way, perhaps by some sign or word from Elijah.

All day long they walked, until they came to a synagogue in another town. When they entered, they found the seats made of gold and silver. The people sat in their seats, but no one rushed to welcome them or to give either one his seat, and not even one person offered to invite them to his home for dinner, as was customary when strangers came to a new town. "Such men can get along well enough with bread and water. There is no need to invite them to our homes," said one of the members of the synagogue to the others around him.

Since no one asked them home for dinner, Elijah and Reb Shmuel remained in the synagogue all night, sleeping on the hard benches in the back. The next morning, as Elijah stood by the door, he said to all the people, "May God make you *all* leaders."

Again Reb Shmuel did not know what to make of all this.

The next evening, they stopped at a small community where everyone was extremely poor. But the people welcomed the two travelers and asked them to stay with them. Everyone began to bring food to the synagogue, and soon there was a wonderful feast with plenty of wine and food. When they left in the morning, Elijah said to the people, "May God bless you with only *one* leader."

Reb Shmuel waited until they were on the road, and

then he turned to Elijah and cried out, "No more! No more! I cannot continue to see such injustices done. Forgive me, but even though I know you will leave me, *please tell me* what you have been doing. I do not understand any of this. It appears to me that you are doing the opposite of what the people deserve." And Reb Shmuel wept.

Elijah replied, "My friend, listen carefully. Do you remember the poor couple whose cow died? The wife was destined to die that very day, so I pleaded with God to accept the cow's death in place of the woman's.

"When we were at the home of the greedy rich man, I straightened the tree which had fallen over. Had I not done that, the man would have found the hidden treasure that lies in the ground under the tree's roots.

"When I wished the wealthy but selfish people in the synagogue to have many leaders, that may have sounded like a good thing. But it was a curse, because any group that has too many leaders cannot agree on anything and can never make any decisions.

"Therefore, when I wished for the poor but hospitable community to have only one leader, that was a blessing, for it is said, 'It is better to have one wise man rule a city than a group of fools.'"

Before Elijah departed, he said to Reb Shmuel, "I want to give you some advice that will be useful to you, my friend. Whenever you see a wicked person who is prospering, keep in mind that his wickedness will ultimately work against him. And if you see a righteous person enduring hardships, remember that he is being saved from something worse. Do not doubt these things any longer."

Elijah departed. And Reb Shmuel returned to his home, seeing once again the wonders and miracles in the world.

Elijah the Builder

Miracles are continually happening all around us: a rainbow appears in the sky, astronauts walk on the moon, a flower grows, people fall in love. We just have to look up and see and hear and feel all the miracles in our world.

Stories about miracles have been told and retold in Jewish life from the beginning of time. The Jewish People have always believed in miracles, even helping to make them happen, and they have passed the wondrous stories along from one generation to the next.

What is a miracle? Sometimes it is an unexplained, extraordinary event, or perhaps a sudden change that helps resolve a difficult situation. It may come from God or be helped along by people. After all, how was David able to fight the giant Goliath and win, if not for a miracle. But David did not just stand there and wait for a miracle to happen. He did something about it. Through the belief in miracles, we keep our hope, our courage, and our wonder.

In this well-known story, we meet Elijah once again. Isaac Bashevis Singer has written a version called *Elijah the Slave*, published as a wonderful children's book with illustrations. The source of the story, however, is the Talmud, a source that many writers, Jews and gentiles, have mined for ideas and inspiration. It can also be found in Ibn Shahin (1557), Cohen (1721), and Farhi (1870).

There is no parallel to this tale in the Aarne-Thompson (1964) Index, but the tale is typed as 730 *B in Jason (1965), written to accommodate roughly the first half of the IFA collection. The index supersedes Dov Noy's Indiana University dissertation on the same subject (Indiana University, 1953, under the name of Dov Neuman) and is itself continued with the organization and development of the IFA and Jason's (1975) work. This special version of "Elijah and the Builder" has a parallel text in IFA 9243.

 here once was a good, pious couple who had five children. But rich as they were in faith and family, so poor were they in wealth. Now the husband had not been able to find work for many weeks.

One day, when they did not have enough bread to put on the table, and the children cried from hunger, the wife said, "Husband, go to the marketplace. Maybe today God on High will help you find some work so you can earn a few pennies. We must not give up hope. God will help you, but not if you just sit at home."

And her husband answered, "Where can I go that I haven't been? What new doors can I knock on that I haven't tried? I have no rich relatives, no rich friends—not that I would bring shame on us by borrowing from anyone."

However, each day the situation became worse, and finally the wife cried, "How can you sit and watch your children die before your eyes? Go, husband, trust in God. May God bring you hope so you may prosper."

Reluctantly, the husband left the house, walked a little way in one direction, then in another, and finally he sank to the ground, looked up at the heavens and prayed: "Great God in the heavens, great and good God. Take pity on us; have mercy on my little children. For their sake, if not for mine, help us. Our hunger is terrible and we ask, we plead with you, O Merciful God, You who created us, hear my

prayers and turn to us in Your mercy and send Your help—
or else let me die now and quickly, so I should no longer see
how my children and my wife suffer."

And then he rose and walked on as in a daze, weeping
and praying. Suddenly, a young man appeared on the road,
walking toward the unfortunate husband. He stopped and
asked the unhappy man what troubled him so. And the man
wept again, as he told his story of misery.

Then the young man, who was Elijah the Prophet in
disguise, said, "Take me to the marketplace and sell me to
the person I will point out to you. When you receive the
agreed-upon price, give me one dinar. That is all you have
to do."

"Good sir, " said the astonished husband, "you are kind
in offering to help, but you look more like *my* master and I
your slave. They will never believe me when I look like this."
And the man pointed to his rags and his bare feet.

But Elijah insisted, "Do as I tell you, and all will be well
with you. Come, and we'll go to the auction."

As they walked through the marketplace, many did
mistake the man for Elijah's slave, but Elijah told them, "No,
he is my master."

It happened that one of the King's ministers had come
riding through to buy slaves for the building of the King's
new palace. Upon seeing the strong young man, the minister began to bid for him as soon as Elijah was called up for
sale. When the King's minister offered the price of 80 dinars,
Elijah said quickly to the man, "Sell me to the one who bid
80 dinars, and do not accept any more bids." The man took
the 80 dinars, and gave one dinar to Elijah as he had promised.

Elijah held the dinar in his hand for a moment and
then said, "Take this dinar now and return home. May it be
for good. You will never suffer from poverty or want again."
And he blessed the man.

When Elijah rode off with the King's minister, the man
bought all kinds of good food and returned home.

After his family had eaten, the wife said, "My husband, you did what I advised, and it seems as if I gave you good counsel. But tell me how this came to pass. How did you earn this money?" And her husband told her how he had met the young man and sold him as a slave. He often wondered what happened to that young man and who he really was.

When Elijah left with the King's minister, he was brought to the King. The King had been planning to build a great palace outside the city and had bought many slaves to haul stones, timber, and other building materials. As soon as the King saw Elijah he asked, "And do you have a particular skill or shall we put you to work with all the slaves to drag stones and cut trees?"

"I am a builder, your Majesty," said Elijah, "and I can work best by planning and directing the work."

"Well then, it is our good fortune that we have purchased you today," said the King, and he explained his plan for the great palace he desired to have built. "Build it for me in six months' time, and I will reward you greatly and also grant you your freedom."

"Your Majesty," replied Elijah, "I will do as you ask in even a shorter time. Have the slaves prepare all the building materials at once."

The King directed all the slaves to do as Elijah had asked.

That night, Elijah prayed that God Most High perform a miracle and build the palace according to the King's wishes.

And a miracle happened. All the angels came down from the heavens and worked together to build a magnificent palace. As soon as it was dawn, the palace was finished and Elijah knew the King would be pleased. And when Elijah saw that the angels had finished their work and returned to the heavens, he, too, disappeared.

In the morning, the slaves arose for the day's work but, to their astonishment, they saw the completed palace. They ran to the King, who then searched for his chief builder.

"He must have been one of the angels," the King said when he could not find Elijah anywhere. "But," he added with a grand gesture as though speaking to the air, "I release you and declare you a free man!"

One day, Elijah met the man who had sold him, and the man asked him, "Tell me, how did you fare when you were brought to the King?"

And Elijah answered, "I could have freed myself immediately; but a promise is a promise, and he had paid good money for me to work. So I built him a great palace as he asked. I did not want him to regret buying me and paying so much gold. I performed a task for him worth many times over what he had paid for me. After I fulfilled my promise, I left."

Then the man understood that this was Elijah and thanked him many times and said, "You have restored us to life."

As time passed, the couple acquired even greater good fortune; and they were blessed for the rest of their lives, grateful to God Most High for all that they now had in their lives.

The Princess and
Her Beloved

King Solomon is the second most popular character in Jewish folklore. According to a study made by folklorist Dov Noy, the six most popular heroes in Jewish folktales are Elijah, Solomon, Maimonides, Moses, the Baal Shem Tov, and Shalom Shabazi, the Yemenite folk hero.

Solomon, whose real name was Jedidiah, became known as Solomon, or Shlomo, which means "peace," because peace and prosperity reigned in his kingdom during his rule. He became king when he was 18 and ruled for 40 years (961–920 B.C.E.). His achievements were many, but perhaps the most widely known were those stemming from his gift for poetry: The Song of Songs, the book of Ecclesiastes, many psalms, and the invention of the parable. (Parables are like riddles and, since Solomon was also famous for posing and answering riddles, perhaps we can rightly conclude that he did shape the first parable.) The greatest of all his superb accomplishments was the building of the Temple dedicated to God in Jerusalem.

Solomon enters into our folklore, however, on a different level. There he appears not only as wise judge and Torah scholar, builder of a state and diplomat, architect of the Temple and proud and mighty King; he's also seen as a wandering beggar, following his confrontation with Ashmedai, the King of the Demons.

There are many Jewish legends about the giant bird, the *ziz*, which is so huge that its feet rest deep in the water while its head reaches the sky and its wings block out the sun. According to legend, the *ziz* was created on the fifth day of Creation and was supposed to rule over all the birds.

This fairy tale, "The Princess and Her Beloved," is a wondrous tale of how, with the help of the *ziz*, a princess meets the man destined to be her husband. It shows us the miracle of love.

The Jewish concept of the predestined mate is the focus of this story, as it is in other stories in this book. Even the great King Solomon, the most successful biblical ruler, is human and, like many parents, could not dictate whom his daughter would marry, at least in legend.

I have not been able to find the name of Solomon's daughter. So in this story I call her "Shloma," a feminine version of Solomon's Hebrew name, Shlomo.

The story can be found in *Midrash Tanhuma* and in Louis Ginzberg's (1909–1938) *Legends of the Jews*. I first read it as a child in the book *Jewish Fairy Tales and Legends* by Aunt Naomi (1921), and it captured my imagination.

"The Princess and Her Beloved" is related to the very well-known *Rapunzel* tale, A-T 310, with a series of added motifs, the most striking of which is the *ziz*, well known in the folklore of the Near East, with parallels in the Egyptian and Persian *Rukh*, familiar from the *Tales of Sinbad*. This telling has a close parallel in type 930*J (IFA) with recorded versions from Morocco to Iran. The *Rapunzel* story is known now all over the world, probably because of the Grimm Brothers collection in which it is found as the twelfth tale, but independant oral versions have been collected from the West Indies through India.

This story also brings to mind the words of Agur, the son of Jakeh (one of Solomon's other names) in Proverbs 30:18–19:

There are three things which are too wonderful for me,
Yes, four which I know not:
The way of an eagle in the air;
The way of a serpent upon a rock;
The way of a ship in the midst of the sea;
And the way of a man with a young woman.

n a faraway kingdom there lived a king by the
name of Solomon and his daughter, Princess
Shloma. The princess, who had long black
hair and shining eyes, was not only beautiful
but wise and clever. Dressing in ordinary
clothes, she would often walk in the marketplace and have
long conversations with the people there. After these talks,
the princess would tell the King what she had learned. She
would even suggest ways to help the people. And the people
loved the princess as much for her smile, which was as
radiant as the sunshine, as for her kindness and her gentle
ways.

Suddenly, or so it seemed, the princess began to smile
less and less, and she became more and more melancholy.
She no longer walked in the marketplace. Her father noticed
this change in his daughter one day and began to ask,
"What is troubling you, my precious daughter?" Each time
he asked, the princess did not answer. She just sat silently
and sometimes sighed deeply.

This was a strange illness, indeed. The princess did not
get thinner, even though she did not eat. The princess did
not grow pale, even though she stayed indoors all the time.
The princess did not cry, even though her heart felt heavy,
as if there was no use in anything.

King Solomon was determined to find out what the
mysterious ailment was that afflicted his daughter. He

summoned his physicians and magicians, wizards, potion makers, and sorcerers and commanded them to solve the mystery of the illness of Princess Shloma. There was the renowned astrologer from Egypt, a little man with a hump-back; the mixer of mysterious potions from China, a long, lank man with piercing eyes; the alchemist from Arabia, a scowling man with his face almost concealed by whiskers; a Greek and a Persian and a Phoenician, each with some special knowledge and each one extremely anxious to display it. They all began to work.

While one studied the stars, another concocted a sweet-smelling fluid, a third wandered into the woods and thought deeply, a fourth made abstruse calculations with diagrams and figures, a fifth asked the princess's hand-maidens, and a sixth conceived the brilliant notion of talk-ing with the princess herself. Then they met in consultation and talked in foreign languages and pretended to under-stand one another.

One said the stars were in opposition, another said he had gazed into a crystal and had seen a glow-worm chasing a hippopotamus, which a third interpreted as meaning that the princess would die if the glow-worm won the race.

Each one had discovered a different reason for this mysterious illness. Soon, they were all trying to convince each other by shouting and stamping their feet, and no one was listening to anyone else.

Finally, the magician exclaimed in the loudest voice of all, "I understand!" Everyone stopped talking. "The princess is just tired. That is a disease which will become more popular and fashionable as the world grows older and peo-ple become richer. She is sick of being waited on hand and foot and bowed down to. Therefore, she is bored with all of this attention from us. She needs a different kind of atten-tion, since she now has reached the age of marriage."

That started them all talking at the same time again. Finally, they agreed to report to the King that the time had come for the princess to marry.

The King agreed, and messengers were sent out far and wide for the princes of the land to come to the palace. Soon

a procession of suitors for the princess's hand began to
file past the princess. They were princes of all shapes and
sizes, of all complexions and colors. Some were dressed in
magnificent clothes with jewels, others were followed by
retinues of slaves bearing gifts. When all the prospective
suitors had been inspected by the King, he said to his
daughter, "Pick the one you love best, Shloma dear."

"None," she answered.

"Then tell me what you do want," the King said with
growing impatience.

"I will not marry any man who is such a fool that he
thinks he is the only person in the world who is of any
importance," replied the princess.

"You do not regard any of these princes," said the King,
trying to find the right words, "as worthy of . . ."

"Listen, my father," interrupted Princess Shloma. "You
have always tried to make me happy, and until recently you
succeeded. I wish to obey you in all things, even in the
choice of a husband. But would you really have me marry
one of these fools? Do not be angry, father. Tell me whether
any one of them revealed a gleam of wisdom or common
sense? Were they not all just ridiculous fops? Let me give
you just a few examples.

"There was a prince who talked only of his wars. I will
not be queen in a land where people cannot live in peace.

"Then there was a second prince who boasted that he
spends all his life with his horses and dogs and falcons in
the hunting field. He knows everything about his animals,
but nothing about his people. I will not be the bride of a
prince who allows his subjects to starve while he enjoys
himself with the slaughter of wild beasts.

"A third prince talked about nothing but his jewels and
his clothes. Another prince knew exactly how many bottles
of wine he drank daily, but he could not tell me how many
schools there were in his city. And still another prince had
not the slightest notion of how the majority of his people
lived, whether by trading, or thieving, or working, or begging."

King Solomon listened intently, and he was impressed with his daughter's wisdom.

"Oh, I am tired," Princess Shloma cried out suddenly with tears in her eyes. "My father, listen. I will not be queen in a land where the King thinks the people live only to make *him* great. I shall be proud and happy to reign where the King understands that it is his duty to make his people happy and his country prosperous and peaceful."

The King left his daughter and, deeply concerned, he sought his advisors. After much mysterious whispering among themselves and consultation with some old books, the advisors informed the King that the stars foretold that Princess Shloma would marry a poor man.

King Solomon's patience was exhausted by this time. In a great rage, he told his daughter what the advisors had predicted.

Her answer was simply, "How nice."

Hearing that, the King swore he would imprison her in his fortress on a tiny island in the sea, and he gave orders at once to have the fortress furnished for his daughter.

And there she was brought secretly one night.

To her father's disappointment, she made no protest, but only said, "At last I shall be free for a while of all the absurd flummery of the palace."

The people were sad when the princess disappeared. She had been good to them. She had understood them and their needs. They did not know what had suddenly become of the princess, but they missed her. All they knew was that the King had become morose and sullen.

Strangely enough, the King began to take an interest in the poor. He began to stroll in the marketplace. He asked the people many questions: How did they earn their money? What were their occupations? Had they any pleasures? And what were their thoughts? The King's interest did make his subjects happier, and the officers of state became very busy with projects for improving trade, providing work, and educating children.

One of the King's subjects who thought deeply about many things was a young shepherd. He loved to listen to the birds chirping and to all the sounds of the fields and the forests. He seemed to understand them. He listened to the murmuring of the brook, which was like a gentle cradle song lulling him to sleep on a sunny day. He could also understand the changes of weather. When the wind howled, causing the water to dash over the rocks, he knew that was a warning that floods might come and he must move his flocks to safer ground. "I wonder," he would think to himself, "if I shall ever learn to read the written word and perhaps to write. I could then write the songs of the brook and of the birds so that others would know them, too."

One day, while he was daydreaming, he fell asleep. He slept longer than usual, and when he awoke, he was alarmed to see that the sun was about to set. Darkness was falling quickly, and he had to get his flocks home safely. All went well until he came in sight of his home. At that moment, a monstrous bird, the *ziz*, appeared in the sky, covering the sun with its enormous wings so that it was suddenly night. The *ziz* swooped down on the cows and sheep. The shepherd tried to beat off the bird with his staff. The frightened animals began to run in different directions. The *ziz*, however, was evidently determined not to be deprived of its prey. It dug its talons deep into the flanks of an ox that had stampeded in the wrong direction, lagging behind the others.

The poor animal bellowed in pain, and the shepherd, rushing to the rescue, seized the ox by the forelegs as it was being raised from the ground. Curling his leg around the slender trunk of a tree, the shepherd began a struggle with the *ziz*. The mighty bird, its eyes glowing like two lanterns, tried to strike at him with its tremendous beak.

In the darkness it missed, fortunately for the shepherd, but the thrust of the beak caught the upper part of the tree trunk, which snapped under the blow. The shepherd had to let go of the tree trunk. He still gripped the forelegs of the ox tightly. With nothing to hold it back, the *ziz* had no difficulty rising into the air. Before he could understand what was happening, the shepherd found himself high above the trees.

Higher and higher the *ziz* rose into the air, spreading its vast wings majestically, and flying silently and swiftly over the land. Since it made the shepherd dizzy to glance down at the ground far below him, he closed his eyes.

When he opened his eyes again after a while, the shepherd was horrified to see that they were now flying over the sea. With a heavy sigh, he gave himself up for lost and began to consider whether it would be better to release his hold and fall into the sea rather than be devoured by this gigantic bird.

Before he could make up his mind, the bird landed, and the shepherd was bumped down on something with such violence that for a moment he was stunned.

When he regained his senses, the shepherd saw that he was on top of a tower in the sea. Beside him was the carcass of the ox. Above them stood the *ziz*, its eyes glowing like twin fires, its beak thrust down ready to strike.

With a quick movement, the shepherd drew a knife, which he still had in his belt, and struck at the opening of the descending beak. The bird gave a shrill cry of pain as the knife pierced its tongue, and it took flight at once. So swift was its flight that, almost instantly, the *ziz* was a mere speck in the moonlit sky.

Exhausted and relieved, the shepherd slept until he was awakened by the sound of a voice. Opening his eyes, he looked up and saw a woman so beautiful that he thought he must be dreaming. He sprang to his feet and bowed.

"Who are you?" asked a surprised Princess Shloma. "And tell me how you came here with this dead ox, so far from the land and so high up as this tower in the sea?"

And the shepherd answered as in a daze, "I do not know for certain. Perhaps I am bewitched or dreaming, for I fear you will not easily believe my adventure." The shepherd then related all that had happened to him.

The princess said nothing. Instead, she motioned to the shepherd to follow her. She led him to the bath chamber. "Wash and put on these robes," she said, giving him some clean clothes. The shepherd did as he was instructed. Then the princess brought food to him, and the shepherd ate. He felt better after washing and eating. The princess kept looking at him for a long time.

"You are a very handsome man," said the princess finally.

The shepherd blushed and stammered in reply, "I thank you for these kind words."

After a while he said, a little more boldly, "Fair Lady, I do not know who you are. You have the beauty and grace of a royal person. I am only a poor shepherd."

"And may not a shepherd be handsome?" the princess replied quickly. "Tell me, who has written a law that says that only royal persons may be fair to behold? I have seen many princes who are ugly to look at."

She stopped suddenly, for she did not wish to betray her secret. They sat in a little room in the tower, unknown to the guards down below. Although the shepherd protested, the princess waited on him herself, bringing him food and large cushions on which he could rest that night.

The next morning, they climbed up to the tower together.

"I come here every morning," said the princess.

"Why?" the shepherd asked.

"To see if my husband comes," was the answer.

"Who is he?" asked the shepherd.

The princess laughed. "I do not know yet. Some mornings, when I have stood here and felt so lonely, I have made a vow to marry the first man who comes here."

The shepherd was silent. Then he looked directly into the eyes of the princess and said, "You have told me that *I* am the *first* man who has come here. I feel that I must tell you how much I love you. I don't know who you are or why you are here—and I don't care. Let us marry and become husband and wife."

The princess gave him her hand. "It is so ordained," she said. And so they pledged themselves one to the other.

"We cannot remain here forever," said the princess. "Husband of my heart's choice, can you think of a way to escape?"

Looking at the carcass of the ox, the shepherd exclaimed, "I have a plan! Listen my love, it is most probable that the monster bird that brought me here will return for his meal. He can then carry us away. If the heavens approve, it shall be so."

That very night, the *ziz* returned and feasted on the ox. While it was satisfying its hunger and not easily distracted, the shepherd managed to attach strong ropes to the legs of the *ziz*. To the ropes he then attached a large basket in which he and his bride made themselves comfortable with silken cushions.

Toward morning, the *ziz* rose slowly into the air, and the princess and the shepherd clutched each other tightly as the basket spun around and around. The giant did not seem to notice its burden at all, and after a while it began a swift flight over the sea.

After many hours, a city became visible, and the shepherd could even see the excitement caused by the appearance of the *ziz*. The bird was getting tired and, having at last noticed the weight tied to its feet, was seeking a way to get rid of it.

Flying low, the *ziz* dashed the basket against a tower. The cords snapped, and the basket rested on the parapet of the tower. Free of its burden, the bird flew swiftly away.

Just as the shepherd and his bride managed to get out of the basket, armed guards appeared. At the sight of the princess, they lowered their weapons.

"Inform my father that I have returned," the princess instructed them, and the guards immediately ran to do her bidding.

"Do you know where you are?" whispered the shepherd in surprise.

"Yes, this is the king's palace," she replied.

Soon the King appeared, and with a joyful laugh he embraced his daughter.

"I am very happy to see you again, my daughter," he cried. "I ask your pardon for leaving you out in the sea fortress. But I see you have managed well. Come and tell me all that has happened."

Turning to the young man at her side, the King asked, "Who is this?"

"My husband and your son-in-law, father," answered the princess joyfully.

"From which kingdom do you come, and are you a prince there?" asked the King.

"He is a prince among men," replied the princess quickly, "a man without riches who comes from the people and will teach us their needs and how to rule them." The princess and the shepherd exchanged smiles.

The King gave a nod of consent, for at last he understood the wisdom of his daughter. He blessed the young couple and ordered a great celebration. Then he appointed them to rule over a province, and there they settled down to work together to make everybody happy and prosperous.

And they all lived in peace.

Solomon's Way of
Getting to the Truth

When Solomon had a choice of what he could ask of God, he asked not for long life or riches or honor, but for "an understanding heart" so he could serve others through wisdom and righteous behavior. Feeling the great responsibility of his powerful position, Solomon's thoughts were not centered on himself, but rather on the people. Solomon had a great knowledge of science and philosophy, and especially Torah. But while he had intellectual knowledge, which Solomon believed generated wisdom, he chose to ask God for an "understanding heart," which would give him compassion and make him sensitive to the people's needs. His goal was to acquire both book knowledge and insight into people. (King David, his father, differed in his opinions about wisdom. David felt that the heart was the main seat of wisdom because it combined feeling *and* will).

King Solomon legends are filled with *hokhme*, wisdom. Whenever there was a serious problem in need of solution, Solomon was the one to turn to because of his knowledge, his wisdom, and his understanding heart. Very often, Solomon appears in Jewish folktales as a judge, and his most famous case, which is mentioned in the Bible (I Kings 3:15; 4:1), concerns two women who appear before him with one living child and one dead one, each one claiming to be the mother of the living child. Solomon's understanding of human nature allowed him to test the women's reactions and arrive at a correct decision. While still a youth, when his father King David was a judge, Solomon often showed his brilliance and resourcefulness in difficult cases and taught many a lesson, even to his father.

There are also a number of stories in which David and Solomon disagree over how to handle a case. Their differing views over the source of wisdom and over divergent approaches to resolving disputes suggest that there may have been a father-son rivalry going on.

Many are the stories about Solomon's settling of a quarrel, proving true ownership of treasure or money, or in one case a sack of flour, solving riddles that tested his wisdom, whether posed by King Hiram of Tyre or by the Queen of Sheba, and especially solving many problems in building the Temple, which had to be built without using tools of iron (which symbolize war).

This tale, which contains a story within a story, is a two-part parable and has been told in many lands where Jews have lived, among them Kurdistan, Iran, and Turkey, where many versions can be found. The Kurdish variant, taken from *A Tale for Each Month 1971* is included in the Israeli Folktale Archives, IFA 9122.

An early version of this tale, in *Asseret Hadibberot* (*Midrash Decalogue*, 15th century), is a commentary on the Eighth Commandment, "Thou Shalt Not Steal." There are variants in *Rabbenu Nissim* 38 and in Jellinek (1853–1878). The tale contains type A-T 926E and has a somewhat similar parallel in the exemplum in Gaster (1924) (426).

 long time ago, three merchants were on their way to conduct some business in Jerusalem. Each merchant carried with him a good sum of money. One evening, they found themselves near a forest. Since robbers roamed the woods in those days, they knew someone might attack them. So they looked for a place to hide their money.

Nearby, the merchants found a cemetery, and one of them said, "Here, under this gravestone we can hide our money, and no one but the three of us will know it is here." And so they hid the money carefully and then went to the next field to sleep.

In the middle of the night, one of the merchants got up and stole the money, thinking to himself, "No one will know it's me. I'll hide it in the meantime under another gravestone and return here sometime later." Feeling very clever about the whole thing, the thieving merchant went back to sleep.

In the morning, when they awoke, the three travelers went quickly to the gravestone where they had hidden their gold coins. When they uncovered the hiding place, they found that the money was gone. Each of the three began to accuse the others of stealing the money, but each one swore that he was innocent. They began to argue and shout until finally one of them said: "Let us take the matter to King

Solomon, the wise King. He will be able to unravel this mystery."

And so they continued on their way to Jerusalem and brought their story of what had happened to King Solomon.

King Solomon listened attentively. After a long silence he said, "I have heard your case and must consider this carefully before pronouncing my sentence on the guilty man. In the meantime, I see that you are clever and successful merchants and would ask your advice on a certain matter." And Solomon told them this story.

There once were two wealthy friends and each one had a child; one had a son and the other a daughter. While their children were infants, the friends betrothed the two toddlers to each other in the expectation that, when they reached the proper age, they would marry each other. Unfortunately, the parents died before that time and left 300,000 gold pieces to each of the children. The young woman was endowed with all good virtues, but the young man was a gambler and soon wasted all his inheritance.

When they reached the age of marriage, the young woman sent a message to the young man, her betrothed, saying, "This is the time for our marriage," and she asked him to prepare himself as the betrothal agreement provided.

The young man, however, sent back a message: "I am now poor and do not wish to drag you into poverty. Therefore, I renounce my right to marry you. Find someone who will be worthy of you."

"Well," sighed the young maiden, "I can't force him to marry me."

In a short time, she found a young student, a poor young man, whom she loved very much. Being an honest young woman, she said to this scholar, "I must tell you that my parents wished me to marry their friends' son, and we were pledged to each other. So before I can marry you, I must go to my betrothed and ask him three times if he will obey our parents' will and marry me. If he refuses, then I will be free to stand under the wedding canopy with you." The young scholar happily agreed to this condition.

The maiden put on her finest velvet and silk clothes and went to her betrothed. "Do not break the will of our parents who wished us to marry," she said to him. "As for money, have no worries; I have enough for us both, and we shall live comfortably, I promise you."

"No, no," answered the young man. "I am a spendthrift, and I cannot change my ways. Your money would be used up in a short time, that's all I can promise you. You will be unhappy with me. I cannot marry you."

The young woman left him and, eight days later, she returned wearing clothes of silver and gold. Again she tried to persuade him to obey his parents' will. And again he refused.

When she went to see her betrothed a third time, after waiting eight days, she wore diamonds and pearls. In answer to her plea, the young man said, "May God bless you and may you have great happiness. Marry the man you love. I cannot allow our marriage; it would only bring you misery. I release you from any obligation."

On the way home, the young woman's carriage was attacked by robbers. The robbers were about to steal the diamonds and pearls she was wearing, when the maiden explained that she was on her way to her wedding. And she told them about the betrothal arranged by her parents and about her new bridegroom.

"Well, in that case," said one of the robbers, "everyone has acted so honorably—the betrothed for giving up his right to his promised bride and the bridegroom who would not marry a woman betrothed to another until she was free. We, too, will not take your jewels. Instead, we return them to you as our wedding gift." And the robbers sent the bride off in peace.

"Now," said King Solomon, "what I am asking you to decide is which of these persons acted most nobly? Which performed the greater *mitzva?*

The first merchant said, "I believe that the noblest of them all was the young man who had the chance to marry such a desirable young woman but refused so as not to burden her with a life of misery. Why, he performed the greatest *mitzva*."

The second merchant disagreed: "The young woman did the most honorable deed by attempting to obey her parents' will. She tried three times to persuade her betrothed to marry her. Even though she loved the scholar more, she honored her parents."

"*No, no, no,*" cried the third merchant with great impatience. "It was obviously the robbers who were the noblest of the three, for they sent this young maiden off without even taking her jewels when they would have stolen a copper penny from their own grandmothers. What fools!"

Then King Solomon pointed to the third merchant and said: "You are the guilty one! You revealed how greedy you are for the jewels you never even saw. How much more, then, must you have desired the gold you did see. Arrest the thief!"

The third merchant was arrested, confessed to the crime, and was sentenced according to the law of the land.

Three Wise Sayings

Advice handed down from generation to generation, whether in the form of a proverb, a maxim, or a story, usually turns out to be good advice, what some may call "common sense." In this legend, King Solomon offers three pieces of advice in the form of three sayings.

The first, to journey only during daylight, is advice Jacob gives to Joseph when he is sent to report on his brothers' wellbeing. According to a *midrash*, "Jacob dismissed Joseph with the injunction that he journey only by daylight." Later in that same story, Joseph dismisses his brothers "as soon as the morning was light," for it is a good rule to "leave a city after sunrise, and enter a city before sundown."

The second rule of conduct is a variant of the proverb, "He who throws himself against a wave is overthrown by it."

The third counsel is one I have changed. In the original version, Solomon's advice is "Never betray a secret to a woman, even to your wife." There are other folktales that include this advice. After the husband receives some "secret" wisdom, he is told not to reveal it to his wife, which causes his wife to nag it out of him, always producing a calamity for both in the end.

I found myself troubled by this approach. It is true that Solomon wrote (if indeed it was Solomon) in Ecclesiastes, "I find more bitter than death the woman, whose heart is snares and nets, and her hands as bands, whoso pleaseth God shall escape from her; but the sinner shall be taken by her" (7:26), and "one man among a thousand have I found, but a virtuous woman among all those have I not found" (7:28). On the other hand, Solomon wrote Song of Songs, a love story that celebrates a woman's emotions. The woman says, "This is my beloved, and this is my friend" (5:16), and "I am my beloved's, and my beloved is mine" (6:3).

Surely Solomon believed in women's good feelings and intelligence. He certainly had models of brilliant women in his mother Bathsheba and his friend the Queen of Sheba. And so I am more optimistic than Solomon was in his later days. Since he understood human nature, he would have known that a man who seeks wisdom would have chosen a wife wisely, and the reverse would also be true.

This story of three wise counsels of King Solomon is in Talmudic legends, a medieval compilation of tales about the wisdom of Solomon, known as *Meshalim Shel Shelomo (Parables of King Solomon)*, as well as in medieval Latin legends. Since Solomon was regarded as the archetype of the wise judge, many tellers of wisdom tales incorporated him into their stories.

This tale contains motifs similar to those found in A-T 910B, especially TMI J21.5 Do not leave main highway, and other pieces of advice found under TMI J21 Good Councils. Compare the variant of this telling with IFA 8608.

ing Solomon was famous throughout the world for his wisdom and his shrewd judgments. Many came to his palace seeking to become wise, perhaps even as wise as Solomon himself.

Once, three brothers came to Solomon and asked:

"How can we become as wise as you, Oh King? May we stay here and serve you and learn?"

The King agreed but only on condition that they stay for three years. The brothers accepted the condition, and so they sat near the King whenever he decided the many cases brought to him and watched him discuss the many complex points of Torah with learned men.

Three years passed, but the three brothers were disappointed. They felt they had not grown wise. One day, they said to the King:

"Your Majesty, we have decided to return home to our wives, since our stay here has not profited us at all."

"Very well," replied the King. "In that case, I release you from my service. Since you are leaving, I offer you each 100 gold coins —— " and then the King paused. "Or shall I offer you each three wise sayings? Which shall it be?"

The King waited as each brother considered the choice, and then each brother, in turn, asked for the gold coins.

They took their horses and rode away from the palace. When they had gone a short distance, the youngest brother regretted his choice and he said, "Brothers, I must return to King Solomon. I don't want the gold. I would rather have the wisdom he offered. When he offered us money, my head was dazzled by the gold. Come, let us return to the palace to ask for his wise words. What else did we work and hope for these three years?"

But his brothers insisted that they continue on their way home. "Give up 100 gold coins for three sayings?" they cried. "Give us your gold and we'll tell you three sayings too!" They laughed mockingly as they rode off.

The youngest brother quickly returned to the palace and was brought before King Solomon.

"O King, I came here to gain wisdom and not gold. Therefore, I regret that I did not accept your wise sayings in the first place. Please take back the coins you have given me and give me your good counsel instead."

The King was delighted at his request, and he answered, "With pleasure! And here are the three wise sayings for you to heed:

"When you travel, journey only by daylight, and find your place to sleep before darkness falls.

"When you find a river swollen with water, wait and do not cross.

"When you meet your wife, confide in her as a friend."

The youngest brother thanked King Solomon and sped off to catch up with his brothers. But when they met again, the youngest brother said nothing about what Solomon had told him.

The three rode along until they came to an inn. Although it was still daylight, the youngest brother, remembering Solomon's advice, said, "Let's remain here for the night."

The brothers, however, protested, saying, "It will still be light for several more hours. Why waste the time when we could be traveling farther. Is this the kind of wise advice you received from Solomon?" they taunted their younger brother. "Stay here if you wish, but we will continue on our journey."

The youngest brother stayed at the inn, and when

darkness fell, he was warm and comfortable and ate a good dinner, while his horse was cared for and had plenty to eat and drink as well.

Meanwhile, the two brothers continued up the mountain when suddenly there arose a snowstorm. The brothers were trapped among the ice-covered rocks and froze to death.

At dawn the next day, the youngest brother set out to continue his journey home. When he reached the mountain pass he discovered his two brothers' bodies. He wept when he saw what had happened to them, recited the mourner's prayer, and tried to bury them as best as he could in the frozen ground, But before he buried them, he took the gold they had received from the King.

When he reached the other side of the mountain, he saw in the distance a river he would have to cross. The river was overflowing, and the waters were rushing and swirling and flooding the banks.

Once again remembering Solomon's advice, the youngest brother decided to remain high on the mountainside and wait until the waters receded.

As he looked down, he saw two men on horseback driving several heavily laden mules toward the river. He tried to shout down to them, "Wait. Don't cross. Stop! It's dangerous." But his voice blended with the wind and was swallowed up by the roar of the waters. Soon the men and the beasts, struggling against the swollen river with all their might, were drowned.

When the waters returned to their usual level, then, and only then, did the youngest brother begin to cross the river. On the way, he found the drowned animals with bags of gold loaded on their backs. He unstrapped the bags and took the gold with him. And he continued on his journey home.

After three days, he returned home, wealthy and in good health. He embraced his wife and, now for the third time remembering Solomon's advice, told his good wife everything that had happened to him and to his brothers.

The brothers' wives soon came to greet him, and they asked eagerly, "But where are your brothers? Why have they not come home with gold as you have?" (For the two wives had seen the many bags of gold he had brought on his horse.)

He was then forced to tell them what had happened to his brothers, their husbands. When they heard how their husbands had died, the women shouted, "You murdered them for the gold! That gold belongs to us. We will drag you to a court of law to be tried and hanged."

"No, no, dear sisters," cried the youngest brother's wife. "My husband is innocent of your charges. He did not kill anyone. He is alive only because he followed King Solomon's good counsel."

The two sisters-in-law became even more outraged and shouted, "Naturally you will take his side so you two can have all the gold to yourselves. Solomon's good counsel, indeed! Perhaps the advice was to follow his brothers and kill them."

"Very well," said the young wife. "Let us go to King Solomon's court for a trial. The King is known for his fairness and honesty. He can see into all our hearts and thoughts."

Hearing that, the two sisters-in-law agreed. They went to the court of King Solomon.

When Solomon heard the case and recognized the youngest brother as the one who had chosen to accept his offer of the three wise sayings, he announced:

"All that this man has told you is true. Your husbands chose the gold. No one murdered them for it. They did not understand the rules of nature and scoffed at my offer of wisdom. The youngest brother asked for the three pieces of advice that helped save his life. However, the gold I gave to each of your husbands shall now be yours."

And Solomon added, "Remember, always seek wisdom, for wisdom is more precious than gold."

Solomon's Gift

The hoopoe bird was called "the wild cock" in the Talmud and identified with the biblical *dookhifat* (Deuteronomy 4:18). This bird with the bright red crest of feathers on its head was the guardian of the *Shamir*, the tiny miraculous worm that was created in the twilight of the sixth day and could cut through rocks, a feat that Solomon made use of when he was building the Temple in Jerusalem. All this is according to legend.

In a description of the hoopoe I found in a fanciful article, Barkton (1937) (identified only as the *nom de plume* of an American rabbi), quotes "the words of one authority" (with no further citation):

> About the size of a thrush, with a long, pointed and slightly arched bill, its head and neck are of a golden buff, the head adorned by a large erectile crest which begins to rise from the forehead and consists of broad feathers, gradually increasing in length, tipped with black, and having a subterminal bar of yellowish white. [p. 157]

This description corresponds to that found in serious books, such as Bertel Bruun's *Birds of Europe*. No doubt the hoopoe got its English name from its characteristic call, "hoo-poo-poo."

This tale is similar to many creation myths explaining natural phenomena, for example, the American Indian myth, "How the Tanager Got Its Colors."

Like many biblical characters whose image is changed in Jewish folklore, the hoopoe has been endowed with special qualities by Jewish folklore. The Bible describes the hoopoe as an unclean bird (not kosher) and one with a strong putrid odor. In our folktales, however, it is an arrogant but helpful and trustworthy bird.

In this story Solomon is once again the great and wise judge. Owing to his folkloristic gift for communicating with animals, Solomon becomes the main character in this tale, which is possibly derived from Arabic rather than Jewish sources. There is also a version of the story of the hoopoe bird written by Hayyim Nahman Bialik.

The hoopoe bird continues to live as a native bird in Israel, and it does, indeed, sport a marvelous crest of feathers to this day.

 wish I had all the gold in the world, and especially gold hair," I once said to my mother. And do you know what my mother answered? "Let me tell you a story."

"When I was a child," my mother said, "I too had long dark brown hair, just like you. My mother would comb it and braid it into two long braids. One day as she was braiding my hair, I said aloud, 'How I wish I had hair made of pure spun gold. How wonderful that would be. I would be the most beautiful person in the world! And everyone would admire and envy me!'

"Then my mother stopped braiding my hair and said, 'I'll tell you a story.' And this is the story my mother heard from *her* mother."

There once lived a great and wise King, and his name was King Solomon. Solomon was known as the King of Peace, and because of that he was given the great honor to build the Temple in Jerusalem. His father, King David, could not build the Temple because he had fought many wars. Only Solomon, a man of peace, could build such a Temple. Well, he built a beautiful Temple, but it took so many years and involved so many details, so many worries: how to get the cedars from Lebanon, how to cut the rock without using tools of iron, how to get enough gold, and on and on. There were many, many problems and difficulties.

Well, you can imagine how tired the King was when the work was completed. So Solomon decided to find a place in the country where he could be by himself, talk to his friends, the animals (for he knew the language of all the birds and beasts), be able to refresh himself and then return to the palace with a clear mind and a stronger spirit.

He found such a place in the country, but it took days to travel there by horseback. Solomon was an extraordinary man, and he did not travel the way others did. Besides he needed the time for rest, and *quiet*, not for traveling. So Solomon got on the back of his mighty eagle and flew to this place in one hour's time. Then, after refreshing himself in the quiet country air, he returned to the palace, again by flying on his eagle.

One day, he was flying to the country place when he began to feel ill and became dizzy. It was a hot sunny day without a cloud in the sky, and since the sun's rays were making him feel more and more ill, Solomon was afraid he would fall from the eagle.

Flying in the distance was a flock of hoopoe birds. When the King of the Hoopoes saw that Solomon was in trouble, he gave a signal, and the birds understood what to do. They closed ranks and their wings overlapped, forming a huge canopy over Solomon and thus protecting him from the blazing hot sun.

In a short time, Solomon felt better because of the cool shade. Then he thanked the birds and said, "You have saved my life, and for that I thank you. To show my gratitude I will grant anything you ask of me. But whatever you decide, you must all agree upon the same thing. Come to me in three days and tell me your request."

The hoopoe birds gathered and began discussing, arguing, debating, deliberating as to what they could ask of the great King Solomon. What could they all agree on?

"Seeds for the rest of our lives," one hoopoe shouted.

"Large bird houses for us all," said another.

"Beautiful feathers," another volunteered.

"Lots of baby hoopoes," still another added.

"To be the smartest birds in the world," a small hoopoe sang out.

"Gold," one hoopoe cried.

Soon all were talking at once and were shouting, hitting, and shoving.

Finally, a strong voice called out: "Hoopoes, Solomon wears a crown of gold. We, too, should have a crown of gold! That way we would be rich and beautiful, and everyone could actually see how smart we are."

All the birds agreed that what they would ask of the great King Solomon would be a crown of gold.

On the third day, as Solomon had commanded, the King of the Hoopoes and his advisors arrived at the palace. Solomon greeted them and thanked them again for coming to his aid.

"And now what request do you have?" Solomon asked.

"Your Majesty, we ask to have a crown of gold," answered the King Hoopoe.

Solomon thought for a moment and slowly, with great concern, replied: "King Hoopoe, are you certain that that is what you *all* wish for?"

"Yes, your Majesty," said the hoopoe.

"Have you discussed this *carefully*?" asked King Solomon.

"Yes, your Majesty," said the hoopoe.

"Have you *all* agreed on this *together*—have you voted unanimously?" again insisted Solomon.

"Yes, your Majesty, we have," said the hoopoe.

But Solomon was not so certain, and he said, "Perhaps you have not considered this seriously enough," and Solomon watched their faces. "But I will grant your request since you ask this of me. But should you ever reconsider or be in trouble, come to me and I will help you."

When the hoopoe birds left Solomon's palace and rejoined the other birds, they all found to their delight the promised crown of gold on their heads. They were overjoyed. When they flew over lakes and streams and rivers, they saw the glitter of the golden crowns and they flew in circles to keep admiring themselves. They couldn't fly as high as before, because of the golden crowns, but they didn't mind that. They could see themselves better when they flew lower anyway.

The Queen Hoopoe stayed on a low branch overhanging a lake, and she never tired of looking at herself all day long.

"Oh, how beautiful I am with this golden crown!" she cried. "I am the most beautiful of all the birds anywhere in this world! Oh, how they must all envy me, those poor birds who have only feathers on their heads. . . ." And on and on she would chatter and laugh.

One day, a fisherman came to the lake to fish—but when he saw the Queen Hoopoe bird, he wanted to catch her, for her golden crown would bring him more money than any amount of fish he could hope to trap in his net in a week. Slowly, he spread his net under the tree branch. Then he carefully placed bowls of water around the net.

When the Queen Hoopoe saw her sparkling golden crown glitter in the bowls of water, she flew down to drink. Just then, the fisherman grabbed the net and trapped the Queen Hoopoe in it. He chopped off her head and took off the golden crown.

Wherever he showed it, other fishermen and hunters wanted such a crown. So they started hunting for the hoopoe birds, with nets, bows and arrows, and even ropes.

When the King Hoopoe saw that his birds were not safe anywhere and that they were being killed, he flew to Solomon.

"King Solomon, save my birds, for they are being killed because of the golden crown," cried King Hoopoe.

When Solomon heard this, he answered, "I was afraid that your request would bring you trouble. After all, a golden crown does not belong on a bird. But since you had saved my life, I will help you this time too."

So what did Solomon do? He turned the golden crowns into crests of feathers, beautiful and colorful feathers—like a regal bird crown. And when the hunters saw the crest of feathers, they stopped hunting the birds because they didn't want feathers. And so the hoopoe birds lived and had more baby hoopoes. And they continue to live even today in the Land of Israel.

When my mother finished telling me the story she had heard from *her* mother, she said, "Your grandmother would turn to me and ask, 'Nu, my child, would you still rather have spun gold hair?' So I will ask you the same question: "Would you still rather have golden hair?"
And can you guess what my answer was?

The Boiled Eggs

The original version of this story shows the greater wisdom of young Solomon over that of his father King David in resolving a dispute about the price of borrowed eggs. The central motif of the Boiled Eggs (TMI J.1191.2) is a well-loved feature of many stories from all over the Mediterranean world, and the judge is not always Solomon. One such version is the Portuguese folktale called "An Expensive Omelette." The story in this form is A-T 920A, sections II and III.

This legend of Solomon, found in Ginzberg (1909–1938) and in Gaster (1924) (in two different variants), has fascinated me because of the cleverness of the counterargument. Other versions can be found in Eisenstein (1915) and in Bin Gorion (1976).

I have transposed the location of the story to a *shtetl*, but boiled eggs are still boiled eggs whether found in Solomonic legends or in your home today. Judge for yourself.

ne early morning, the *balagola* was driving his wagon through the countryside. He had just taken a customer to the train station and was returning home. While he rode, he spoke aloud, as was his habit — to himself, to his old horse, and always to God.

As he was driving by a small inn, Motl realized he was very hungry. He had left his house before sunrise, rushing to make sure his customer would not be late for his train. After tying his horse to a post and making sure the animal had some hay and water, Motl entered the inn for breakfast. He ate four boiled eggs with a thick slice of bread and butter, and drank a glass of sweet tea, expertly breaking the piece of sugar between his teeth. But when Motl reached into his pocket for his change purse, he realized he had lost his money through a hole in his pocket. As a result, he could not pay for his breakfast.

"I will stop by when I come this way again," Motl promised the innkeeper. What could the innkeeper do but trust Motl to keep his word for half a ruble?

Months went by and Motl still did not have any occasion to drive by that inn.

In time, he forgot about his debt.

As it happened, Motl decided to go to America, where so many of his relatives had gone. They had written to him about America in such glowing terms: "a golden land," "a place where the streets are paved with gold," "a land of golden opportunity." So Motl went to America too. And he had good fortune, because in no time at all, he made a great deal of money.

With all his wealth, Motl still longed for his home in the old country. So one day, Motl decided to return to his village.

When Motl arrived at the train station in his village, it was already Friday afternoon. He hired a *balagola* to drive him to his former home. On the way, just as he was passing the inn, he suddenly remembered about the breakfast he had eaten there several years before. He quickly shouted to the *balagola*, "Stop here for a moment. I must repay a debt I owe."

Motl entered the inn and immediately recognized the innkeeper, although the innkeeper did not recognize Motl, who had now become a rich man and dressed like one. He looked like a real nobleman.

Motl approached the innkeeper. "I have come to pay my debt for a breakfast of four boiled eggs I ate here a few years ago," he said. "At that time, I had no money and so now I want to pay what I owe you." Motl took out his purse and handed the innkeeper half a ruble.

"A half ruble!" exclaimed the innkeeper. "What do you mean by paying only half a ruble? Let me give you a complete accounting of what you owe me," said the innkeeper. To himself the innkeeper thought greedily, "Here is a way to make some extra money from this newly wealthy peasant who wears such fine clothes."

"Let me see," continued the innkeeper aloud, "four eggs would have hatched four chickens, and they would each have hatched sixteen chickens each, which makes sixty-four. They in turn would have hatched 1,024 chickens, each producing 4,096 chickens. . . ."

The innkeeper went on rapidly calculating the amount

until he finally said, "and so you owe me not a half ruble, my friend, but 16,285 rubles."

"What? How is that possible?" cried Motl. "Do you take me for a fool? How can I pay that amount when I don't even have that much with me?"

The innkeeper insisted on payment or else he would call the police and have Motl arrested for not paying his bill.

Since it was almost Shabbos, and it was too late to go for a policeman in the next village, the innkeeper asked the *shammes* of the *shul* to put Motl up as a guest until after Shabbos, when they would go to the judge's house to decide the case.

As you can imagine, this Shabbos was not as joyful as Motl had expected. He tried to enter into the Shabbos spirit, but he was not able to forget, even for the day, his outrage over the injustice of the innkeeper's demands.

By the afternoon, the caretaker's young and clever daughter Doba-Leya could see there was something bothering their Shabbos guest, and she asked Motl what was troubling him. As they sat in the little cottage drinking a glass of tea, Motl told her the whole story. Doba-Leya listened and replied, "You are right to feel upset. But don't worry any longer, for I have a plan." She smiled reassuringly at Motl.

The next day, the innkeeper and Motl drove in a carriage to the judge's house. As the judge listened to the innkeeper's case, about how much Motl owed him for the four boiled eggs, the door opened and in came Doba-Leya carrying a sack filled with roasted chestnuts.

"Here they are," she said abruptly to the innkeeper, handing him the sack. "I will begin planting tomorrow."

The innkeeper, surprised, exclaimed, "What's this? What are you planting?" The innkeeper quickly opened the sack and burst into loud laughter. "Oh, this is a good one! Do you take me for a fool? These chestnuts are boiled, you foolish girl. Chestnut trees don't grow from cooked chestnuts!"

"So they don't," answered Doba-Leya, "but neither can boiled eggs be hatched!"

The judge smiled and agreed. "All that Motl owes is half a ruble for the breakfast of four boiled eggs."

And that is all Motl paid the innkeeper.

The innkeeper's reputation for greed spread, and no one ever stopped at the inn again.

The Bird's Wisdom

Wisdom stories have been part not only of the Jewish heritage, but also of other cultures. There is a web of translations, adaptations, and variants crisscrossing the continents. So many tales have been borrowed and transformed that it is difficult to know the origins of some stories. What is more important is that the tales always retain their original bit of wisdom—if we can find it.

This tale, A-T 150 "Advice of the Fox (Bird)," is known all over Europe and Asia and is perhaps best known from the forms found as fables. The Greek verse version by Babrius tells the same story with a wolf and a fox instead of a man and a bird and is listed in Perry (1952) as number 159. The version with the bird, usually a nightingale and often called Philomela, is first known in Europe in the collection of Odo of Cheriton (12th century), and from there found its way into the canon of *Aesopica* throughout Europe and the East (it is listed in Perry [1952] as number 627). The motifs in the story: K604 Man releases bird if the latter will give him three counsels, J21.12 Rue not a thing that is past, J21.13 Never believe that which is beyond belief, and J21.14 Never try to reach the unattainable, all of which counsels are proved wise by experience, are found in earlier forms as early as the *Jatakas*, stories in oral tradition connected with the birth of the Gautama the Buddha, but which were in oral tradition almost certainly before. Other versions are listed in Campbell's (1960) "The Three Teachings of the Bird," and other studies are listed under the tale type index and the fable index in Carnes (1985). As a teaching tale, it is to be found in Jacobs (1966), Benfy (1859), and *The Arabian Nights*. It was eventually translated into many languages, especially during the Middle Ages, and found its way into Jewish oral sources.

Sometimes, the bird is a nightingale or a quail or just "a wise Bird." Its treasure is a jewel or pearl as big as an ostrich egg, or an eagle egg, or a goose egg. In Jewish lore, the bird knows the seventy languages of mankind, a common Jewish motif. (See "Kindness Rewarded.")

One version, "The Three Counsels of the Cock" (IFA 7663), was collected by Zvi Moshe Haimovitz from Yerahmiel Feler (Cheichel 1968). There are variants in *Haggadot Ketuot* (1923), in Ginzberg and colleagues (1912–1922), in *Ben Hamelekh Vehanatzir* (1557), and in Gaster (1924). There are also two versions in Bin Gorion (1976).

The three wise sayings that the bird teaches the prince are, indeed, good counsel. If only we could remember and apply them.

 proud young prince was walking in the palace garden early one morning. He admired the cedar and cypress trees standing guard like royal servants over the olive trees, the pomegranate trees and the other blossoming fruit trees. Passing by the flowerbeds, he noted a great buzz of activity: the bees, the butterflies, the insects, were busily flitting from flower to flower.

The prince was enjoying all of this when *suddenly*, as he turned down another path of this wondrous garden, he saw on a low branch of a pomegranate tree the most exquisite bird he had ever seen. In fact, he had never seen a bird like this one before. It was a small bird, bearing a crest of feathers that reflected the colors surrounding it—the blue of the sky, the white of the clouds, the green of the leaves, the orange-red of the flower, the wine-red of the fruit.

"Ah," thought the prince, "this crest will surely make a perfect feather in my cap. I must have it, for it is a royal crest and everyone will admire it but no one else will have one like it." Standing under the tree, the prince reached up quick-as-lightning and grabbed the little bird, holding it in a fierce grasp.

The bird, trembling, as you can imagine, began to speak. "Do not kill me, gentle Prince. After all, if you kill me only for my crest of feathers, all you will have is a feather that can blow away in the wind. But if you let me live, I can give you something more useful and longer-lasting than a feather." Struggling for a little more air, the bird continued, "Since I know seventy languages, I have stored in me many worthy thoughts and wise counsels that have been passed along for generations. I can teach you something that you can use for the rest of your life, but only if you will set me *free.*"

The prince, hearing this, replied, "Very well, my handsome little bird. I am curious enough to heed you." And the prince loosened his grip on the captive bird. "Teach me your secrets first, wise one, then I *will* set you free."

"Listen well," said the bird, "for here are three rules of conduct that will be a good guide throughout your life. Guard them, and they will serve you well.

The first one is, "Never regret what you have done."
The second one is, "Do not seek what is unattainable."
The third rule is, "Do not believe what is impossible to believe."

"Remember them well, and you will thank me for these words. They are more precious than treasure."

Satisfied with the bargain, the prince released the bird as he had promised. But no sooner had the bird flown to a high branch of a nearby tree, when it sang out, "Fool of the world that you are, my prince! You let me go free, but you have no idea what you lost by doing so! But now it is too late!"

Confused, the prince shouted, "What do you mean, *lost*? Explain yourself, you arrogant bird!"

"Why my prince, if you had killed me as you had planned to do in the first place," said the bird, "you would have found a large pearl, as big as an ostrich egg, inside me. Then you would have had not only your desired feather, but a good fortune to spend besides."

Regretting that he had released the bird, the prince said, "Sweet little bird, beautiful bird, come down to me, dear little bird. I am sorry we could not talk more so that I could better *understand* what you were trying to teach me. I need to learn more wisdom from you. Come to me, and I will offer you my sweetest fruit and berries and a marvelous place to live in. I shall guard you like the apple of my eye. My word is my pledge, gentle bird." The prince said all this in a sweet and soothing voice, hoping the bird would be beguiled by his words.

"Oh no, my prince," said the bird. "Come to you? That I will not do. But you have forgotten my advice much too quickly. My advice to you was not to regret anything you have done, and already you are regretting giving me my freedom."

With a burst of anger, the prince began to climb up the tree as the bird flew to a still higher branch. Suddenly, as the prince climbed higher, he fell, broke his legs, and was in great pain.

The bird flew closer and again called out, in a mocking tone, "Dear prince, I taught you that you should not seek what is unattainable, and yet you tried to climb up this tree to capture me again. And finally, listen well, my prince, you were given the good counsel not to believe what is not worthy to believe. Is it possible for a pearl the size of an ostrich egg to be in a small bird's body, a body that fits in the palm of your hand? So next time my prince, be less foolish and heed well the lessons I have taught you."

The little bird nodded its head, forming an arc with its regal crest, and it flew away—far away. It was never again seen in that garden, no matter how much the prince searched for the wise little bird.

Wisdom for Sale

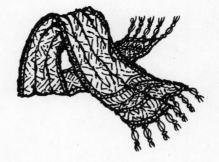

As a child, I loved to hear the legends "David and the Frog" and "David and the Spider," in which King David learns that everything God has created—even the croaking bullfrog and the web-spinning spider—is unique and precious—that everything in our world is beautiful, after all. The second wise saying in "Wisdom for Sale" echoes the lesson I learned from the King David legends.

As for the third saying, that recalls my mother's warning about restraining one's anger. The story she used to drive home that warning appears in the introduction to this book.

"Wisdom for Sale" appeared in *The Jewish Child* in 1915 but, as with any folktale, I have changed it in the retelling.

n a small village, in a certain country, there once lived a husband and wife. Although they worked very hard, there was never enough food, never enough money for clothes, and certainly never enough for *tzedaka*; there were so many charity funds in the village—for the poor, for penniless brides, for the old, for the synagogue.

Early one morning, the husband decided to journey far away from home and try to earn enough money so that when he returned in a year or two, they would have a more comfortable life and perhaps even have enough for *tzedaka*.

And so he traveled and worked, worked and traveled farther and farther from home. Finally, after eighteen years of hard work, he had saved three bags full of money—one filled with gold coins, one with silver coins, and one with copper coins—and he started on his return home.

On the way, he came to a town where a fair was under way. "Perhaps I will be able to buy something for my wife," he thought. So he began to walk through the fair in search of an unusual gift. He examined all kinds of objects and listened to the various merchants sing the praises of their wares, but he found nothing that pleased him.

As he was about to leave the fair grounds, the man noticed an old woman sitting quietly, with a large, beautifully woven shawl on her lap.

"That shawl pleases me," said the man. "How much does it cost?"

"No, no, this shawl is not for sale," answered the woman.

"What, then, do you sell? Are you not a merchant too?" asked the man.

"I am a merchant, but I sell something unusual—not the customary fare, for not everyone wants to buy what I sell," replied the old woman, smiling.

"You speak in riddles, good woman," said the man. "But I am looking for the unusual to bring as a gift to my wife. So perhaps I will be the right customer for you."

"In that case, I will tell you. I sell wise sayings," the old woman said.

"Wise sayings?" asked the man in surprise. "And how much do you charge for this wisdom?"

"A bag of copper coins," answered the old woman.

Fascinated by what he had heard, the man handed the bag of copper coins to the old woman and said, "Tell me what wise saying this bag of coins buys."

The old woman put the bag of coins in her shawl and told the man, "Always follow the main road, though it take longer."

The man waited for the *important* piece of wisdom. When he realized that the saying was all there was, he turned to the old woman and said, "But where is the wisdom?"

"You will see," answered the old woman. "This advice will be useful some day."

The man now became even more curious and said, "Here is a bag of silver coins. Sell me more wisdom."

"Very well," answered the old woman. Taking the bag of silver coins and carefully placing it in her shawl, she said, "What is called ugly is also beautiful."

Now the man was even more confused. "You speak in riddles but I am not Solomon," cried the man. "My two bags of coins, which took me so many years to earn, have been given up for two useless riddles."

Even though he wanted to leave, to run away from this place, the man was more than ever intrigued by the old woman, and he thought, "Maybe, just maybe, I can get some wisdom from her that will *really* help me."

And so, the man told the old woman that he had one more bag, a bag filled with gold coins. "Sell me something worthy of this gold," he pleaded.

And the old woman took the bag of gold and replied:

"Beware of anger in the evening — but rather wait until morning."

The man turned away, not knowing whether to be angry or sad—and when he turned back to where the old woman had been, there was only a basket with a loaf of bread and the beautiful shawl.

The man began to cry, "What have I done? I've given away my hard-earned fortune for three sayings. What shall I do now?" Mumbling miserably to himself, he decided to take the shawl he had admired so much and the bread.

As he gathered up the shawl, he noticed it was heavy, heavier than such a shawl normally is. To his surprise, he found the three bags of coins wrapped up in the shawl. He looked around for the old woman, but she was nowhere to be found. When he inquired about the old woman, the other merchants laughed at him, "What old woman? You must be crazy."

Puzzled by the disappearance of the intriguing old woman but joyful about his restored earnings, the man continued on his way home.

He walked a long way, and when he had grown tired and hungry he stopped on the side of the road to eat. As he was eating a piece of the old woman's bread, two carriages carrying merchants came down the road. Seeing this lone traveler, the merchants stopped and invited him to ride with them to the next town. The man accepted the offer gladly.

As they were driving along, they came to a divided path. Both roads led to the same town, but the path on the left was shorter. As the merchants were about to go to the left, the man riding in the carriage suddenly noticed the shawl in his pack, and he recalled the first piece of advice the old woman had sold him, "Always follow the main road though it may take longer."

The man stood up and shouted for the drivers to stop. When he directed them to stay on the main highway, the merchants began to argue with him. Only when he was about to step down from the carriage did the merchants in his carriage agree. The merchants in the other carriage, however, refused to travel the longer distance. They were anxious to get to the next town and sell their goods.

When the man and his fellow passengers reached the town, they discovered that the other carriage had not yet arrived. "Perhaps they had a broken wheel or, even worse, were held up by robbers," the merchants said.

"We must go help them," insisted the man. So they got back into the carriage and returned along the shorter path. As they entered a wooded area, they saw that robbers had indeed stopped the second carriage. When the robbers saw the first carriage approaching, they fled into the woods. The merchants were so grateful to the traveler that they gave him a bag of gold coins and wished him godspeed on his way home.

A few weeks later, the man was about to enter a big city. Wherever he walked, he heard people laughing at their once powerful and beloved King.

Wherever he looked, he saw people looting and robbing, since they no longer held any regard for the King's laws.

When he entered the courtyard of the King's palace, he saw all the servants and guards pushing and poking at a shriveled-up man who looked more like a wild animal than a human being. He had an oversized head and bumps and scales growing everywhere on his body. His hands and feet were twisted, and his voice was no longer a human-sounding voice but sounded more like the cry of a wounded animal. Everyone was shouting, "Get away, you ugly beast!

Of course you are a King—the King of ugliness!" They kept taunting and chiding this creature.

When the traveler came closer for a good look at the tortured man, he remembered the advice of the old woman: "What is called ugly is beautiful."

"Yes," he shouted, "You are beautiful, for everything that God has created is beautiful."

When these words were spoken, the shriveled-up man was suddenly transformed, and he became the handsome, tall King he had once been. With tears of gratitude, he thanked the traveler and told him how a demon had put a curse on him. Only when someone would call him beautiful could the curse be lifted. And because the traveler had saved the kingdom, the King gave him many bags of gold and jewels and the clothes of a nobleman.

When the man finally arrived in his own village, night had fallen and he did not want to frighten his wife at such a late hour. Instead, he went to an inn nearby. As he was led to his room, he noticed that the servant was his own wife. But she did not seem to recognize him. She looked at him but without a smile of recognition.

The husband's joy turned instantly to disappointment. "Could it be because of my rich clothes? Have I changed so much?" He sat in the room, becoming more and more upset and angry.

"What! I traveled and worked thinking only of returning to my wife and my home—and now here I am and my own wife has forgotten me!"

The anger struck at him in torrents and he hastily picked up his bags, determined to leave town and never to return. As he did so, the shawl dropped out, and the man remembered the third bit of wisdom he had bought: "Beware of anger in the evening—but rather wait until morning."

And so the man restrained his anger and waited impatiently—but he waited until it was light.

In the morning, as he was about to leave, the servant, his wife, met him at the door and she exclaimed, "Excuse me, sir, if I stared at you last evening, for you reminded me of someone I once knew."

"And who is that?" asked the man.

"It was my husband, who left here eighteen years ago," she replied softly. "I fear he must be dead, for I have received no news of him for many years, but it is hard to forget someone you love."

"My dear wife," said the man, "forgive me for not telling you who I was last night. *I* thought *you* had forgotten *me*. I have returned to you, and with good fortune besides."

And so the husband and wife were reunited, and they lived in happiness, with wisdom and wealth for the rest of their lives.

A Question of Sharing

My father had a wonderful sense of humor, a beautifully dimpled smile (although he rarely smiled in photographs), and he enjoyed witty conversation.

The only joke I remember him telling, besides humorous *midrashic* or wisdom stories, is the one about two boys who are so poor that they have to share everything. And so when a bride is proposed for one of them, the question he asks is not out of place. I have taken this joke, which I loved to hear, and turned it into a story—to be shared.

inkhus the tailor and his wife, Leah, lived in a small town in Lithuania. He earned a good living by working hard, and he was known for the good work he did. He never wasted cloth and, when a piece of material was left over, he would say to his customer: "This is not my cloth to keep. If I need something, God will help me. But to take from someone what is not mine, no!" Then the tailor would add "And wear it in good health!" as he handed back the extra cloth along with the suit or dress or coat he had made.

Honest and pious, this tailor lived happily with his wife, and the couple was blessed with twin sons, the older by a few minutes, Yankl, and the younger, Yosl.

As the children grew, they saw that no matter how noisy or hurried everything was during the week, on Shabbos there was a change in the house. The tailor would go out early Friday morning to the marketplace, even before the morning service, and he would bring home, in honor of Shabbos, the best fish and fattest chicken, candles, and wine, and always two sprigs of flowers or sometimes only myrtle leaves.

"Why *two* bunches of flowers, Papa?" the young sons would ask each week, and Pinkhus would always answer, "One to remember the Shabbos and one to observe the Shabbos. Two for us to share in the delight of Shabbos."

And Leah would be busy cleaning and cooking and baking two *hallas* for Shabbos.

"Mama, why do you bake *two* loaves of *halla*?" the boys would ask together, or sometimes one echoing the other. "To remember the double portion of manna God gave to the Israelites in the desert, my sons, we share two loaves," their mother would answer, as she continued her work to make everything ready for Shabbos.

Just as the sun was at the level of the tree tops, Leah would light the Shabbos candles—always four candles—and recite the blessing. "Why *four* candles, Mama?" the boys would ask. "One for each of us in the family, my children—two for your Mama and Papa—and two for you, my twins," their mother would answer joyfully and patiently. "And this way we can all share in the light of Shabbos."

At the table, the tailor would recite the *Song of Songs* to his wife as she sat, smiling modestly in a new dress her husband had sewed for her, and feeling the peace and love of the Shabbos in her home—for no one would think to quarrel on the Shabbos.

Each week, the boys would ask the same questions. Each week, the parents would give the same answers. And so it was for several years.

But the wheel of fortune turns, and the tailor and his wife became poor. They tried to save enough money to buy special foods for Shabbos, but it was very difficult. There came a time when Pinkhus could no longer buy two of everything for Shabbos. He would buy only one sprig of flowers and split it into two. His wife would have enough dough for only one *halla*, but she divided it into two smaller loaves. And the boys no longer asked their questions, but stood silently and watched. There was barely enough money for candles and wine, so the tailor bought only two candles and wine enough for *kiddush*. And if there was no wine, then he would recite the *kiddush* over the *halla*.

And as for clothes for the boys to wear, everything had to be divided and shared. When the twins were old enough to understand, Pinkhus said to them, "My sons, you are brothers. Give to each other and God will give to you. If you have an apple, cut it in two so each of you can enjoy at least a little piece. Don't be selfish, and don't fight over anything. What can I do? We have to make the best of what we have."

The boys had one pair of shoes between them and one suit of clothes, and since they had to share, they took turns going to *shul*. Yankl would go one week wearing the suit and shoes and Yosl would go the next week. Sometimes, whoever put his foot into the right shoe first got to wear the pair that day to school—for they both knew it was bad luck to put the left shoe on first. And they had one book to learn from, one hat, one coat, one of everything—everything the twins had was shared. Yankl had nothing just for himself— and Yosl had nothing just for himself.

One Friday evening, years later, Pinkhus sat at the table with his family. He looked at his now grown-up sons and said to the oldest one, "Yankl, you know that each of the days of the week has a partner. Sunday has Monday, Tuesday has Wednesday, and Thursday has Friday. So Shabbos became jealous and said to God, 'Why did you give a partner to all the days but not to me? I am alone.' Well, God saw that Shabbos was right and said, 'Shabbos, you too will have a partner. The Jewish People will be your partner.' Well, my oldest son, it is now time for you, too, to have a partner. And so I have arranged a *shiddukh* for you with a fine young woman. What do you say to that, Yankl?"

Yankl looked bewildered for a moment, and he looked at his brother Yosl.

He looked at the one pair of shoes, the one suit of clothes, and once again at Yosl. Then he turned to his father and asked simply:

"But, Papa, do I have to share her too?"

Pinkhus and Leah looked at each other and burst out laughing. Then together they raised their cups of wine and said, "*Lehaim*," as they continued to share the joy of Shabbos.

The Wedding Blessing

When two of my friends were getting married a few years ago, they asked me to tell a story during the wedding ceremony. I searched for a story. It had to be short, but it had to be right. I asked a former student of mine at Stern College (who is now also a storyteller), Rachayl Eckstein Davis, if she knew an appropriate story. She referred me to a page of *Gemara*. The kernel of the story comes from the Talmud (*Gemara*, *Taanit* 5). It has become a special story that I have told at several weddings and other *simkhas*.

When a youngster has a Bar or Bat Mitzva, the traditional blessing to the parents is "May you live to bring your child to the *huppa*." When a young person grows up and marries, then the blessing again looks ahead to when the couple will have children. Judaism certainly has a positive "plan-ahead" philosophy.

May it be God's will that you also have many opportunities to tell this story at *simkhas* of all kinds.

 storyteller once attended the wedding of two friends. At a certain point in the ceremony, while they were still under the *huppa*, the couple turned to the storyteller and asked: "Would you give us your blessing?"

"Yes," replied the storyteller, "but a storyteller gives a blessing by telling a story." And this was her story.

Once, a man was making a journey across a desert. Soon he became hungry and thirsty, as you can imagine, and weary too. He looked around to see if there was any place where he could stop and rest. There before him was a tree, with wide branches and leaves and beautiful fruit. Beneath the tree was a flowing stream. The man ate of the fruit and drank of the water. Then he sat under the branches to rest in their shade, and soon he felt refreshed and strong.

When he was ready to continue his journey, the man said to the tree: "O Tree, Tree, *Elan, Elan,* How shall I bless you? *Bameh avarekhekha?*

"Shall I say, 'May your fruit be sweet?' Your fruit is already sweet. 'May your shade be pleasant?' Your shade is cool and pleasant already. 'May you have a stream of flowing water beneath you?' But you already have a flowing stream that refreshes and feeds both you and the traveler! *Elan,*

Elan, Tree, O Tree, How shall I bless you? May it be God's will that all the offshoots taken from you be like you."

אילן אילן במה אברכך

משל. למה הדבר דומה?

לאדם שהיה הולך במדבר

והיה רעב ועייף וצמא.

ומצא אילן שפירותיו מתוקים,

וצילו נאה, ואמת המים עוברת תחתיו.

אכל מפירותיו ושתה ממימיו וישב בצילו,

וכשביקש ללכת אמר:

אילן אילן במה אברכך?

אם אומר לך שיהיו פירותיך מתוקים,

הרי פירותיך מתוקים!

–שיהא צילך נאה,

הרי צילך נאה!

–שתהא אמת המים עוברת תחתיך,

הרי אמת המים עוברת תחתיך!

אלא יהי רצון שכל נטיעות

שנוטעים ממך יהיו כמותך!

(מסכת תענית ה:-ו.)

"And so, my dear friends, bride and groom, I too ask, with what shall I bless you?" asked the storyteller. "You already have the fruit of friendships made sweeter by helping others, and giving others a sense of comfort. You have beautiful branches that reach out to each other to offer protection with your feelings, thoughts—and silence. You also have flowing water, your sense of spirituality and wisdom.

"Then how shall I bless you?

"May it be God's will that all the works that you create together and the children that you have and love together will all be like you. May it be God's will."

The Bride's Wisdom

Ever since I read Isaac Loeb Peretz's beautiful story, *Messiras Nefesh* (*Devotion Unto Death*), I have been fascinated by the powerful image of the bride who confronts with courage and wisdom the Angel of Death, when the latter comes to claim the soul of her bridegroom. I recalled my surprise at discovering this turn of events in a Jewish story.

After years of reading Jewish folklore, I found that the motif of "The Youth About to Die on his Wedding Day" occurs in the folktales of many nations and is used repeatedly in Jewish folk stories (IFA 27). The IFA types this tale as 934 *F, but the tale has elements of A-T 934B and the TMI M341.1 Prophecy of death on wedding day. There are many parallel tellings of this popular tale in the IFA, in versions told from Morocco to Afghanistan.

It is interesting to note that the Babylonian Talmud (*Berakhot* 54b) and Rashi's commentaries stress that both bride and bridegroom should be carefully guarded at the wedding and on the wedding night. The Evil Eye lurks everywhere at such times, and one must be careful so that the Angel of Death does not become jealous of the groom and of the great joy felt at the wedding party. Weddings are especially perilous occasions for young couples.

Other versions of this story can be found in the Apocryphal *Book of Tobit* and in Ibn Zabara (1912). "The Bride's Wisdom" is in *Midrash Tanhuma, Haazinu 8*.

The Talmud and the Midrash have many stories with the same theme as this tale, and they have influenced Islamic literature and the literature of many nations. This story of faithfulness and love has continued to be retold among Jews throughout the ages. It appears in Cohen (1721), Gaster (1924, 1934), *Yalkut Sippurim Umidrashim* (1923), and Bin Gorion (1976).

here once was a wealthy man whose wife was not only beautiful but wise. Together, they taught their only daughter, Deborah, Torah, the laws of *tzedaka*, and kindness. Since the daughter loved to study Torah, she also learned to question what was not right or not just. Deborah and her father and mother—oh yes, her mother was also very learned—often talked late into the night and on Shabbos about the interpretations of the Law using examples and stories and quotations from the Torah.

As she grew older, Deborah's mind became quick as the wind, as deep as the waters, as solid as the earth, and as brilliant as fire. Her parents were proud of their daughter, of the way she acted and the way she spoke.

When Deborah became a young woman, her parents arranged a marriage for her. She had many suitors, since she was beautiful and wealthy; but the young man her parents chose attracted her particularly because of his ability to refute a statement of law. (What she never heard from him was the positive side, but she never realized this.) So she consented to the marriage and they were wed. As happy as she was on the day of the wedding, so great was her sorrow when, that night, the bridegroom died a sudden, unexplained death. The bridal gown had to be changed for a gown of mourning.

Time passed, and once more Deborah was betrothed to a young man who was drawn to her wealth. Once again, the young bridegroom died on the wedding night.

After a while, the young woman married a third time, and this time also the bridegroom died. The wedding night turned into a morning of bitter grief.

Then Deborah resolved that she would never marry again. "Three times have I wed," she cried, "and three times have my bridegrooms died. Where is your great pity, Oh God, to cause such young men to die? Enough! If this is how it is to be, then I will remain alone, not just as a widow but as an *aguna*, so I cannot marry any more. And I will remain an *aguna* until You in your Heavens will see our suffering and sorrow and will have mercy."

And so Deborah remained alone for a long time.

Deborah's father had a brother who lived in another country, and his brother had a wife and ten sons. Every day, the young woman's uncle and his eldest son went into the forest to collect firewood. They would sell the wood and thus earn a living for the large family.

As it happened, one day when they went to the market-place to sell their wood, no one came to buy. That night, they returned home with no money and no food. This bad luck continued until, one night, the father's eyes filled with tears and he said, "My son, let us remain in the forest to sleep tonight. I cannot bear to see how my wife and children cry for food and how they suffer because of me."

And the eldest son, whose name was Sholom, also wept.

The next day Sholom said, "My father, you have often told me about your brother, who is a wealthy man and a kind one. Let me go to him and perhaps find some work. In that way, my father, I can help you and the family." His parents saw that Sholom was determined to go. What else could they say to him, what reason could they offer him not to go? So they gave him their blessing, and Sholom set out on his journey.

When Sholom arrived at his uncle's house, he was welcomed with great joy. After he had rested and eaten, Sholom's relatives asked about his father and mother and his brothers.

When Sholom related how poor his family had become and how hard life was for them, his uncle gladly agreed to give the young man work, and he also sent cartons of goods and money to his brother.

After seven months had passed, Sholom approached his uncle and said, "You have been very good to me and to my family, my uncle. But with everything I have now, I would ask one more request of you which would bring me the greatest happiness. If you do not grant it, then I fear I shall have to return to my home."

The uncle was puzzled and said, "I don't understand. Tell me what you mean."

"Promise me that you will grant my request, Uncle," Sholom said.

"My dear nephew, I have grown to love you like a son. You would never ask for anything that is not according to the Law. So Sholom, I promise with all my heart to grant your request."

After a long while, Sholom said, "My uncle, I would like nothing more than to marry your daughter Deborah. I want to make her my wife."

The uncle began to weep. "Don't do that, my son. Don't, my child. I cannot grant it. Ask anything else of me, but not permission to marry my daughter. I love you as my own son, as I love my brother. Three times she has married, and each groom has died on the wedding night. What has happened must have been on account of my sins, so I cannot keep the promise I have just made. I would be leading you to your death."

"Uncle, Uncle, I know what has happened," said Sholom. "I also know you have given me your promise, your word, to grant whatever request I made. You have given your word, Uncle, and I ask that you keep it."

"Don't marry her, Sholom," commanded the uncle. "I'll give you plenty of silver and gold. You are a wise young man with a good head. Don't put yourself in danger."

"No, it's not for your money that I want to marry Deborah," said Sholom. "What is money compared to the love I have found? Uncle, you have sworn an oath to grant my request. I have faith in God's love, that He will help us and protect us. He watches over Israel, just as a person watches over the apple of his eye. Isn't that what the Bible says?"

The uncle then realized that he would have to give his consent. Immediately, he went to his wife and to Deborah to tell them about his promise. When Deborah heard the proposal, she began to weep, and she cried out bitterly, *"Ribon Haolamim*, Lord of all the world, better You should turn Your hand against me, but do not cause others to die because of me. My love for Sholom is so great. Do *not* take him away from me."

Hearing this, her parents wept together with Deborah and they prayed to God, asking Him to guard the young couple from evil.

Then they began the wedding preparations. A great feast was planned, and all the people in the town, from the most important elders to the poorest of beggars, were invited to join in the wedding celebration. No one was left out.

It was the day of the wedding. Deborah was dressed, once again, in her wedding gown. Her tears of joy mingled with tears of fright and pain, and she prayed silently to God as she waited to be led to the *huppa*.

In another room sat Sholom with the men, praying and singing—and also waiting.

Suddenly, there appeared a stranger who motioned Sholom over to him and said, "My son, I am here to give you some good counsel, and you must follow it exactly." This stranger was *Eliyahu Hanovi*, Elijah the Prophet, may he be remembered for good.

And Eliyahu continued, "At the feast, a poor man will approach you. You will know who he is, because he does not resemble any other person in the whole world. His look will be wild. His clothing, black and torn. He will be weary. When you see him, get up from the table and place him next to you. Feed this stranger with the best foods and give him the finest wine. Serve him with honor and with your heart. Do not forget to obey everything I have told you. I wish you well, as I must leave you now." And Eliyahu disappeared.

After the marriage ceremony, the guests sat down for the festive meal. The bride and bridegroom sat at the head of the table, both happy in their love for each other. As everyone was eating and drinking, a stranger, a poor man bedraggled beyond description, appeared at the door. When Sholom saw him, even from a distance, he knew that this was the man he had been told to expect. As the man approached the table, Sholom stood up and invited him to sit next to him. And the bridegroom served this guest with honor and with his heart, as he had been counseled.

At the conclusion of the feast, the poor man called to the bridegroom, "I must speak with you for a moment." The bridegroom followed him into a room and the poor man began, "My son, I am the Messenger of God, the Angel of Death, and I have come to kill you and to take your soul."

"My lord," replied Sholom, "if it is God's will, then I can only obey. But give me a year, or even half a year, to share just a short span of time with my bride. Then I will go with you."

"No, I regret that I cannot grant even a moment more," answered the Angel of Death.

"Give me thirty days then, or let me enjoy just the seven days of feasting as is the custom for a bride and bridegroom," pleaded Sholom.

"Impossible," responded the Angel of Death. "*This* moment is *your* time to come with me. I cannot delay what I have come for."

"Very well, I will come with you, but allow me to bid farewell to my dear wife," said Sholom. "At least wait for me just a few more moments. Will it matter so much?"

"You have been hospitable and kind and have shown me great honor," said the Angel of Death. "Therefore, in return for this good deed, I will grant you a few moments more. But be quick, for I must return with your soul on schedule."

When Sholom returned to the feast, he saw that his bride was not at the table. He went to the bride's room, where Deborah was sitting, alone, weeping and praying to God. Knocking gently on the door, Sholom called out her name. When Deborah came to the door and saw her husband, she embraced him and asked in a frightened voice, "My beloved, why have you come?"

"I have come to say good-bye to you, because the Angel of Death has called me to go with him," replied Sholom.

"*You* will *not* go with him!" she said with such force that even she was surprised. "*No,* my love, *you* stay here and *I* will go to him. *I* want to talk to him *myself.*"

And Deborah went and found the Angel of Death waiting impatiently outside the room, and she asked, "Are you that angel who has come to take the life of my husband?"

He answered, "Yes."

"Well, he cannot die now," declared Deborah, "because it says in the Torah: 'And what man is there that hath betrothed a wife, and hath not taken her, let him go and return unto his house, lest he die in the battle and another man take her.' So it's clear that when a man marries, he must stay with his wife. You cannot take my husband at this time."

"I must. I have been sent by God as His messenger. But you do have a good argument," replied the angel weakening.

"Furthermore," continued Deborah, "it is written in the Torah: 'When a man takes a new wife, he shall not go out in the host, neither shall he be charged with any business. He shall be free for his house for one year, and shall cheer his wife whom he hath taken.' Well, this would become a feast of mourning if my husband died now. Is this what God calls cheering and rejoicing? But God is true and His Torah is true. If you take my husband's life, then you will make a sham out of the Torah. So, if you accept my words, good. If not, then I will take you to a *Beit Din,* to a rabbinical court, and we'll let the rabbinical judges decide. God would not break His own Laws."

And Deborah stood there looking at the angel eye-to-eye.

The angel, feeling pity for the young couple, looked

away as he said, "I will go and consult with God." The angel flew directly up to Heaven.

That evening, the bride and bridegroom consecrated the marriage and slept peacefully.

The parents of the bride, however, could not sleep that night because of the dread of what might happen to their daughter's husband. All night, they wept and prayed and, in the middle of the night, they got up and prepared a grave. At dawn, as the sun was rising, they entered the house again and, to their great surprise, heard sounds of joyful laughter filling the house.

When the young couple opened the door of their chamber, the parents saw that the young husband was alive and well. The faces of the bride and bridegroom shone with such beauty and love.

Well, as you can imagine, those seven days of feasting were truly days of rejoicing for the whole family.

As for the Angel of Death, when he presented the bride's argument before God in the Heavens, God had to agree that the bride was right. So instead he sent the angel on other missions. The angel did not visit the bride and bridegroom for many, many, many years. And when he did, it was their true time to go with him.

The Innkeeper's Wise Daughter

Whenever I tell this story, I think of my mother. I suppose this is so because my mother was a very clever and resourceful woman. Her father was not an innkeeper, but a peddler of shoelaces in New York City's Lower East Side, a man who once owned a grocery store in the White Russian village of Lepl. In any case, she had the same marvelous woman's logic (a nonlinear logic) shown by the innkeeper's wise daughter.

Stories based on riddles have always been popular. But do not all stories contain riddles? There is something mysterious, something hidden, in both riddles and stories. Certainly both are imaginative and playful, and when we enter the creative play of "solving" riddles, a sort of delicious joy comes over us.

This tale, A-T 875, "The Clever Peasant Girl," is extremely popular in European versions and has been collected from China to Western Europe. It is included in the Grimm collection in very nearly this form and is very common in Jewish tradition as well. Gaster (1924) has a parallel form (number 196), and there is a somewhat similar retelling in Bin Gorion (1916–1921) (IV, 108), with the addition of motifs from 875D. Some of the non-Jewish versions are "Clever Manka," a Czechoslovakian tale, "The Riddles," a Turkestan tale, and "The Maiden Wiser than the Tsar," a Serbian tale (the last two found in Shah (1979)).

In Jewish literature, the last episode of this story can be found as part of a story in the *midrashim* on the Talmud (*Pesikta*). The story is about a couple who, after ten years of marriage, have no children and the husband wants a divorce. The rabbi asks that, just as they began their marriage with a feast, so they should end with a feast. At the farewell dinner, the husband tells the wife to take the dearest thing in the household before returning to her father's home. Of course, the wife takes the husband. The couple realizes their love for one another and, after a time, they are blessed with a child.

There are 25 versions of "The Clever Maiden" tale type in the Israel Folktale Archives, such as "The Dearest Thing"

(IFA 9254) remembered by Yeshayahu Shaltiel from Yemen (Noy 1972).

Versions that include a more expanded story involving riddles, in addition to the *midrashic* core, can be found in over 80 IFA parallels from Palestine, Egypt, Yemen, Bukhara, and so on. One version of this story was included in Cahan (1931) under the title, "The Innkeeper's Daughter." It is similar to a Yemenite tale (IFA 6699), in which the King of Yemen asks his Jewish counselor three questions:

What is swifter than a bird? (The eye.)

What is fatter than a hog? (The earth.)

What is sweeter than honey? (A person's soul.)

These were probably stories told by women as they sat together doing embroidery or other needlework or plucking goose feathers for quilts and pillows. Tales of Clever Women would certainly be a favorite type of story.

any years ago, in a small village in Russia, there were two friends, a tailor and an inn-keeper. One day, as they were drinking glasses of tea, they began to talk about their philoso-phies of life. As their discussion went on, they began to argue more and more intensely—each one claim-ing to know more about life than the other one—and they almost came to blows. They realized that neither one would win the argument, so they decided to bring the matter to the local nobleman, who was respected for his wisdom and honesty and who often served as a judge in disputes. The two friends finished their tea in silence and set out to see the nobleman.

When the nobleman heard the case, he said to the two men, "Whoever answers these three questions correctly will be the one who knows more about life: What is the quickest thing in the world? What is the fattest in the world? And what is the sweetest? Return in three days' time with your answers and I will settle your disagreement."

The tailor returned home and spent the three days thinking about these riddles, but found no answers to them. When the innkeeper returned to his home, he sat down holding his head in his hands. Just then, his daugh-ter saw him and cried out, "What's wrong, Father?" The innkeeper told her about the three questions. She an-swered, "Father, when you go back to the nobleman, give him these answers: The quickest thing in the world is thought. The fattest thing is the earth. The sweetest is sleep."

When three days had passed, the tailor and the innkeeper came before the nobleman. "Have you found answers to my questions?" he asked. The tailor stood there silently.

But when the innkeeper gave his answers, the nobleman exclaimed, "Wonderful! Those are wonderful answers! But tell me, how did *you* think of those answers?"

"I must tell you truthfully that those answers were told to me by my daughter," replied the innkeeper.

"Since your daughter knows so much about life, I will test her further. Give her this dozen eggs and see if she can hatch them all in three days. If she does so, she will have a great reward."

The innkeeper carefully took the eggs and returned home. When his daughter saw him carrying a large basket, and she also saw how he trembled, she asked him, "What is wrong, Father?" He showed her the eggs and told her what she must do in order to receive a reward and prove her wisdom again.

The daughter took the eggs, and she weighed them, each one, in her hands. "Dear Father, how can these eggs be hatched when they are cooked? Boiled eggs indeed! But wait, Father, I have a plan as to how to answer this riddle." The daughter boiled some beans and waited three days. Then she instructed her father to go to the nobleman's house and ask permission to plant some special beans.

"Beans?" asked the nobleman. "What sort of special beans?" Taking the beans from his pocket, the innkeeper showed them to the nobleman and said, "These are boiled beans, your honor, that I want to plant."

The nobleman burst out laughing and said, "Well, you certainly are not wise to the ways of the world if you don't even know that beans can't grow from boiled beans—only from seeds."

"Well then," replied the innkeeper, "neither can chickens hatch from boiled eggs!"

The nobleman immediately sensed the clever mind of the innkeeper's daughter in the answer. So he said to the innkeeper, "Tell your daughter to come here in three days. And she must come neither dressed nor undressed, neither walking nor riding, neither hungry nor overfed, and she must bring me a gift that is not a gift."

The innkeeper returned home even more perplexed than before. When his daughter heard what she had to do in three days' time, she laughed and said, "Father, tomorrow I will tell you what to do."

The next day, the daughter said to her father, "Go to the marketplace and buy these things—a large net, some almonds, a goat, and a pair of pigeons." The father was puzzled by these requests, but as he loved his daughter and knew her to be wise, he did not question her. Instead he went to the marketplace and bought all that she had requested.

On the third day, the innkeeper's daughter prepared for her visit to the nobleman. She did not eat her usual morning meal. Instead, she got undressed and wrapped herself in the transparent net, so she was neither dressed nor undressed.

Then she took two almonds in one hand and the pair of pigeons in the other. Leaning on the goat, she held on so that one foot dragged on the ground while she hopped on the other one. In this way, she was neither walking nor riding.

As she approached the nobleman's house, he saw her and came out to greet her.

At the gate, she ate the two almonds to show she was neither hungry nor overfed.

Then the innkeeper's daughter extended her hand showing the pigeons she intended to give as a gift. The nobleman reached out to take them, but just at that moment the young woman opened her hand to release the pigeons—and they flew away. So she had brought a gift that was not a gift.

The nobleman gave a laugh of approval and called out, "You are a clever woman! I want to marry you, but on one condition. You must promise never to interfere with any of my judgments."

"I will marry you," said the innkeeper's daughter, "but I also have one condition: If I do anything that will cause you to send me away, you must promise to give me whatever I treasure most in your house." They each agreed to the other's condition, and they were married.

Some time passed, and one day a man came to speak with the young wife, who had become known for her wisdom. "Help me, please," the man begged, "for I know you are wise and understand things in ways your husband does not."

"Tell me what is wrong, for you look very troubled, sir," she answered. And the man told her his story.

"Last year," said the man, "my partner and I bought a barn which we now share. He keeps his wagon there, and I keep my horse there. Well, last night my horse gave birth to a pony under the wagon. So my partner says the pony belongs to him. We began to argue and fight, so we brought our dispute to the nobleman. The nobleman judged that my partner was right. I protested, but to no avail. What can I do?"

The young woman gave him certain advice and instructions to follow. As she had told him to do, he took a fishing pole and went over to the nobleman's well and pretended he was fishing there. The nobleman rode by the well, just as his wife had predicted, and when he saw the man, he stopped and asked, "What are you doing?" The man replied, "I am fishing in the well." The nobleman started to laugh, "Are you really so stupid that you do not know that you can't catch fish in a well?" "No sir," said the man, "not any more than I know that a wagon cannot give birth to a pony."

At this answer, the nobleman stopped laughing. Understanding that his wife must be involved in this case after all, he got out of his carriage and went looking for his wife. When he found her, he said, "You did not keep your promise not to interfere with my judgments, so I must send you back to your father's home."

"You are right, my husband. But before I leave, let us dine together one last time." The nobleman agreed to this request.

At dinner, the nobleman drank a great deal of wine, for his wife kept refilling his cup, and, as a result, he soon became very sleepy. As soon as he was asleep, the wife signaled to the servants to pick him up and put him in the carriage next to her, and so they returned to her father's home.

The next morning, when the nobleman woke up, he looked around and realized where he was. "But how did I get here? What is the meaning of this?" he shouted.

"You may remember, dear husband, that you also made an agreement with me. You promised that if you sent me away, I would be able to pick whatever I treasured most in your house to take with me. There is nothing that I treasure more than you. So that is how you come to be here with me."

The nobleman laughed, embraced his wife, and said, "Knowing how much you love me, I now realize how much I love you. Let us return to our home."

And they did go home, where they lived with love and respect for many happy years.

The Promised Betrothal

This is a well-known story found in the *Gemara* (*Taanit* 8a) and in *Tosafot* and Rashi's commentaries. A longer version of this story is in *Sefer Arukh Hashalem.* The story found its way into *Ein Yaakov* in the beginning of the 16th century, a book of talmudic stories collected by Jacob ibn Habib. *The Exempla of the Rabbis* (Gaster 1924), which contains the largest number of post-biblical tales, and *The Maase Book* (Gaster 1934), a book of Jewish tales and legends translated from Yiddish, also include versions of "The Story of the Well and the Weasel." The striking element of the weasel and the well called to be witnesses is also found in Bin Gorion (1916–1921) (I, 122). The IFA types this tale as 930*F (compare the somewhat similar A-T 842B*), and it does not seem to have close parallels outside the Jewish tradition.

This tale has traveled well as a folktale, but it was also the basis of Abraham Goldfaden's Yiddish play *Shulamis*, or *The Daughter of Jerusalem*, a romantic operetta set in ancient Judea, and written in the early 1880s. Goldfaden, 1840–1908, known as the father of Yiddish Theater, wrote several plays based on Bible, Jewish history, and legends. Like many other writers, Goldfaden went to the Talmud and to Jewish folklore for inspiration in many of his works.

Here is a summary of the play, taken from *Vagabond Stars: A World History of Yiddish Theater* by Nahma Sandrow:

> Absalom rescues Shulamis from a well in the desert. They fall in love and vow to be faithful forever, calling as witnesses to their pledge the well and a wild desert cat; these will avenge any betrayal of their love.
>
> Absalom continues on his way to Jerusalem, where he was going on a pilgrimage to the Temple, and there he meets another woman. He forgets poor Shulamis, marries, and has chidren. But years later his two children die, one drowned in a well and the other killed by a cat. He remembers his pledge and returns to Shulamis,

who has been waiting for him all along, fending off
suitors by pretending to be mad. [p. 62]

A production of *Shulamis* played to full houses in Warsaw shortly before World War II broke out in 1939. The
director, Zygmunt Turkow, writes: "Every day, chorus
members disappear, and actors. But we go on playing. Till
the play is interrupted. One of the first German bombs over
Warsaw falls on our theater. It is transformed into a ruin."
(Sandrow 1977, p. 336).

Like so many other tales from the Talmud, this one
teaches us a moral lesson: Keeping a promise and being
truthful are high on the scale of Jewish values.

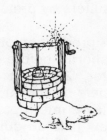

any years ago, in another time and another place, a young woman went for a walk in the countryside. Wearing a gown of gold and silver, she looked as beautiful as a princess in a fairy tale. Near her home there was a woods. As curious as she was beautiful, she decided to enter the woods and explore a place she had never been. She wandered deeper and deeper, along paths she had never before taken. Her gown caught on some branches as she walked, but she did not care. After a while, she came to a well.

"Good!" she said aloud to herself. "I am so thirsty. I will seat myself in this bucket and lower myself down to get some water." So she lowered herself down into the well, sitting in the bucket, and she drank of the cool well water. But when she tried to raise herself in the bucket, she could not pull the rope hard enough. She tried time and time again. Each time the rope burned her hands, and she could not raise herself up to the top of the well.

What did she do then? She began to cry and shout, hoping someone would pass by and hear her. And she prayed.

After what seemed like a very long time, a young man, walking nearby, heard those cries. He listened and then ran over to the well, looked down, and saw a strange form draped in gold and silver. He called down, "Are you a human or a demon?"

"I am a human," she answered emphatically. "Pull me up for I have no more strength."

"Swear to me that you are human," said the young man. "And if you are, then when I raise you up, you must marry me."

"I am a woman, and please pull me up quickly, for I am very cold down here," pleaded the young woman.

The young man pulled on the ropes, and soon the young woman was standing next to him. And when she saw the young man in a better light, close up, she saw a handsome young man with a wonderful smile.

"Now that I have saved you," declared the young man, "I see you are more beautiful than you seemed when I saw you in the well. You must agree to marry me immediately."

"Who are your people?" asked the woman guardedly.

"Be assured that I am a Jew from a respected family and a *Kohen*," he answered quickly.

"First let me thank you for saving me," said the young woman, "but I cannot consent to marry you before you meet my mother and father and ask their permission, as is our custom."

"I will wait, then, until I meet your parents," the young man replied. "Give me your word that you will marry no one else, and that will assure me of our pledge to each other."

"My word as a pledge of our betrothal? Why, how can we pledge without witnesses?" the young woman asked with a smile. Then she looked around and added, "Look, there is a weasel. And here is the well from which you rescued me. Let us declare the weasel and the well to be witnesses and, besides, we have the stars in the heavens above us as witnesses."

"Agreed," answered the bridegroom-to-be with a laugh. Accompanying the young woman until they reached the edge of the woods, he promised to come to her parents' home soon. And once again swearing their love and promising to be true to each other, they parted.

Each day, the young woman waited for the young man, but he never came. The days soon turned into weeks, the weeks into months, and the months into years. Yet she remembered his smile, his strength in lifting her up from the well, his promise. Each time a doubt entered her thoughts, she dismissed it by saying, "Perhaps he will come just before this Shabbat."

But each Shabbat came without the promised visit.

With time, more and more suitors appeared who wanted to marry her. At first, she refused each one, giving one excuse after another. For she wanted to keep her pledge and remain faithful to the young man.

As time passed, it became more difficult to refuse to marry. She had not spoken of her pledge to anyone, not even to her parents, whom she loved very much. And they did not understand her mysterious behavior, nor did she explain why she was acting so strangely. She began to dress in an eccentric manner and to feign madness, tearing out her hair and bursting suddenly into song or else remaining silent for days. It was not long before everyone in town was talking about how the beautiful young woman had gradually lost her mind.

After a while, no one came anymore to inquire about her hand in marriage. The young woman was glad of that, as she preferred being left alone. But how bitter her nights were, when she cried into her pillow as she thought of the young man, of his promise to her, and of the weasel, the well, and the stars that had been their witnesses.

And what happened to the young man, you ask? He returned to his city and did not remain faithful to his pledge. He married another, and before long they had a son. One day, when the child was three months old, he fell asleep in the garden, and his throat was pierced by a weasel's fangs. The sorrow in that home was great.

After a while, the bereaved couple had a second child, also a son. The mother watched this child carefully, especially when he slept, and she never left his side. He was strong and healthy.

One day, when the child was three years old, he ran out into the garden and quickly climbed to the top of the well. In his haste, the boy lost his balance and fell into the well. When his parents heard his scream, they rushed to the well but they could not save his life. When they brought the child up from the water, he was dead. The mother let out a soulful sound and fell to the ground. She could not be consoled and repeated the same question over and over again: "Why? Why?"

When the period of mourning was over, the grieving wife came to her husband and said in a quiet tone, "Our children, both of our sons, have died in a strange manner. One death was caused by a weasel, and the other by a fall into a well. There must be a reason for this. My husband, can you tell me why this has happened to us?"

The husband would not look at his wife. And still she persisted: "Husband, have you hidden something from me? Have you ever broken a pledge? There must be a curse on us for all this to have happened. We cannot bring our children back to life, but perhaps by telling me the truth, you can help us prevent more unhappiness."

When the husband heard his wife's words, he realized he would have to confess all that had happened, for he was, after all, responsible for causing this grief.

He fell on his knees and wept. Then he sat next to his wife and revealed what had happened on the day he rescued the young woman from the well in the woods.

His wife listened carefully. Then she got up from the chair, walked to the window, and looked up at the stars. They seemed to be giving her counsel, for after a few moments she knew what to say. And this is what she said: "We must go and get a divorce. And then you must find the young woman to whom you gave your sacred word to marry. Only then can we all find happiness and peace in our lives."

When the young man arrived in the town where his betrothed lived, he asked about her. Wherever he went, people told him the same thing: "That young woman? Why do you want to see her? She's crazy. No one would want her for a wife. She sits alone in a room all day and babbles or sings or else she sits in silence for days."

After a while, the young man was directed to her house, and he asked to see her. At first, the family would not allow him to see her, making up excuses why he could not visit her.

But when he said, "Bring three witnesses. I promise to take her with whatever defects she has," they allowed him to enter her room.

When the young man saw his betrothed, he was shocked by the change in her appearance. When he first met her, she was a beautiful young maiden in a dazzling gold and silver gown. Now, she looked like a wild woman of the forest. Yet he saw, even now, traces of her loveliness and of her smile, and he loved her.

He approached her and softly whispered, "I have brought three witnesses; but I have also brought with me the memory of our original and true witnesses—the weasel, the well, and the stars in the heavens."

When the young woman heard these words, she looked up at the young man. Her eyes became clear and bright, her loveliness returned, and she spoke slowly with her true, clear voice. "I have stayed with my promise to remain faithful to you, for once a sacred oath has been taken, it cannot be broken."

Upon hearing these words, the young man wept. Then he told his betrothed what had happened in his life since he last saw her.

"What happened to my children was because of my broken promise, and for that I must atone. But now, my love, if your love for me remains as strong as my feeling for you, let us be married." And he quickly added, "after I ask your parents for permission."

The parents, hearing this story, wept with a mixture of sorrow and joy. They granted the young man permission to marry their daughter, if she gave her consent.

So she did, and they were married. They had many children together and lived a life filled with happiness and contentment.

The Magic Pomegranate

Stories like "The Magic Pomegranate," known as cumulative tales, are great fun because they involve a reasoning and sifting process. They flourish in the folklore of every nation. Stories like "Anansi the Spider" (Africa), "The Skillful Brothers" (Albania), and "Tales of a Parrot" (Afghanistan) are prime examples of the genre. There are such stories in Japan, Germany, and Italy; in Grimm's fairytales and in *The Arabian Nights*. In some cultures, where audiences hear these stories over and over, they are often asked to supply an answer to the puzzle presented by the storyteller.

"The Magic Pomegranate" and the many Jewish versions of it are uniquely Jewish, because the kernel of these stories is the talmudic teaching that the greatest *mitzva* is performed by the person who gives of himself or herself—or who gives up something of his or her own. Only such a person deserves the reward, in this case, to marry the princess. Without exception, the youngest brother is the one who deserves and gets this reward. (Think of all the Bible stories where the youngest wins out. And the same is true in all folklore.)

What is important in tales like these is not just the need to find the answer to the question that is posed, but the attempt to understand why a specific answer was given. Why did the listener or reader choose the wrong brother, often for valid reasons? Or why did the reader decide that no one should win the reward, because they *all* helped to solve the problem. (See "The Golden Watch.") Questions are always more important here than are the answers. And important, too, are the *reasons* behind the answers. With his answers, the listener becomes the storyteller.

Usually, stories of this type include three elements: a magic carpet or a magic airplane, a magic glass or mirror or jewel, and a magic potion or apple. In *Faithful Guardians*, there is a story (told by Eliyahu Wakhba from Egypt, IFA 5118) whose title indicates which three gifts are involved: "The Telescope, the Aeroplane, and the Wonderful Remedy."

I have heard one interpretation that says that "the remedy which cannot be used up" is a euphemism for the Torah, which is constantly renewing itself, nourishing us, and healing us, as a good remedy should.

I have changed the third element to the marvelous pomegranate, one of the choice fruits of the Land of Israel. This fruit has a great deal of symbolic meaning in Judaism. It is a symbol of fertility and plenty. The shape of its crown was said to have influenced the design of King Solomon's crown. I especially love the saying from *Song of Songs Rabba* (6:11): "Children, sitting in a row studying Torah, are compared to the compact kernels of a pomegranate." What an image!

Have you ever cut open a pomegranate and looked at all that wonder! There are supposed to be 613 kernels for each of the 613 *mitzvot* that a Jew is to perform.

But more than all this, the flower and the fruit are so magnificent that they are more magical for me than any magic apple. However, there may be a close connection because pomegranate means *seeded apple* from Middle French (*pome garnete*).

Among the many Jewish versions of this story are "Who Cured the Princess?" (Noy 1963) and a Yemenite tale entitled "The Mute Princess" (Schwartz 1983). A third Jewish version, from Greece (IFA 10091), was collected by Attias (1976). There are about 20 IFA versions from Morocco, Libya, Tunisia, Egypt, Yemen, and Poland. Tale Type 653 in Aarne-Thompson is a close version of this tale, but the IFA listing of 653*C, with three versions from Iraq to Yemen, is the epitome of this telling. There are versions in Gaster (1924) (330) and in Bin Gorion (1916–1921) (I, 303).

nce there were three brothers who loved adventure. One day they decided to go on a journey, each one to a different country, and to meet again on a certain day ten years later. Each brother was to bring back with him an unusual gift.

The oldest brother decided to go to the East. When he arrived in a certain Eastern town, he was fascinated by what he saw there: Magicians, dancing girls, jugglers, and acrobats were everywhere. As the brother was watching the entertainments, he saw one magician hold up a magic glass through which he could see to the distant corners of the kingdom.

"Ah!" thought the oldest brother, "I would like to have that glass, for that would certainly be an unusual object to share with my brothers." He asked the magician, "Tell me, how much is that glass? I should like to buy it from you." At first, the magician would not part with his magic glass, but after much pleading by the older brother, and some bargaining, they agreed upon a price and the magician sold the glass to the oldest brother.

The second brother traveled to a country in the West. Wherever he went, he kept his eyes open, and his mind as well. He was always on the lookout for the most unusual gift he could bring back to his brothers.

One day, he was attracted by the cries of an old carpet seller, who called out, "Carpets for sale! Beautiful! Wonderful! Carpets here!" The brother approached the carpet seller and began to examine his carpets, when suddenly he saw the carpet at the bottom of the pile begin to move. It seemed to be moving by itself! "What kind of carpet is this one?" he asked, pointing to the bottom one, which was quite visible by then.

The old merchant motioned for him to bend down and whispered in his ear, "This is a magic carpet. Buy it, and it will take you anywhere you want to go—and quickly too!" The second brother and the carpet seller finally settled upon a price, and the brother took the magic carpet with him, satisfied that he had a most unusual gift.

The youngest brother went South, and when he arrived in a certain country, he traveled far and wide to see what he could find to bring back to his brothers.

Now, this was a country noted for its many forests. One day, the youngest brother was walking in a grove of trees, when he noticed something strange—a tree that was of a different shape from the hundreds of other trees around it. It was covered with orange-red blossoms, and it was so beautiful!

As the younger brother came closer, he saw that there was only one red pomegranate on the tree.

"This is strange indeed," thought the young man. "A pomegranate tree with only one pomegranate." He approached the tree slowly, laughing to himself and thinking of the story he would tell his brothers about the pomegranate tree full of blossoms with only one fruit on it. As he reached for the pomegranate, it fell into his hand even before he could pluck it from the branch. As soon as that happened, another pomegranate burst from one of the blossoms. When the brother saw this, he looked at the pomegranate in his hand and said to himself, "This must be a magic pomegranate. It was the only one on the tree, and yet as soon as it fell into my hands when I was about to reach for it, a new pomegranate appeared suddenly. But what kind of magic does it perform, I wonder?"

The youngest brother examined the pomegranate, marveling at its beauty. "The shape is so perfect," he thought, "crowned with the crown of King Solomon." He walked away from the tree looking at his mysterious new treasure. When he looked back to see the pomegranate tree once more, it was no longer there. It had disappeared. "Now I know this is a magic pomegranate, and so this is what I will bring to my brothers."

Ten years passed, and when the three brothers met as they had planned, they embraced with delight. They eagerly showed each other the unusual objects they had brought back from their journeys.

The oldest brother said, "Let me look through my glass and see what I can see." When he held up the glass, he saw, in a far-off kingdom, a young princess lying ill in bed, near death.

"Quickly, dear brothers, get on my magic carpet and we'll fly there!" said the second brother. In what seemed like seconds, the three brothers arrived at the far-off kingdom.

In the royal palace of this kingdom, the King, whose daughter lay ill, was grief-stricken. He had sent for every doctor in the country to cure the princess; but they had all failed and there was no hope left for the princess. Finally, the King had sent a messenger throughout the country saying, "Whoever can save my daughter, the princess, will have her hand in marriage, and half the kingdom!"

As if in a dream, the youngest brother heard a voice whisper inside him, "The pomegranate!" The youngest brother approached the King and asked, "May I try to cure the princess?" The King agreed and led the young man to the princess' chambers.

When the young man saw the princess, he approached quietly and sat by her side. Then he took the pomegranate from his pocket, cut it open with gentle care, carefully cut each kernel from its place, and then fed the juicy red kernels to the princess. In a few moments, the princess felt stronger, and the color returned to her cheeks. Soon, she sat up in her bed, fully restored to health.

The King was overjoyed. He hugged his daughter and, turning to the three young men, he announced, "The man who saved my daughter will marry her."

The three brothers began to quarrel, each one claiming to be the one who should marry the princess.

The oldest brother said, "If it were not for my magic glass, we would never have known the princess was ill in the first place. So, since I discovered this first, I deserve to marry the princess."

"But, brothers, it was because of my magic carpet that we could arrive so quickly," argued the second brother. "Otherwise, the princess would have died. I deserve to marry the princess."

Then the youngest brother said, "It was my magic pomegranate that actually healed the princess. I deserve to marry her."

Since the three brothers could not decide which one should marry the princess, the King tried to decide. He looked at the three clever young men, but he could not decide who deserved to marry his daughter.

The King finally turned to the princess and asked, "Who do you think deserves to marry you, my daughter?"

The princess answered simply, "I will ask each of them a question." She turned to the oldest brother and asked, "Has your magic glass changed in any way since you arrived in this Kingdom?"

"No," replied the oldest brother. "My glass is the same as always, and I can look through it and see to every corner of this kingdom."

The princess then asked the second brother, "Has your magic carpet changed in any way since you arrived in this kingdom?" And the second brother answered, "No, my carpet is the same, and I can fly anywhere on it, as always."

Turning to the youngest brother, the princess asked, "Has your magic pomegranate changed in any way since you arrived in this Kingdom?" And the youngest brother answered, "Yes, princess, my pomegranate is no longer whole, for I gave you a portion of it."

The princess turned to the three young men and said, "I will marry the youngest brother because he performed the greatest good deed—because he gave up something of his own."

The brothers and the King all understood the wisdom of the Princess. A lavish wedding was arranged for the princess and the youngest brother.

And the King appointed the princess and all three brothers to become his royal advisers.

The Iron Chest

This story always brings to my mind a passage in the *haftora* for *Shabbat Hagadol*:

> And he shall turn the heart of
> the fathers to the children,
> And the heart of the children
> to their fathers. (Malachi 3:24)

"He" is Elijah the Prophet, whom God will send to bring about reconciliations between parents and children. Only then can the hearts of parents and children be turned to God.

In Jewish folklore, Elijah is not only the great reconciler and the messenger who will announce the coming of the Messiah; he is also a healer, a helper, and a peacemaker. (For more about Elijah, see the introduction to "Elijah and the Three Wishes.")

This story was popular in Eastern Europe and is included in Cahan (1931). There are at least 25 variations of the tale.

The Iron Chest follows similar lines to A-T 745A, but with parts of A-T 947A. The IFA listing of 745*B, with versions from Turkey, Yemen, and Kurdistan, covers much of the tale, but the closest version in the IFA seems to be 7735, found in *Twelve Folktales from Sanok* (Hebrew) (IFA 7735), collected in Yiddish by Pipe (1967). A-T 745A, "The Predestined Treasure," and other related tales are well known in Slavic lands, which might be the connecting link to the Jewish tradition. There are parallel tales in Gaster (1924) (423) and Bin Gorion (1916–1921) (II, 106).

 here was once a rich man who was riding home from a fair. Although night was falling, he decided to continue his journey rather than stop at an inn. Riding through the forest, he saw the figure of a tall man pushing a cart. The tall man's white beard reflected the light of the moon and shimmered in the dark, as if lighting his way. As the rich man came closer, he saw that the tall man was pushing a large iron chest and had stopped at the side of the road.

"Good evening," said the tall bearded man to the rich man as he approached.

"Good evening to you," answered the rich man. "What are you planning to do with that iron chest at so late an hour?"

"Bury it," replied the tall man.

"And what does it contain?" asked the rich man cautiously.

"Gold coins," the tall man answered simply.

"Gold coins! And whom will these gold coins belong to after you bury them?" asked the rich man greedily.

"To your son-in-law," the tall man said.

"My son-in-law? But my daughter is a young girl, too young even to be betrothed," declared the rich man in puzzlement. "Well then," he continued, "perhaps you can exchange a few coins with me?" And he noted well the spot.

The tall man readily agreed and, in exchange for 40 coins, he gave the rich man three gold coins from the iron chest. As the rich man rode away, he looked back, but the tall bearded man with the iron chest had disappeared.

Several years later, the rich man's daughter had grown to be a *kalle moid.* She had reached the age of marriage, but no matter who was presented, she would not consent to a match. Her father grew impatient with her, but there was nothing he could do to change her mind.

One evening, as the rich man was walking in his gardens, he looked up at the moon and was suddenly reminded of his nighttime encounter with the tall bearded man in the forest and the three gold coins he had been given. "The gold coins will belong to your son-in-law," he remembered the tall man telling him. And that gave him the idea for a plan.

The next evening, the rich man placed one of the gold coins near the door of the *beis medrash.* "Whoever picks up the coin will become my daughter's husband," he said to himself.

When the rich man arrived at the *beis medrash* the following morning, he saw that the coin was gone, so he put a second coin in the same place. The next morning, it, too, was gone.

The rich man did the same with the third gold coin, and the same thing happened: the next morning it was gone.

The rich man did not know who had picked up the gold coins, so he decided that on Shabbos he would ask that whoever had found those coins should come to him for a special reward.

In this town there was a *treger,* a porter, who voluntarily brought water every night to the *beis medrash* so that the scholars would have something to drink while they studied. He himself was not a learned young man, but this was his way of being helpful to the rabbi and the students and, at the same time, perhaps learning a few words of Torah or hearing an interesting *moshl* (parable). On his way to the *beis medrash* on each of those three evenings, this young man had found one of the three coins.

On Shabbos, when the young man heard the rich man's announcement—that whoever had found the coins should come to him for a special reward—he immediately went up to the rich man and told him, "I found your three coins, and I'll bring them to you after *havdala.*"

The rich man could not believe what he had heard. "This poor young man cannot become my son-in-law," he thought to himself.

"How could this ignorant, penniless youth be my son-in-law? Impossible!" But he would wait and see. Perhaps the porter had not picked up the right coins, after all. And he brightened at that possibility. "Maybe the one who found my gold coins could not come to *shul* this Shabbos," he thought, hoping that this was indeed the case.

Soon after *havdala,* the rich man heard a knock on the door and, yes, the poor porter was there. And, yes, he had found the right gold coins. What could he do? A promise is a promise.

"You shall marry my daughter," said the rich man finally. "But before you are married, you must study. I will hire a teacher for you." And that is what he did. The young man studied and learned well. He came to live in the rich man's house, and the rich man's daughter and the poor young man became fond of each other.

The rich man waited each day for the tall man in the forest to arrive with the chest full of gold coins as a sign that this young man was really the *basherter* for his daughter. After a time, the daughter grew impatient and said, "Father, we want to be married. I have given my consent. Let us wait no longer."

And so a wedding was prepared, and the young couple was married. (A tall man was present at the *huppa,* but he disappeared afterwards and no one noticed him.)

Time passed, and with each day the rich man grew even angrier that the promised fortune had not yet arrived. Perhaps he had been tricked.

One day, the rich man said to his son-in-law: "Come, let us ride into the forest. Bring a shovel, for there is something

there that we must try to find." Together they rode to the
place where the rich man remembered meeting the tall
stranger with the iron chest. Since the place looked different by the light of day, he picked a spot near a large tree and
told his son-in-law to dig. But wherever he dug, the son-in-
law turned up only dirt or rocks—no iron chest. After many
hours of digging and finding nothing, the rich man and his
son-in-law gave up and went home.

From then on, everything his son-in-law said or did
caused him to speak sharply to the young man.

Since they were living in the same house, the two men
saw each other constantly, and there was great unhappiness in the house.

One day, the young man again unwittingly displeased
his father-in-law, and the older man shouted, "Leave my
house. I have had enough of you. You are a poor ignorant
water-carrier, and you will always remain a poor ignorant
water-carrier!"

What could this poor young man do? He left, but his
wife, the rich man's daughter, went with him, for they loved
each other very much. They found a small room to rent and
in this room they lived and opened a small shop of odds and
ends, junk, and tools. In this way, they earned a meager
living.

One Friday, a tall peasant entered the shop and asked
for a certain item. The young woman gave him what he
asked for, and the peasant told her, "I do not have money to
pay for this, but I have an old iron chest. Will you accept it as
payment?"

Yes, the couple agreed; they would be happy to take the
iron chest. Immediately, the tall peasant rolled in the iron
chest. It was covered with spider webs and dust. As soon as
he had put it in the room, the tall peasant left in a hurry.
The couple looked at each other and decided to open it up.
They would have to do it quickly, as Shabbos was approaching. The husband opened the bolts easily, and when they
lifted the cover, they found, to their astonishment, a chest
filled with the same gold coins that the poor young man had
found at the *beis medrash*.

The young couple ran out into the street to find the tall peasant, asking everyone if they had seen him, "a tall man—a peasant with a long white beard—wearing a crushed hat—pushing a cart."

But no one had seen such a man.

After Shabbos, the couple went to the rabbi, and they told him everything that had happened. "Rebbe," they said, "we want to use this money to build the finest *beis medrash* in our town. We will supply whatever money you need, but we will do so only on the condition that, until the building is completed, you will not reveal who gave you the money."

The rabbi agreed, and the building of the *beis medrash* began. It took three years for the building to be finished according to the plans. When it was completed, the congregation gathered with great excitement. Everyone had a seat assigned. Even though a great crowd had come, two seats remained empty—one in the men's section and one in the women's section. The young couple, meanwhile, remained in the back, among the poor congregants.

Then the rabbi went up onto the *bima*. As soon as everyone was quiet, he began his talk. When he was finished, the young couple walked to their seats—to the two empty places.

Everyone watched and wondered. The rabbi then announced, "These are the two people who built our beautiful *beis medrash*."

Upon hearing this, the rich man ran over to his son-in-law and fell to his knees to beg forgiveness. The son-in-law forgave his father-in-law, and the two men told the congregation the whole story, exactly as it happened.

The rich man then approached his daughter and asked her to forgive him also. And she did. The three made peace with each other, and from that time on they remained good friends. The young couple lived in comfort and dignity for the rest of their lives.

Zohara

This is an unusual story: Instead of the usual wicked step-mother found in many folk stories and fairy tales, it has a wicked stepfather.

In another version, found in Gaster (1924) and in Bin Gorion (1916–1921), it is Akiva's second wife who pays a man to kill Akiva's daughter, her stepdaughter. The man, however, saves the stepdaughter's life, although he leaves her in the same condition as the heroine of this story. Instead of a fairy godmother, Elijah the Prophet appears in time to help the person most in need of help.

"Zohara" is the Jewish version of the famous international tale type, A-T 706 "Maiden without Hands," known especially from the Grimm Collection, where it is the thirty-first tale. This telling is an exact match for the standard tale, which is known especially in Europe and Latin America. The IFA Type 706 is known in over a dozen close versions throughout the IFA collecting area. The Maiden without Hands type is known from as far afield as Japan and central Africa. This version of "The Persecuted Girl and Elijah the Prophet" is from Gamlieli (1978) (IFA 5450), as told by Ezra Cohen. The story comes from Yemen, and it is part of the Israel Folktale Archives, which include many variants: IFA 7073, IFA 7941, IFA 8127, IFA 8901, and IFA 9280.

nce there was a couple who had an only daughter, and they named her Zohara, for she was as beautiful as the sun. When Zohara was still a child, her father died. Years passed, and Zohara's mother remarried. Zohara, now a young woman, longed for her father, but her mother told her, "Zohara, my child, nothing can bring back your father. We must continue with our lives. My new husband will be like a father to you, and you must obey him in all that he asks, just as you would your own father."

"I will try to do that to please you, Mother," replied Zohara wisely, "for whoever is dear to you is dear to me, too."

Her stepfather was kind enough to Zohara as long as she did as he commanded. Often, she had to go to the market with him. At other times, he would give her his clothes to wash in the river while he sat nearby and watched her work.

One Friday afternoon he said to Zohara, "Come, let us go to the forest to cut some firewood and perhaps find some flowers for Shabbat." Zohara agreed, and they walked into the woods, deeper and deeper.

"Oh here is some good firewood," said Zohara.

"No, no," replied her stepfather, "let's walk further along, so we can cut some of the thicker trees."

It was quiet in the deep forest—only the song of a bird

or the rustle of leaves in the slight breeze could be heard in the heavy silence.

The stepfather stopped in a small clearing. As Zohara was looking at the trees, he suddenly grabbed her by the waist and embraced her, not the way a father embraces a child, but rather as a hungry, rough lover would do after he had been away at sea for many years.

Although taken by surprise, Zohara quickly understood what was happening, and she pushed and kicked at him with all her strength. She bit and spit and screamed, although there was no one in the woods who could come to help her. Finally, disgusted that he could not have his way with her and thinking that perhaps she was possessed by a demon who enabled her to fight back so powerfully, the stepfather threw Zohara to the ground and quickly cut off one hand and one leg.

"This will be the end of you," and he laughed with a cruel sneer. "You will have no way to return home, so you won't be able to tell anyone. The animals in the forest will have a good dinner tonight. That will teach you to disobey me." And the stepfather left the forest alone.

When he returned home, his wife asked: "Where is Zohara?"

"I don't know," he answered sharply. "She is a willful child and often goes off by herself." What could the mother do? Her heart gave her other messages, but she had no proof that anything was wrong. Only when her daughter did not return home for Shabbat did she know that something evil had happened to Zohara.

When Zohara regained consciousness, it was almost dark. She quickly took her kerchief and her apron and wound them tightly around her leg and arm. Then she reached for a low branch of a nearby tree and pulled herself up slowly from the ground. Using a sturdy stick she found nearby, Zohara hopped through the woods, in the opposite direction from her home, until she could see the lights of a village through the trees.

Near the edge of the forest Zohara saw a cottage. As quietly as she could, she reached the door and listened. Inside, she heard someone reciting a blessing over candles, then a blessing over wine, then another blessing over bread. And at the end of each blessing, Zohara murmured, "Amen."

In that cottage lived a Jew. He was a jeweler who dealt in silver and gold. As it happened, he was the only Jew in this village, and he lived alone most of the year. His mother and father and sister lived in another village several days' travel away, and when there wasn't much work for him, the jeweler went to visit them. On this *erev* Shabbos, he was in the cottage, and in the quiet moment after each blessing, he heard "amen" whispered, like an echo, after his own "amen."

"That's strange," he thought to himself. "I am the only Jew in the village. And if I am the only Jew in the village, who could be repeating 'amen' after me? Perhaps only a demon?" And the jeweler was frightened.

Just then, he heard a knock on the door, and he froze with fear. Out of the darkness he heard a pitiful, weak voice calling, "Let me in. Please, please open the door."

The Jew opened the door slowly and saw no one. But when he looked down, he saw a young girl with bloody wounds, lying on the ground.

Without a moment's hesitation, he picked her up and brought her into the house. Quickly, he washed her wounds and wrapped clean cloths around them. He gave her some warm soup and wine to drink. Then she slept while he watched over her all night.

On Shabbos, she awoke late in the morning. At first, she was frightened when she saw the strange man, but he calmed her and comforted her and said, "Do not be afraid. I will care for you until you become stronger." She felt safe and told the jeweler all that had happened to her; but she did not tell him that the man who had attacked her was her stepfather.

Each day, Zohara grew stronger and her wounds healed. Then one day, the jeweler said, "I will make you a new hand and leg out of silver." And he fashioned for her a silver hand and a silver leg. With the silver leg, she could now walk without the stick. She was very grateful.

The jeweler had become fond of Zohara, and he asked her to marry him. She agreed, and they became husband and wife.

Soon after, Zohara became pregnant. When the time came close for her to give birth, the jeweler took Zohara to his mother's house so that she could watch over Zohara and help her care for the baby.

Before returning to his work, the jeweler said, "Mother, if a son is born, send for me and I will come to perform the *bris*. If a daughter is born, then do not bother to send any message and I will come when I can."

Alone with her mother-in-law and father-in-law and sister-in-law, Zohara felt their coldness and hatred. The two women were disgusted by the way Zohara looked, and they often insulted and shamed her. They called her "the half-woman" and other terrible names. Worse, they tried to harm her and treated her like a wild animal, without any concern for her feelings.

One day soon after, the baby was born—and it was a boy. But Zohara's mother-in-law did not send a message to her son. She did not even make any preparation for the *bris*.

"Did you send a message to my husband?" Zohara would ask, but no one even bothered to answer her. Instead, they took her silver hand and leg and hid them. Zohara, feeling alone and fearful that they would take her child away, decided to leave.

One night, when everyone was asleep, Zohara took her child and ran away.

After a while, although he had not received any message, Zohara's husband came to visit her, thinking that by now she had given birth to a girl. To his surprise, his mother told him, "She left in the middle of the night with your son—for no reason at all."

The jeweler realized that his mother and sister had not

been very kind to Zohara, although he had no way to prove it. He was certain that was why she had run away.

During the night, Zohara had jumped and crawled away from the house as best she could, until she and the baby arrived at the bottom of an isolated hill. There she fell into a deep sleep. In a dream, an old man with a long white beard appeared, standing in a bright light. He said to her in a kind voice, "Here, my daughter, take this bottle of liquid. Before you is a pool of water. Pour the liquid into the pool and dip yourself in the water of the pool seven times. Do as I say and you will be blessed."

Zohara moved as if to take the bottle and suddenly woke up. As she looked up, she saw the old man from her dream, smiling, handing her the bottle of liquid. As she took the bottle, she saw the pool of water in front of her. While the old man, who was Elijah the Prophet, held the baby, Zohara poured the liquid into the pool and dipped herself in the water seven times.

When she emerged from the pool, a miracle happened. The hand and leg that had been cut off were restored, and she was whole.

Overjoyed, Zohara thanked Elijah for his blessing. Then Elijah performed the *bris* and blessed the baby. As he gave the baby back to Zohara, he said, "In this city, there is a big house for sale that no one wants to buy. There is good reason for that: Whoever has lived in that house has died. Buy that house at whatever price they ask for it, and I will help you. Then turn the building into a house of welcome for anyone who is poor or sad or needs help. If you follow what I say, you will be blessed."

Zohara went to the city, bought the house as directed, and waited. Elijah came to her and said, "Fill the water barrel and place it near your door. Then you and your son must go and remain in the house. Keep the doors locked and do not answer no matter who knocks on the door and no matter what time of day it is. Do *not* open the doors."

Zohara did everything that Elijah told her to do. At

midnight, she heard a loud knocking. Remembering what Elijah had told her, she did not open the door. The knocking continued. And who was doing the knocking? A large snake trying to break down the door and kill the inhabitants of the house. Finally, since no one was opening the door, the snake went to the water barrel and drank all the water. Then he threw up all the water back into the barrel. But now it was filled with the snake's poison.

"Ha ha ha," laughed the scheming, treacherous snake. "Tomorrow the people will drink this water and die."

The next night, again at midnight, the snake returned to knock on the door. Again Zohara remained locked inside the house. When the snake still could not succeed in entering the house, he again drank the entire barrelful of water, swallowing the water he hoped would poison the people. Instead, he drank his own poison, and he could not even vomit it out of his body. The poison caused him to swell up until he grew so swollen that he exploded into a thousand pieces.

The next morning, Zohara, who had heard the explosion, opened the door and collected the pieces of snake. She put them into a big pot of boiling water. After a while the flesh melted and in its place seven jewels as bright as the sun appeared in the pot.

Zohara removed the seven jewels and placed one under her tongue. In her mind's eye, she then saw a treasure hidden under the floor of the house, under the very place where she was standing. Digging in that place, she found an enormous treasure and she became rich.

With her newfound wealth, Zohara bought more houses, repaired and furnished them, and opened them up as houses of welcome to all the poor and needy. Poor people came, and so did orphans and widows. She fed and housed them, supported them, and cured them of their illnesses. Soon Zohara became known throughout the land, not only for her charity and her cures, but also for her wise judgments. People came for her good advice and for her just decisions.

One day, many years later, two families of poor wanderers came to Zohara's house. She immediately recognized who they were: her mother and stepfather and her husband with her mother-in-law. But they did not recognize her. She took them in, actually giving them better treatment than all the others around them. She cured them of their ills and offered them generous hospitality.

At times, she heard them discussing some matter in very excited tones. Once, as they were arguing, Zohara asked: "What is it that you are quarreling about so heatedly?"

Zohara's stepfather replied, "My stepdaughter disappeared from home one Shabbos, many years ago. And my wife, her mother, keeps accusing me of having caused this."

Then Zohara's mother-in-law said, "My daughter-in-law suddenly left my house in the middle of the night, taking her baby boy with her. My son, her husband, keeps accusing me of having thrown her out."

After presenting their disagreements and telling their unhappy stories, the two families said to their generous benefactor, "Perhaps you can help us solve these disputes, since you are known to be such a wise judge."

And Zohara replied, "This daughter, daughter-in-law, and wife is actually here. I'll call her to come and be a witness. Then we can all know the truth about what happened in both these cases."

When the families heard this, they were shocked and surprised. They waited in suspense for Zohara, looking to the right, to the left, and in every direction—some in fright, and some with happiness.

Finally, Zohara spoke again. "You are all waiting for Zohara to appear. But she is here in front of you, the same woman who spoke to you. I am Zohara and this young man standing next to me is my son." Seeing their reactions, she wisely added, "But do not be afraid, for I do not plan to punish you. I have forgiven all of you a long time ago for everything you have done to me. Instead, I will help you now and continue to support you, because God has helped me out of all my suffering."

When the stepfather heard this, he trembled so violently that he died. The mother-in-law became ill and died not long after. Zohara's mother stayed with Zohara and was overjoyed to be reunited with her daughter. And Zohara's husband asked for forgiveness and lived with her and their son, working together to help the people who came to their house. They had more children and, in time, grandchildren who continued the good work of their parents.

May we be like them, too!

The Two Bridegrooms

One bride and two ardent suitors—how does one decide which one should be chosen? Well, one could change the law and marry both men, but in folktales, a contest of some kind is usually set up. Sometimes it involves sending the young men to complete certain tasks, with the one who completes the tasks winning the hand of the bride; in other cases the young men must bring back the most precious gift they can find, and so on. The youngest of the contestants always wins the bride.

In this story, however, the rivals are two cousins, and age is not a factor. So how can the bride decide who is the more worthy one to marry? The bride is wise and she sets up a contest, of course. Although in this story the young man does not heal the young woman in order to "win" her, as in "The Magic Pomegranate" and its variants, he does perform a wondrous healing action, which advances his chances considerably. This is another story in which Elijah the Prophet lends a helping hand.

The resolution, in this story, also contains a Jewish wish fulfillment. To say more would be to give too many clues to what actually happens.

This story is found in Eisenstein (1915), Gaster (1924, 1934), and the French journal, *Revue des Etudes Juives XXXIII*. A slightly different version is included in Bin Gorion (1976).

nce upon a time there lived a wealthy and respected rabbi and his wife and their only daughter, Sarah. This child of theirs was the apple of their eye. She was beautiful, yes; but, more important, she was learned and wise. She was the child of their older years, so that when she reached a marriageable age, her parents were quite old.

One day, the rabbi said to his wife, "My good wife, we are both old and our daughter is so young. What will happen to her when we die? We must prepare to bring her to the *huppa* soon, so that she will have a suitable companion for life."

"But who shall become her husband?" asked the rabbi's wife.

The rabbi answered with great care, "My dear wife, I have been giving this matter some thought. I feel that it would be best to marry Sarah to my sister's son, Joshua, who is wealthy and is a good person."

His wife interrupted him, saying, "I would rather marry her to my brother's son, Benjamin, for he is an excellent student and a virtuous young man, although his family is poor. After all, we have enough of a fortune to leave our daughter so that she will not want for anything."

Since they could not decide who should marry their daughter, the rabbi and his wife went to speak to the young woman herself. They told her of their dilemma, certain that she would know how to choose wisely between the two young men.

When the daughter heard the arguments for each of the young men, she said, "My worthy parents. Both cousins please me greatly, and both have good qualities to consider. Since you have asked me to choose between them, I must have some time to consider what to do. I will let you know my decision tomorrow."

The next day, Sarah went to her parents and said, "My dear parents, this is a difficult task, as I do not want to offend either of you by rejecting one or the other of the young men. Therefore, give each cousin 200 shekels and send them on a journey. Whoever uses the money in the best way—by buying merchandise, or however he wishes to use it—he will become my husband. But they must be gone no more than one year. We will have a wedding at the end of a year."

The parents found this decision to be indeed wise and agreed to carry out their daughter's plan. They called their two nephews to them and said, "My children, you are both worthy to marry our daughter Sarah. But if you wish to be considered as a possible husband for her, you must do what we ask of you. We will give each of you 200 shekels. You will go out into the world and use them for whatever merchandise, or anything else, you deem worthwhile. Whoever uses the shekels most wisely will marry our daughter at the end of one year. May God be with you both in your travels."

The two young men happily accepted the 200 shekels and went off peacefully together, each one certain he would win the contest and the bride.

The two cousins traveled to a far-away city and found their way to the marketplace. Joshua immediately began to buy some golden silk cloth, beautiful hand-woven rugs, and other wonderful merchandise—and soon he had spent the entire 200 shekels. Benjamin, on the other hand, decided to purchase jewels, for he reasoned that they would always keep their value. Then the pair started on their journey homeward.

On the way, they stopped at an inn, where they attracted the attention of some other guests who showed a sudden interest in the affairs of the two cousins. They were scoundrels, up to no good, and they began to question the young men about their purchases. In the middle of the night, the thieves stole into their room and took the jewels and money from Benjamin's bag and some of Joshua's merchandise.

In the morning, when the young men discovered the theft, they were very distressed, and Benjamin most of all because he had nothing left.

"I shall return home without delay," said Joshua to Benjamin. "Will you return with me?" But Benjamin was too ashamed to return home without even a shekel. "No," he answered, "I will stay here awhile."

When Joshua arrived home, everyone asked after Benjamin. "I don't know where he is, because he took another route," he told them.

The rabbi and his wife agreed that if Benjamin did not return by the end of the year, Joshua and Sarah would marry. The rabbi's wife and Benjamin's parents were very sad to have no news of Benjamin, and they prayed to God for his safe return.

Meanwhile, Benjamin was considering his next move. "I cannot go back now," he thought. "I have still almost a year left before the wedding takes place. Perhaps God has something else in mind for me. As long as I am here, I will go to the great yeshiva in this city to study." Benjamin entered the yeshiva, and although he was a learned young man, he pretended that he was not since he looked so poor and ragged. He sat behind the stove and listened all day and slept there all night.

One day, the rabbi was discussing a difficult passage in the Talmud. He then read a sentence and told his students to explain it to him on the next day. All night, Benjamin studied the passage, sitting at a table in the *beis medrash.*

Suddenly, Elijah appeared to the young man and

taught him everything he needed to know in order to understand the passage. By morning Elijah had left, and Benjamin wrote an explanation of the passage and left it on the
rabbi's desk. In the morning, the rabbi found the paper and
asked the students who had put it there. No one knew, and
Benjamin said nothing.

The next day, the rabbi read another difficult passage
and again asked his students to study it and explain it.
None of the students could understand it. That night, Elijah
again taught Benjamin, and in the morning the rabbi found
a written explanation on his desk. Still, not one of his students had come forward to say he had written the note.

The rabbi was determined to find out who was leaving
the written notes on his desk, notes that showed such
wisdom that he was moved to say, "How fortunate is the
teacher who learns from his students." So on the third day,
the rabbi read an even more complex passage, one that very
few of his students would ever understand.

That night the rabbi sat in a room next to the *beis
medrash* and, through a crack in the wall, he watched to see
who would put a paper on his desk. He waited all night and,
toward morning, he saw that it was the poor young man
who sat all day behind the stove, Benjamin, who had written
the explanations. And the rabbi wondered how the young
man had understood these passages so well.

The next day, the rabbi acted as though nothing had
changed. But when he came to the unusually difficult passage, he called upon Benjamin to explain it. "Dear learned
rabbi, do not ask me," pleaded Benjamin. "I cannot give you
an answer." But when the rabbi pressed him, insisting that
he speak, Benjamin stood up and spoke with such beauty
and clarity that everyone was amazed. The rabbi then admitted that he had watched Benjamin write the note the
night before.

A short time later, Benjamin realized that the end of the
year was getting closer, so he decided to leave the yeshiva
and continue on his journey. He thanked the rabbi and all
the students for allowing him to study with them during his
stay. They gave him some food to take with him and accom-

panied him to the edge of the forest, wishing him well on his way.

For three days and three nights Benjamin walked in the forest. All his food was gone and he was famished. On the fourth morning, he saw an apple tree laden with beautiful fruit. He reached up and took one apple. As soon as he had eaten it, he became leprous. He was in pain and filled with grief at what had happened to him. "Perhaps," he reasoned, "if I eat another apple, I will die. That is my wish." So he picked an apple from another apple tree, one that was next to the first one—and he was instantly cured, becoming even more handsome than before. "God works in strange ways," he mused, as he thanked God for curing him.

"Let me gather some apples from the first tree as well as from the healing tree. Maybe this will serve me in a way I don't yet understand." And he took equal amounts of apples from each of the two trees and continued on his journey.

He soon arrived in a big city, but when he tried to talk to people, he saw they were all sad. Everywhere he looked, he saw sorrowful faces. "What is distressing you in this city?" he asked them. "Oh stranger, our good King has become leprous and no physician in the land has been able to cure him. All hope is lost for our benevolent ruler," they told him.

"Take me to see your King," said Benjamin. "With the help of God I will be able to cure him." They put little trust in this young man's words, but one of the people said, "Come with me and I will lead you to the King. Everything else has been tried without success. Perhaps God has sent you here for a purpose."

The young man was brought before the King. The King gave his permission to speak by greeting him and asking, "Do you think you can help me, young man?"

"Your Majesty, peace be with you," said Benjamin. "I may be able to cure you with God's help, but you must do as I say and not ask any questions."

"If you cure me, then I shall give you half my kingdom," said the King. "But my life now is so dark that I prefer to die."

Benjamin then took an apple from the first tree, cut a slice, coated it with honey, and commanded that the King eat it. Instantly, the King became violently ill. "Have patience, Your Majesty," urged Benjamin, "for before you are cured, you must endure more pain. But now, Your Majesty, eat this apple and you will be healed." And Benjamin cut a slice from the healing apple, coated it with honey, and gave it to the King.

As soon as he had eaten the second slice, the King was cured and became more handsome than before. All the people rejoiced but no more than the King himself.

The King thanked the young man and, with a grateful heart, said, "Whatever you desire will be yours up to half my kingdom."

"Your Majesty, it was God's work that cured you. But I would ask the King to give me the town where my parents live as a gift, so that I may govern there, if that is Your Majesty's wish."

The King announced, "You will now be in charge of that town. And when you are ready to return home, 400 horsemen will accompany you there." And the King put a golden chain around Benjamin's neck and gave him a great reward as well.

When the people of Benjamin's town heard that the new governor was arriving, they rode out to welcome him with great ceremony.

The Jews of the town also wanted to meet the new governor, and they hoped he would act justly and kindly with them. So the rabbi, the father of Sarah, was chosen to be the Jews' representative. He went to meet the governor with gifts collected from the Jewish community. Of course, he did not recognize that the governor was his nephew. How could he ever imagine that such a thing was possible?

"Fear not," said Benjamin-as-governor to the rabbi. "I grant all the Jews my protection. Continue to live according to your laws and customs."

The rabbi thanked the governor, but as he was about to leave, Benjamin added, "And rabbi, I ask only one thing of you. When you plan to hold a wedding, let me know and please invite me to come."

The rabbi answered, "As it happens," replied the rabbi, "I am holding a wedding in a few days. We will be honored to invite you, and you will be welcome. I wish you long life and happiness, Your Honor." And the rabbi happily reported to everyone that the governor would deal well with them.

The rabbi and his wife began the preparations for the wedding of their daughter Sarah to their nephew Joshua. The only unhappiness that marred this celebration was the fact that no one knew what had happened to Benjamin, and many townspeople feared the worst.

On the day of the wedding, the governor sent a message to the rabbi that he would accept the invitation with great pleasure, and he asked the rabbi to wait for him before beginning the marriage ceremony.

The rabbi prepared a special seat for the governor next to the wedding canopy, so that he would have a fine view of the religious ceremony. The governor arrived, this handsome young man, wearing clothes of gold silk and the golden chain the King had given him. He sat in the seat prepared for him.

Just as the ceremony was about to begin, the governor stood up and said, "Wait! I have something to tell you. This is my bride, for I am Benjamin, the other nephew you sent away with 200 shekels. Now judge for yourselves who has made use of the money more wisely." And Benjamin told them all that happened to him as a student and about the apples and the dying King.

When he heard Benjamin's story, the almost-bridegroom, Joshua, shook hands with his cousin and wished him well, although he was obviously ashamed and disappointed at losing the bride. The new bridegroom, Benjamin, took his place under the canopy, and Sarah and he were married with great joy.

With Sarah next to him always, and their children and their children's children, Benjamin continued to govern the city with wisdom.

The Snake Son

A childless couple who desperately wants to have a child is the subject of many stories in the Bible and in Jewish folk literature. We are familiar with the stories of Sarah and Abraham, Rachel and Jacob, Hannah and Elkanah—and how God finally blessed them with children.

In this story from East European folklore, collected by Cahan (1931), there's another universal motif that forms the core of the story, namely, the birth of a snake as the son. Some may find this a surprising element in a Jewish story. While such transformation stories are found in the folktales of other countries (e.g., Africa, India, China, Italy), they do not seem to fit into a Jewish context. As a matter of fact, there are a number of Jewish variants in which the offspring born to humans are in animal form—a bear, a bull or, more often, a serpent. But in all these cases, the Jews see the story through Jewish eyes and introduce Jewish values and behavior in these psychologically important "passage of life" stories.

There is a Moroccan variant of this tale (IFA 4497), told by Avraham Eloz to Yaakov Avitzuk in Noy (1963). This story tells of a King who has 99 wives but not a single child from any of them. He then marries a young woman (wife number 100) who becomes pregnant. In a dream, the King learns that she will give birth to a snake. And so she does. But while everyone else calls her a witch, the King is kind to her and to their "child," and he cares for them. The story line changes somewhat, but the Moroccan version remains a transformation story in the Jewish oral tradition.

"The Snake Son" is related to the International Tale Type 425, but is best defined by the IFA type 425*Q, known from several tales collected in those archives. Whether from Morocco or Eastern Europe, this transformation story is a love story—between parents and child, and between man and woman—but a Jewish love story.

n a certain town, there lived a wealthy couple who had everything—a mansion, jewelry, gold. The only thing missing in their lives was a child. The husband, Avrom, gave large amounts of money for charity, always hoping and praying they would be blessed with a child, but Sarah, his wife, did not become pregnant.

Avrom traveled to great rabbis near and far asking for help. Wherever he was, Avrom gave charity willingly to everyone in need. But still his wife remained barren. One day, Sarah went to the rabbi to ask for his advice once more.

"Dear rabbi," said Sarah, "tell us what we must do to have a child? We have prayed and hoped for so many years for a child to be born to us. We have given charity and we have supported the synagogue. We have lived as Jews should. If I do not bear a child, then my husband can rightfully ask for a divorce. Then it would be impossible for me to live, as we love each other so much. Help us. Tell us what to do."

The rabbi, a wise and patient man, said to Sarah, "With God's help, Sarah, you will have a child soon. On *Rosh Hodesh*, invite everyone to a celebration meal. Invite all the poor as well as the rich, and place any stranger who comes to your house at the head of the table. All will be well if you do as I say."

Sarah rushed home and, with great excitement, told her husband what the rabbi had advised.

At the time of the new moon, Sarah and Avrom held a great feast and invited everyone in the town, including strangers. The tables were set with the finest silver, crystal, and china. The wine decanters were filled. The food was plentiful and delicious. And every chair was taken. At the head table in the places of honor sat the dignitaries of the synagogue and the wealthiest men of the town. As everyone was eating and drinking, an old man with a long white beard, a stranger in town, arrived at the celebration and asked to talk to the host. Avrom came over to the door to greet the guest and brought him to the table where the poor people and beggars were seated.

"Put me at the head of the table," the old man demanded.

"You are a wanderer, perhaps a beggar. Look at your ragged clothing. How can I ask the wealthy heads of our synagogue to make room for you. Should I disgrace them for you? Here, take this place," Avrom repeated, pointing to a small crowded table. "You will have fine food to eat, good wine to drink, and the celebration is the same."

"Bring me to your wife," demanded the old man. Avrom guided the stranger through the tables to another room where all the women sat. At the entrance, he stopped and said to a servant, "Ask my wife to come here, as someone wishes to see her."

In a few moments, Sarah came to where her husband and the old man waited.

"My wife, this stranger has asked to see you," said Avrom.

The old man turned to the couple and said, "You have forgotten to follow the rabbi's advice—to seat the stranger at the head table. Nevertheless, I shall bless you with a child, but the child born to you will be a *snake*." And the old man disappeared.

Soon after that, Sarah found that she was bearing a child, but the couple's happiness was mixed with fear aroused by the old man's strange blessing.

Time passed—nine long months of waiting—and in Avrom and Sarah's house there was great sorrow at the time of the birth, when the midwife indeed delivered Sarah of a snake. The mother wept and the father tried to console her.

"Sarah, my wife, this is our child. We will care for it and love it. Perhaps God will be good to us and give us another chance—a human child—next time. We must not harm this child of ours. I will build a special box for it to live in—and we will care for him as we would a son. You are my beloved wife and now you must be strong and get well."

When Sarah heard her husband's words, she wiped her tears and felt stronger in what she had to do, knowing of her husband's love and concern.

Every day, the mother and father fed the snake and watched it grow. The snake was gentle and harmed no one, and they loved him very much. Often, the snake would leave the house and go into the woods for days. At those times, the parents worried and wept, but there was nothing they could do.

Thirteen years passed, and one day the snake asked for *tefillin* and a *tallis* to be prepared for him. The father had a special set made and left them for his son. The snake came, took these items, and left.

When five more years had passed, the snake came home and said, "I am now old enough to be married. Choose a bride for me, and I will return in one month's time for the wedding."

Now the parents did not know what to do. The snake had become part of their lives. They cared for the snake themselves, because no servant dared come near it even though the snake would harm no one.

Again they went to the rabbi for advice. "This time, we have a terrible dilemma," they told the rabbi. "How can we fulfill the *mitzva* of marrying off our child whom we love and who has asked for this marriage, when we are afraid that no one will accept him. They will be repulsed or laugh or who knows what. Dear rabbi, have mercy, what should we do?"

The rabbi answered, "God created a solution to every problem—even before the problem arose. Sometimes we have to search for an answer far from home. So go to this certain town a few days' ride from here. Now, when you arrive on Friday afternoon, seek out the poorest man in the town and spend the night there in his home. Eat the Shabbos meals at this person's house. Whatever you see that puzzles you, ask no questions. There you will find your son's *basherte*."

"But rabbi," said Avrom hesitantly, "should we marry this woman to the groom as he is? As a *snake*?" He almost whispered the word "snake."

"Yes," answered the rabbi. "God will take care of all that happens later on."

The next morning, Avrom started on a journey to that certain town and arrived on Friday afternoon. People everywhere were hurrying to prepare for Shabbos. Avrom stopped and asked, "Who is the poorest man in town?" Each person he asked named Yankev as the poorest man. "And where does he live?" Avrom asked. "Oh, you don't want to go there," people said. "It's a hovel. What do you want with him?" And people laughed and went their own ways.

Finally, Avrom found Yankev's house and knocked at the door. Yankev came to the door and asked in a surprised tone, "What do you want?"

"I would like to stay here tonight and to spend Shabbos with you."

"And where would a guest sleep?" asked Yankev. "There is not an extra bed even. And as for food, there is no food for Shabbos."

"My good friend, don't worry. I will be happy to sleep on the floor. And as for food, I will be delighted to buy the food and share it with you."

The poor man saw that the guest was insistent, so he agreed.

On Friday night, as they sat down to eat, Avrom noticed that the man prepared seven platefuls of food. Five he took to another room and two he placed on the table for them to eat. Avrom was puzzled, but he remembered the rabbi's warning not to ask any questions.

At the second meal on Shabbos, the same thing happened—seven plates were prepared, five were brought to another room, and two were served. When the same thing happened at the third meal, Avrom could no longer restrain himself, and he asked where the five plates were being brought.

Yankev replied that Avrom was not allowed to know this. But Avrom pleaded with him to tell him. Seeing that he insisted on knowing, Yankev agreed and said, "I have five daughters who are in the next room. As they have only rags to wear, they are ashamed to come out and meet a guest."

Avrom laughed with relief and shouted, "In that case, here is some money. Buy them decent clothes and bring them here, for I want to meet them." After Shabbos, Yankev took the money and went to buy the clothes. Then the daughters came out of the room, dressed in their new dresses, and Avrom saw that they were all beautiful.

Avrom asked the eldest daughter first if she would return home with him to marry his son. She refused. And one by one the daughters refused. But when he asked the youngest, she said, "Yes, I will go with you." She wanted to leave this terrible place and decided that even the unknown would be better than what she had here.

Avrom gave a lot of money to Yankev as a gift and drove off with the youngest daughter.

Preparations for the wedding began as soon as Avrom returned with the bride. A beautiful gown was made for her, and wedding clothes were ordered for everyone.

The day of the wedding arrived, and still the young bride had not met the groom. As she was finishing dressing for the wedding, she turned and suddenly saw a snake climb in through the window. He closed the shutters and instantly ripped off his snake skin. There stood a handsome young man in a wedding suit. It all happened so quickly that the bride stood speechless, too astonished even to be afraid.

"Do not be frightened," said the young man, "for I have come to tell you that I am to be your husband. But I came to you in my snake form. I was born that way because my father did not give the seat of honor to a certain poor stranger at the head of the table as the rabbi had told him to do. The poor old man, the stranger, was Elijah the Prophet, and it was he who told my parents that they would have a child, but that child would be a snake that they would have to care for. Every night, I study Torah with Elijah in the woods. When we stand under the *huppa*, I may be in the form of a snake, but be assured, my bride, that I will become a man after we are married."

The young man then begged her not to reveal to anyone what she had seen. And in the blink of an eye, the groom, as a snake, slithered from the room back to the woods.

When everything was ready, Avrom and Sarah brought the bride directly to the *huppa*. They were amazed to see the bride so happy, for usually at her own wedding a bride is nervous or even fearful. At this wedding, however, it was the parents who were nervous. But this was not to be the usual wedding.

At a nod from the rabbi, Avrom and Sarah went to the separate room to bring their son to the *huppa*. When they opened the door, they saw a handsome young man wrapped in a *tallis* and praying. The young man stopped praying, stood up, and smiled as he said, "Come, my mother and father. I am ready." Faint with joy, the parents embraced their son and led him to the *huppa*. The wedding turned into a great *simkha* for everyone, and Elijah himself performed the wedding ceremony.

The young man became a great scholar, and he and his wife lived happily until the end of their days.

Her Wisdom Was
Her Beauty

In this love story, a child is, in a sense, the matchmaker and peacemaker between his parents. Jews enjoy love stories, but this one differs from most in that the young heroine has a serious blemish: the face of an animal. (In other Jewish stories it is usually the young man who takes the form of an animal, often a snake or a bear. There are several such tales in this book. See "The Snake Son" and "The Fisherman's Daughter.")

But while the woman of our tale is not the usual beauty, she is a great Torah scholar. Throughout Jewish history, there have been women noted for their interpretations of Torah, among them Hannah Rohel Werbermacher, a learned *tzadeikes* from the Ukrainian town of Ludomir. Jews flocked to hear her learned discourses and to seek her counsel. (Her story can be found in *The Jewish Woman in Rabbinic Literature*.)

This tale, from Morocco (IFA 4510), is in Noy (1963). The Israel Folktale Archive types this tale as 873*A and lists at least five other versions. The tale is not well known outside of the area collected by the workers of the Israel Folklore Archives and is not recorded in this subtype anywhere else. Variants of this tale can be found in Farhi (1870) and Bin Gorion (1916–1921, 1976).

Eight parallels of this story come from Yemen, Iraq, and Eastern Europe.

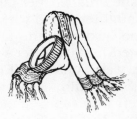

nce upon a time there was a girl who was born with the face of a beast. So hideous and frightening did she look that her parents hid her from the world. They could not bear to see how people would grimace or laugh at their child, nor could they bear the thought of the cruel things people would say about her.

"We must protect our daughter from such evils," they decided. And so, out of love for her, they kept the child at home, cut off from the outside world. When visitors came to the house, the daughter would stay in her room alone.

As she grew older, the girl began to ask questions and to listen to her father studying out loud. She eagerly absorbed everything she heard and asked more questions. Soon, she was reading and learning Talmud, studying the *Mishna* and the *Gemara*. Once, when her father began to ask her questions, he found, to his surprise, that he could learn something from his daughter.

One day, a particularly difficult passage of Talmud was being discussed in the synagogue and no one, not even the rabbi, was able to interpret it to everyone's satisfaction. When the father returned home, his daughter saw that he was deep in thought, and she asked him, "Father, what did you discuss in the synagogue today?"

The father told her of the Talmudic passage and the

difficulty everyone had in understanding it. The daughter then began a discourse that made that passage crystal clear. When she finished, her father blessed her and thanked God for a daughter gifted with such wisdom.

The next day, the father went to the synagogue and presented his daughter's wise words. The men in the synagogue were amazed. "Elijah must have visited you in a dream," they said. "No woman could be as wise as that when not even our rabbi could understand how to solve this problem." But the father swore that the wisdom he had uttered came directly from his daughter. This experience was repeated many times, and everyone soon knew of the young woman's great wisdom.

One day, a young scholar came to this town in search of wisdom and knowledge. He had heard of a certain woman whose words were "pearls of wisdom," and when he came to the synagogue, he asked about her: Could he meet her? Where could he find her? He was told that he could only meet her father, and through him, he could ask any question, no matter how complex, and the daughter would give him the answer, but again only through her father as mediator.

So the young scholar asked her father to ask his daughter about a certain difficult problem. And the next day, the father brought his daughter's answer to him. The young man was amazed.

The young scholar asked two more questions, and each time the young woman unraveled the mystery and gave a clear explanation.

After the third answer, the young scholar said, with tears in his eyes, "I have been looking for such a woman to marry—one who is learned and wise. I would like to have such a companion to study with. I see I have much to learn from such a woman, for her wisdom is like that of Deborah the judge. I would be greatly honored if you consented to this marriage."

At first, the father refused to consider this proposal, not that there were any others. Then the father hesitated. Perhaps he would consider it. The man persisted, even after being told that the young woman was different, that she had a blemish that marred her womanly presence.

"No, I will have none other for my bride," the young scholar insisted. "Her wisdom is her beauty." Upon hearing this, the father decided to give his consent. And so the wedding took place.

That night, the bridegroom saw his wife for the first time, and her face startled him. The bride wept upon seeing how she had shocked him, and she said softly, "You mock at the work of the Creator, which no creature can change. But whatever could be learned, I have learned. Was it not Joseph's wisdom that brought him out of his prison, while his beauty caused him harm?"

Moved by his wife's words, the young scholar remained that night with her. But at dawn, leaving his ring and his *tallit* on the table, he left the house.

Months passed, and in time the young woman gave birth to a son. Her joy was mixed with bitter tears. As the child grew, it became more and more difficult to keep him hidden in the house. So one day the grandparents took the child to school, claiming that he was their own son. And that is what the child believed, too.

Once, the child overheard someone say, "Those old people could not be his parents. They are surely his grandparents. His father must have come and gone in the night." And they laughed.

The child returned home and said to his grandfather, "Tell me the truth. Are you really my father?" At first his grandfather lied, but the youngster kept doubting his replies.

Finally, the boy's mother decided to answer her son's questions. "I will tell you the truth," she said. "You are old enough now and we cannot, we must not, keep it from you." And she told her son, in a gentle voice, everything that had happened. "And here is your father's ring and the *tallit* that belongs to him."

"Where is my father?" asked the boy. And the mother told him the name of the town her husband had come from. It was far away, in another land.

The boy took the ring and the *tallit.* He kissed them and held them close and said, "I will go find my father."

The boy took the ring and the *tallit* and set out to find his father. Months passed, and he finally came to the town where his father lived. He went directly to the synagogue and asked for his father by name. One old man heard the boy asking about the young scholar, and he said, "I am his father. Who are you, and why do you ask for my son?"

The young man stared at this old man, and finally he said, "Your son married my mother and then left her after the wedding night. I am your grandchild." The old man looked at the boy, not believing what he had heard, and yet, the child, strangely enough, resembled him. It was like looking into the mirror of years ago, so much did the child resemble the old man in his youth. "Tell me, my child," said the old man slowly, "do you have any proof of this?"

The boy took out the ring and the *tallit* to show the old man. "These my father left with my mother."

The old man recognized the ring and the *tallit,* gifts he had given his son many years before. He embraced his grandson and in a trembling voice said, "Come my child, I will introduce you to your father."

When the old man and the boy came to the house, the old man said, "Wait near the door, and let me go inside alone." He entered and saw his son sitting at the table. "My son," he began, "do you remember the ring I gave you many years ago? Well, could this be the ring?" And when the old man showed the ring, his son gasped. The old man knew then that the boy had been telling the truth. And he continued, "So this must be your *tallit?*" And the old man turned to call in the boy, saying, "And perhaps you will also recognize that this is your son."

The boy, now reunited with his father, said, "Father, we must return home. My mother is the most beautiful mother who ever lived and also the wisest. I love her so. And I love you, too. Let us become a true family." After much pleading, the father agreed to return home with his son.

When they entered the house, the boy's mother was sitting at the table absorbed in a volume of the Talmud. Only when she heard a voice whisper, "*Mother?*" did she look up. A smile came over her face when she saw her son, and she was very beautiful.

"You see, Father. Look well and see how beautiful my mother, your wife, really is," cried the boy. "Look, Mother, see whom I've brought home with me. My father! Your husband! Now we can be happy together," shouted the boy.

The boy's father stood at the door, not daring to enter in case his wife would not welcome him. When she looked up and he saw her face, he held his breath, for she was very beautiful. He waited, hoping she would invite him in.

As soon as the woman looked to see who was standing at the door, she recognized her husband. They looked at each other for a very long time, she sitting at the table, he standing at the door. Then she nodded, giving him permission to enter. So the husband and wife and their child joined hands in a blessing of thankfulness.

From that time on, the wife kept the ring next to a mysterious bottle with a few drops of water in it. Whenever the son asked his mother about the bottle, she would laugh and say, "It came from Elijah the Prophet." "And what kind of water is inside it?" the boy would ask. And his mother's answer was always the same: "Miraculous water that washed away the veil from my face." And she would laugh, a bit sadly, and add, "I keep the ring next to it as a reminder of the miracle that brought us together again—your love for us both."

The reunited family lived in great happiness and wisdom.

So may we all.

The Clever Young Man

This story echoes other folkstories, such as the King Solomon legend "The Princess and her Beloved," in which the princess is brought to an island or tower in order to change her destiny. But in this tale, it is the young prince who is placed on an island in order to protect him from the evil eye.

Another mirror-parallel is the sudden appearance, "out of the blue" and also on a bird, of the woman who becomes the prince's love. These wonderful magical occurrences create marvelous images. They remind me of the Yiddish love song lyric, "You sent me a gift from heaven" (*"fun himl a matone host du mir tsugeshikt"*) from the song *Shein Vi Di Levone* (*Beautiful As the Moon*).

The story is interesting for many reasons, not least among them the three questions put to the prince by the young woman's father to test his worthiness. He must *do* something in order to earn the daughter's hand in marriage. How he answers these questions is part of the mystery—for all stories contain mysteries we must unravel and answers we must search for.

The name of the princess in this tale is Shemshiya, which in modern Hebrew means a parasol that protects one from the sun. In folktales, the main female character often has a name suggesting a sense of purity or beauty or light. (Among the more famous ones are Snow White, Sleeping Beauty, Beauty of "Beauty and the Beast.") In Jewish stories we find such names as Zohara, which can be translated as radiant light or glow; Krasavitza, meaning beauty; and Shemshiya (from the Hebrew word for "sun," *shemesh*), which could be translated as "Sun Bright."

This tale combines a number of motifs from a series of tale types, and although each element is well-attested in other contexts, no tale with just these elements is recorded. This Iraqi story comes from *The Beautiful Girl and the Prince* (Noy 1965) (Hebrew, IFA 1928), as told by David Eliyahu.

nce there was a great Sultan who had many wives and many children. But his wives had given him only daughters and not one son to inherit his throne. The Sultan became very sad, and lamented, "What reason is there for my life without an heir to the throne?"

His advisors agreed that the Sultan had a problem, but they said to him, "It is forbidden to despair. The King would do well to have faith and to take one more wife. The merciful and compassionate God will favor you, O King, with a son."

Among the viziers of the court was a very clever one who suggested that the Sultan take a tour around the countryside. The Sultan agreed and set out with his vizier. On the way they passed the cemetery where the Sultan's father was buried. The Sultan went in and stretched himself out on his father's grave. As he did so, he heard a voice from the grave saying, "My son, take a wife from among the common people, and she will bear you a son."

The Sultan heeded this voice from the grave and agreed to marry a woman from among the common people. At the end of a year, the woman he had chosen did, indeed, give birth to a son. The Sultan was overjoyed as he watched the child grow into a wise and handsome youth.

As the years went by, the Sultan's joy became clouded by fears that something might happen to his son—that the evil eye might not be turned away in time.

Once again, the clever vizier advised the Sultan: "Prepare a palace on one of your islands in the middle of the sea and bring your son there to be attended to by faithful servants. In that way, Your Majesty, you will be able to guard him against the evil eye."

The Sultan considered this advice carefully and thought it wise. So he had such a palace built on one of the beautiful but wild islands in the sea. And when it was completed, the Sultan's only son was brought there to live in great comfort.

One evening, the young man was on the roof of the palace looking at the stars when, suddenly, he saw a bird flying over his head, and riding on the bird was a beautiful maiden. He closed his eyes, and when he looked again, the bird and the maiden had vanished.

"I am dreaming," he thought, "but what a beautiful dream."

However, night after night, he saw the same bird and maiden. "My imagination is creating an illusion, but it seems so real," he said aloud to the stars. "Tomorrow I must find a way to catch them." So he asked his servants to bring him a large fishing net, telling them that he intended to catch fish with it. But that night he stood again on the roof of the palace waiting for the bird and its passenger.

Suddenly he felt a breeze, and he quickly threw the net into the air, catching both the bird and the young woman.

"Let me go, Abdul Rahman!" the young woman cried out.

"How do you know my name?" asked the astonished son of the Sultan. "I won't let you go until you tell me who you are!"

"I cannot tell you, because it would bring you trouble and danger," she answered.

"For you, I am prepared to fight and even to die. I must know who you are," replied the Sultan's son.

"If that is true, then I will tell you. My name is Shemshiya. My father, the King of Yemen, has decided that he will marry me only to the man who can answer three clever questions. But if anyone tries and fails, he is put to death," the young woman said.

"I am certain I will be able to answer your father's questions in a way that will satisfy him," said the young man. "Tell me the three questions, Princess."

"Very well," said the princess. "Consider them carefully before you answer, my prince. These are the three questions:

Is it possible to fill a bottomless pitcher with a thimble? Is it possible to overturn, with one blow, a house in which dwell the King's enemies? Is it possible to bring down from a high treetop, without a ladder, the nest of birds whose eggs are used to make medicine for a certain eye sickness?

The Sultan's son released the bird and the princess, saying, "I will soon find the answers to those questions and we will be married!"

"That will be good," the princess shouted back as the bird carried her higher and farther away.

The Sultan's son began to think about the three riddles and soon realized that they were more difficult than he had thought at first. Day after day, night after night, he could think of nothing but the three questions and the princess, and he longed for her. He stopped eating and drinking. Then one day, he became too weak to move from his bed.

The servants became alarmed and sent a message to the Sultan that his son had become mysteriously ill. The Sultan ordered the best doctors to come and cure his son. But no matter what medicines or treatments they prescribed, the prince remained ill and his condition grew worse and worse.

Distressed and angry, the Sultan threatened to execute the doctors if they did not save his son from death.

Upon hearing this, the prince whispered, "Father, do not harm the doctors. My sickness cannot be cured by medicines. Only permission to let me go and find the love of my heart will help me."

When the Sultan understood what was causing his son's illness, he agreed to the young prince's request.

The next morning, the Sultan's son boarded a royal boat to take him off the island. When he reached the mainland, he began to walk through a forest. No sooner had he entered the woods, when he heard shouting. He ran in the direction of the voices and saw three men in the midst of a terrible quarrel.

"Stop," cried the Sultan's son. "What is the reason for this terrible argument? Surely you can resolve your differences in a calmer manner. Will you tell me your problem?"

"It is a question of sharing that is causing our quarrel," replied the brothers. "Perhaps you can help us in this matter, after all. We are brothers, and when our father died, not so long ago, he left us three wondrous objects, each with a magical characteristic. The problem is how to distribute these objects between us."

"Can I know what these wondrous objects are?" asked the Sultan's son. And the brothers answered:

"The first is a magic cloak which can lift you up to the heavens like a bird when it is around your shoulders.

"The second is an enchanted hat which makes you invisible when it is on your head.

"The third is a brass ring which fulfills any request asked of it by its owner—and it does so instantly and precisely.

"So now, tell us, how do we know which object each of us should choose?"

"This is an inheritance that cannot be divided," replied the Sultan's son. "You can never know which object will bring any of you a greater benefit. But I have a solution. Sell *me* your three objects and divide the money you receive equally."

The three brothers agreed to this suggestion, but they asked for a large amount of money. After some negotiation, however, the Sultan's son, who had received a handsome sum from his father, paid what the brothers asked, and they made the exchange. The brothers were happy, for now they had enough money for the rest of their lives; the Sultan's son was happy because he knew at once how to make use of the first object at least.

The prince wrapped himself in the cloak and flew to the distant land of Yemen. When he reached the capital of the country, Sana, he went directly to the palace.

At the heavily guarded entrance, he put the magic hat on and became invisible, passing through the doors and hallways until he reached the princess' chamber. He took off the magic hat and opened the door. When the princess heard someone enter the room, she looked up from the book she was reading and was startled to see the young prince.

Somewhat frightened, she asked, "How did you come here, and how did you enter the palace without the guards and servants accompanying you here?"

"Love brought me to you," the prince answered with a smile.

"Oh?" said the princess returning his smile. "And are you also prepared to answer my father's three questions?"

"Of course!" the prince replied simply.

"Very well, I will announce to my father that you want him to ask you the three questions, and we shall see how prepared you are," the princess said.

When the King heard that a young man had arrived to ask for the hand of the princess in marriage, he commanded, "Bring him to me."

The Sultan's son entered the royal chamber, and soon he was conversing with the King in several languages on various subjects. The King was impressed by the young man's wisdom as well as by his handsome appearance. "This is a man worthy to marry my daughter," the King thought to himself. "Let me see how he answers my questions."

Turning to the young man, the King posed the first question. "Here is a pitcher without a bottom. Can you fill it with water using only this thimble?"

The young man put on the hat that made him invisible and quickly exchanged the bottomless pitcher with an identical looking pitcher filled with water and then gave it to the King.

"Ah hah!" cried the King. "You are clever. But now for the second question! Across the fields stands a house where my greatest enemies live. Can you overturn this house with one blow?"

"I can," answered the Sultan's son. He whispered something to the brass ring, and in a distance they could hear the house of the King's enemies fall into ruins.

"Marvelous," declared the King. "And now the last question. Can you bring down from a high treetop in the King's garden, but without a ladder, a certain bird's nest with all the eggs in it?"

"Certainly," replied the Sultan's son. And once again he whispered to the brass ring. And there next to the throne appeared the nest with its eggs.

The King laughed happily and, turning to his daughter, he announced, "My daughter, this young man is clever— and wise besides. If you agree, he will become your husband."

The princess agreed, of course. Then the young man introduced himself and told them where he came from. Messengers were sent to invite the parents of the prince to the wedding. And there was a great celebration in the city of Sana.

The young couple lived a life of happiness, love, and respect until the end of their days.

The Fisherman's Daughter

Many folktales deal with a fisherman and his wife or with a fisherman and his child. The background of the sea opens up many mysteries and many possibilities. In Jewish literature, there are many "fish" stories, such as the biblical "Jonah and the Whale," and the well-known story of "Joseph the Sabbath Lover," in which a poor but pious man, who always buys the best fish in the marketplace for the Sabbath, buys a fish that has swallowed a great jewel.

There are "fish" stories told by Jewish fishermen from the Mideastern countries. Many of these tales have been brought to Israel and to other countries where Jews live.

The theme of this story, that of a woman redeeming an animal lover, has probably been used in folktales for 2,000 years. A type of "Beauty and the Beast" story, it can be found in many places, including the Scandinavian countries, India, Africa, Russia, and Greece.

Essential psychological and spiritual needs are fulfilled by the telling of a tale such as this. Nevertheless, I was surprised—and excited, too—to find this tale from the Jewish oral tradition of Persia (IFA 7152) in Mizrahi (1967).

The theme of "metamorphosis" appears to reflect deep-rooted fears and hopes, for it occurs repeatedly in the folklore of every nation, and it can be found as well in Jewish folktales.

There are other motifs in this story as well, making it a richly layered tale with symbols, images, and metaphors—a tale to hear many times over and to think about.

Above all, it is a love story.

 nce there was a fisherman whose wife had died and left him with their young child. This child, named Esther, grew to be a beautiful young woman, and she loved her father very much. She helped him in every way she could, especially by doing what needed to be done in the house. Every day, the fisherman went down to the sea to fish. Then he would sell his catch in the marketplace and use the money to buy any provisions needed for himself and his daughter.

Near their house lived a poor widow who often chatted with Esther. One day, the widow said, "You should urge your father to marry so you would have a mother to help take care of the house. A young girl should not have to work so hard without someone to help her. Why not suggest to your father that he marry *me*. I will be a good mother to you and do all the housework. You will be like a true daughter to me."

That evening, Esther said to her father, "Dear Father, I do all the housework with a glad heart. But sometimes it becomes so difficult and lonely for me to work alone all day while you are fishing." And the daughter suggested that perhaps her father would consider the neighbor-woman. "After all, she is alone too, Father, and together we could become a family. I know she will be good to us and take care of me and help me."

The fisherman had been reluctant to marry for fear that a new wife would deal harshly with his daughter. But Esther pleaded with her father until finally he agreed to marry the widow.

In the beginning the widow acted kindly to the daughter, but slowly, slowly, she became more demanding and soon left all the housework for Esther to do.

When the father saw how his daughter grew sadder and sadder, he realized what was wrong. So one day he said, "Esther my child, come with me to the seashore. I am not as strong as I was before, and I need your help in my work." From then on, Esther went with her father every day. The two enjoyed being together, and Esther was even able to help her father sometimes. And so it went, day after day.

One day, the fisherman cast his net but could not pull it in, for it was too heavy. Even though Esther helped, they could not succeed in pulling it in. So the father said, "Hold the ropes, my daughter, and I will run for some strong men to help me."

As Esther was holding the ropes, she heard a melodious voice calling from the depths of the sea, "*Let me go and I will do you much good. I will also fill the net with the best fish.*"

Esther was surprised to hear the voice and listened to the strange request, but she held the ropes tighter than before, as her father had instructed her to do. After more pleading, Esther released some of the net's ropes.

Suddenly, a beautiful mermaid-princess arose from the sea, and she said to Esther, "*Take some of my hair. Because of this favor to me, I will reward you. If you ever need my help, burn a single hair and I will come to you immediately and do as you ask.*"

Then the mermaid-princess disappeared, and in her hand Esther held some of the mermaid's long strands of hair.

When Esther's father returned moments later with several men, they managed to pull in the heavy net and saw that it was filled with the best fish, which they sold at a great profit.

Esther's stepmother hated her for going off with her

father every day and not helping her at all. And she grew
more and more jealous every time she heard the fisherman
talking and laughing with Esther as they left to go to the
seashore each morning or on their return home each
evening.

Time passed, and the stepmother vowed to herself to
find a way to be rid of her stepdaughter.

In that kingdom lived a Queen who loved to walk along
the seashore collecting shells and listening to the sound of
the waves breaking against the shore. One day, at a time
when the Queen was expecting a child, she was enjoying
the sea air. A magician suddenly appeared and swore his
love for the queen. The Queen rejected his advances and
shouted, "You act like a snake, not a gentleman."

The magician, hearing this, replied, "Oh, my Queen, a
snake?" And he disappeared as quickly as he had appeared,
but not before turning the child in the Queen's womb into a
snake. (The Queen, of course, did not know what was happening. How could she know?)

When it was time for the Queen to give birth, they
brought the midwife to the palace. As she was attending the
queen, the midwife suddenly fell ill and died. Each midwife
that came close to the Queen died. The King declared, "Whoever can successfully attend the queen in this birth will be
richly rewarded."

Esther's stepmother, hearing the King's proclamation,
thought to herself, "I will send the fisherman's daughter to
the queen. This will put an end to her life, and I will be rid of
her."

So the stepmother sent a message to the palace that
Esther, the fisherman's daughter, was an expert midwife.
The King's messenger brought Esther to the palace. When
she arrived, Esther changed her clothes and, remembering
the mermaid's offer of help, burned one of those long hairs
she kept with her.

Immediately, the mermaid-princess appeared and said,
"*Do not be afraid, but follow all that I say. Ask the King for*

*a large pot filled with honey. Put the pot on the fire and,
while it is heating, bring the Queen into the room and
close the door. When the pot of honey boils, the smell will
entice the infant to come out of the womb. Know that the
infant will be in the skin of a snake, but do not be afraid of
it. And, above all, refuse any gift from the King."*

Esther did all that she was instructed to do. The queen
gave birth to a child in the skin of a snake, and she began to
nurse it. Esther refused to accept any payment from the
King and returned home.

The child grew, and when he was five, the King hired a
tutor to instruct him in Torah and royal manners. But as
soon as the tutor came near the child, he immediately fell
dead. The same fate befell each of his tutors. So the King
proclaimed throughout the kingdom, "Whoever can teach
my child Torah and wisdom will be greatly rewarded."

Again the stepmother sent a message to the palace:
"The fisherman's daughter," she said, "is an excellent
teacher." Esther was brought to the palace, where she
changed her clothes and burnt another of the mermaid's
hairs.

The mermaid-princess appeared and said, *"Fear not.
Ask the King for two rooms adjoining one another. Place
rare and delicious fruit in the first room. In the second
room place the Torah and books in the seventy tongues of
the world. When the prince enters the first room, feed him
some of the sweet fruit. Then bring him to the room with
the books. Whatever book you give him, he will learn easily. Soon he will know all the languages, and he will be
wise in the ways of Torah. But remember, do not accept
any gift from the King."*

Esther did as the mermaid told her to do, and the
prince learned well. Although the King offered her great
rewards, she refused to accept anything and returned home.

The child grew and became a wise and kind young
prince. When he turned eighteen, his parents began to seek

a wife for him among the nobility. But every girl who came near him immediately fell dead. The King and Queen were upset by their son's fate and they proclaimed, "A great prize will be given to the woman who succeeds in forming a union with our son."

Esther's stepmother hastened to inform the palace, "The fisherman's daughter would like to wed the prince."

The King's emissary brought Esther to the palace. As before, she changed her clothes and burnt one of the mermaid's hairs. The mermaid-princess immediately appeared before her and spoke.

"*Do not be afraid for, although the task before you is difficult, you will succeed if you do as I say.*

"*Ask the King for three adjoining rooms which will be closed to everyone but you and the prince.*

"*In the first room, light a wood fire in the fireplace.*

"*In the second, prepare a bathtub full of lukewarm water.*

"*And in the third, place a bed with a mattress of ostrich feathers.*

"*Put on seven more dresses, one on top of the other, and go with the prince to the heated room. Remember, and this is important, instruct the King and Queen that no one is to come into the room, even if they hear the prince screaming. And you, too, must not pay any attention to the screaming.*

"*Then command the prince, saying, 'When I take off one of my dresses, you must take off one of your skins.' After his screams fade, he will shed his first skin. Then immediately take off a second dress and command the prince to cast off a second skin. Each time he will scream, but he will shed one of his seven skins. Finally, only your own dress will remain. Take the seven dresses and seven skins and burn them in the wood fire.*

"*Then go into the second room and command the prince to bathe in the tub of warm water. Scrub him and wrap him in a large robe. Then take the prince into the third room and command him to lie in the bed. And you lie down, too, but remain fully clothed and keep a pillow between you. All will be well if you do all that I have told you."*

Esther followed the mermaid's instructions, and the prince shed all his seven snake skins, while screaming terribly. No one dared enter the room, and everything happened as the mermaid had predicted.

The next morning, the King opened the door and found his son and the young woman lying in the bed. Instead of the snake, he saw a handsome young man whose face shone with beauty. And the young woman, who the King feared was dead, was not dead at all, but more alive and more beautiful than ever.

The two young people were dressed in royal garments and brought before the King and Queen. The King and Queen embraced their son and, with hearts full of gratitude, they warmly thanked the fisherman's daughter for all the help she had given their son through the years.

During this time, the prince had fallen in love with the wise and beautiful Esther. He spoke to her with words of love and asked his parents for consent to marry her.

"No," replied Esther, "I thank you for this great honor, but I am a fisherman's daughter. I am not fit to be the wife of a prince."

"If, as you say, you are not fit to be the prince's wife only because you are a fisherman's daughter," said the prince, "then I now appoint your father to be my vizier. You are no longer a fisherman's daughter, but the daughter of a vizier."

Since the King and Queen were very fond of this wise young woman, they gave their consent.

And Esther, who loved the prince, then gave her approval, too.

When the fisherman's wife, whose jealousy of her stepdaughter had been so great and whose schemes to get rid of Esther had all failed, heard all this, she ran into the sea and drowned.

Esther, the vizier's daughter, and the prince were married in a majestic wedding, and they lived long and happy lives filled with love and wisdom and joy.

The Dream Interpreter

Dreams have played an important role in Judaism. The most famous Jewish story concerning dreams is that of Joseph, in which we have not only dreams but a master dream interpreter, Joseph himself. Jacob dreams a beautiful dream of the ladder and the angels. In many tales, Elijah appears in a dream and helps someone solve a problem. (See "Zohara.")

In other tales, a deceased relative appears in a dream and shows the way to achieve a desired result. There are the prophetic dreams of Miriam, the dreams of Rebecca, of Laban and of Moses, and stories about their significance. A dream plays a central role in the Hasidic tale "The Dream and the Treasure" and in "A Question of Balance."

In this story, a dream gives rise to an urgent search for an interpreter of dreams. What is unusual here is the person who turns out to be the dream interpreter—a peasant's daughter (or, in other variants, a farmer's daughter, or a village girl). She is a *hakhama*, a wise person who can read dreams. Judaism extols the virtues of the *hakham*, a person who is wise, but also honest, truthful, and righteous, and yet remains connected to life. So, too, we value a *hakhama*, a wise young woman.

This Oriental-Sephardic story, adapted from Ibn Zohara (1912), can also be found in Bin Gorion (1976).

The questions that the chamberlain in the story asks the peasant as they ride along (for example, "Who shall carry whom?") can be found in a tale called "He Who Has Found a Wife, Has Found a Great Good" (IFA 11,459), collected by Kenny Shuler from Mazal Yakobi of Persia in Noy (1979). However, in this Persian tale it is the old man's daughter who answers the King's questions, posers similar to those in "The Dream Interpreter," riddles that have intrigued folk and have been woven into our tales. This tale combines elements from a series of stories, for example the motifs of the Clever Peasant Daughter (TMI J111.4) found in A-T 875 and 921, but this tale is unique in its combinations.

here once was a wise and powerful King who had many wives and concubines. One night, he had a dream. This is what he saw in his dream.

An ape from the land of Yemen was jumping on the backs and necks of all the women in his harem.

It was a strange dream that disturbed him greatly, and all day and night, and for many nights, he could not sleep. He thought only of that dream.

"What could it mean?" he wondered. "Could it mean that the King of Yemen will attack me and take my wives and concubines for his own?"

Seeing that the King was so restless and distressed, his chamberlain asked him, "What is the matter? Perhaps I can be of aid. Tell me, O King, confide in me, so that your sadness will be lightened."

The King then told his chamberlain about the dream he had dreamed. "It is a dream that has caused me great suffering, giving me a taste as bitter as death. Do you know of an interpreter of dreams as wise as Joseph was?"

"Your Majesty, they say there is a wise man who understands all dreams. He lives three days' journey from here. Tell me your dream and I shall find this dream interpreter so he may unravel its meaning. Then calm will return to your soul."

The King agreed to this. He told the chamberlain everything he could remember of his dream and said, "Peace be
with you."

The chamberlain went home, made some preparations,
mounted his mule, and started on his journey to visit the
interpreter of dreams.

On the following day, he met a peasant riding on a
donkey.

"*Sholom aleikhem*," the peasant greeted him.

"Peace be with you," responded the chamberlain. "You
who till the earth are also earth and eat earth."

The peasant laughed when he heard these words.

The chamberlain asked, "Where are you going?"

The peasant replied, "I am returning home."

"So am I," said the chamberlain. And then he asked,
"Well, then, who shall carry whom? Shall I carry you, or you
me?"

The peasant once again laughed, not knowing what to
make of these strange remarks, but then he said, "Surely
you jest. How can either of us carry the other? You are
riding on your mule, and I am on my donkey. The animals
are carrying us."

They rode for a while without speaking. Then, as they
passed a wheat field, the peasant spoke. "See how beautiful
this field is, and with such full ears of wheat."

"That is so," replied the chamberlain, "if only the wheat
has not already been eaten."

They traveled on until they came to a tower built high
on a rock cliff.

"Look at this magnificent tower. It is strong enough to
be a fortress," the peasant said with pride.

"It looks strong enough on the outside, if it is not weak
inside the walls," answered the chamberlain.

After another silence, the chamberlain observed,
"There is snow on the mountain."

Once again, the peasant laughed and thought to himself, "Snow? What snow? Where snow—when it is the middle of the summer?"

Just then, a funeral procession passed by. The cham-

berlain said aloud, "Do you think the person in that coffin is
dead or alive?"

The peasant shrugged his shoulders and thought to
himself, "What a fool this chamberlain is, but a fool who has
fooled himself into thinking he is so wise. Heaven keep us
from such 'wisdom' as his."

By now it was twilight.

The chamberlain said, "It is getting dark, and I must
find a place to stay. Is there an inn nearby?"

"Actually, we are now very close to my house," said the
peasant. "Do me the honor of being my guest tonight."

The chamberlain accepted the invitation. After feeding
the animals, they sat down to a good meal. Then the chamberlain was shown to his bed, while the peasant with his
wife and young daughter went to their room to sleep.

As they were about to go to bed, the peasant said to his
wife and daughter, "Our guest is such a stupid man. We
rode together all day, and he has mixed up my brains with
his words. I couldn't make any sense out of them. A fool of
the highest order!"

"Tell us, Father, what did he say?" asked his daughter
with great curiosity. And the peasant told them of the
chamberlain's strange remarks.

"Father, you shouldn't call him a fool," said the daughter, "for he seems to me very wise. You did not understand
the meaning of his words. Listen, and I will explain them to
you, and then tell me if he isn't clever.

"When he told you that you who till the earth are also
earth and eat earth, he was telling you the truth. After all, we
cultivate the soil and eat the food that comes from it, but we
are made of earth. Is it not written, 'For dust you are, and
unto dust you shall return?'

"And when he asked who shall carry whom, what he
meant was which one of you will entertain the other, because when you tell stories and riddles and sing songs on a
journey, traveling becomes more pleasant. You don't think
about the hardships of the road much, and you feel as
though you are being *carried along.*

"What he said about the wheat fields could mean that

possibly the owner is a poor man who may already have sold the crop to pay his debts.

"When he said that the fortress tower was strong outside, but weak within, he was also right. There might not be enough food and drink inside the tower to sustain the people protected by its outer walls.

"And when he spoke of snow on the mountain, he meant that the hair on your head was white—and you should have replied, 'Time has done this to me.'"

"But when he saw a coffin, how could anyone who is wise ask if one lying in it is dead or alive?" asked her father.

"Father, when someone has children, then he is never dead, for his memory is kept alive. That's what he was asking: Did that person leave any children?"

All this time, the chamberlain was listening to the conversation, and he marveled at the young woman's wisdom.

In the morning, the daughter said to her father, "Father, take this tray of thirty eggs, a bowl of milk, and a whole loaf of bread, and bring it to our guest. Ask him the following: 'How many more days before the end of the month? Is the moon full, and is the sun complete?'"

The father, puzzled at this request, did as his daughter asked. But first he ate two eggs, a piece of bread, and drank some milk. Then he brought the tray to the chamberlain and asked him the questions.

The chamberlain then replied, "Tell your daughter that two days are missing in the month, and neither the moon nor the sun is full."

When the peasant returned to the kitchen, he laughed and said, "I was right. This man is stupid. It's the middle of the month, and yet he says we have only two days left in the month."

"Father," said the daughter, "did you eat any of the food I gave you for our guest?"

"Yes," answered the father. "I ate two eggs, a piece of bread, and some milk."

"O Father, our guest is a wise man!" replied the daughter.

Just then, the guest came into the room and said, "May I speak to your daughter?" And the peasant consented to this request and introduced the young woman.

The chamberlain then told her who he was and the reasons for his journey. "Now that I hear your wisdom, I hope you can interpret the King's dream as well as you explained my words. Listen." And he described the King's dream as the King had told it to him.

"I understand this dream," said the young woman. "But I will interpret it only to the King himself."

After her parents had given their consent, the young woman traveled to the palace with the chamberlain, and soon she stood before the King.

When the King saw the young woman, he was pleased by her appearance, and he spoke to her kindly. When they were alone, he asked her to tell him what the dream meant.

"Your Majesty, I assure you that the dream contained no evil prophecy," declared the young woman. "Do not fear. But I hesitate to reveal its meaning, because it may bring you shame and sadness."

"I ask you to speak," said the King. "No one is here, and I must know what this dream means."

Finally, the young woman answered, "Very well, Your Majesty. Search your harem. There you will find a young man disguised as one of the women, but he is their *lover*. He is the ape you saw in your dream."

The King searched the harem, and he did, indeed, find a handsome young man wearing woman's clothing. The King had the man executed and sprinkled his blood on the faces of the women who had sinned with him. And those women were banished from the palace forever.

After all this was done, the King asked the peasant's daughter to marry him. She gave her consent gladly—but only after the King swore to be faithful to her and her alone.

And she wore the royal crown wisely.

Kindness Rewarded

The story of Hanina is found in rabbinic literature about Adam and Lilith, a female spirit who bore Adam a son. This son could change into a frog or a scorpion or any other animal, and he would also perform miracles as a reward for kind treatment. The rabbis told such fanciful stories to teach the lessons and values of the Torah. This story must have been very popular with the people because of its imagery and its fantasy quality. In some versions the animal that rewards Hanina, or Johanan as he is called in some Hebrew versions, is a scorpion. In another version, it is a frog, not the frog-son of Adam and Lilith, but a frog who is actually a bewitched princess whom Hanina marries after many adventures. Though there are differences in the versions, the theme of "reward for kindness and hospitality" remains the essence of the tale, a significant theme found in folk stories around the world.

This tale and the one that follows are connected by a number of common motifs. "Kindness Rewarded" is not found among International tale types, but uses TMI D217 Animal languages learned and B215.4 and B580 Animal help to humans. The tale has a number of features of A-T 554 "Grateful Animals," but shares these with the next tale, "Kindness Returned." Sources of this story are found in Eisenstein (1915), Bin Gorion (1916–1921, 1985), and Gaster (1924, 1934).

I first read this story in a favorite book when I was a child, Aunt Naomi's (1921) *Jewish Fairy Tales and Legends*. I have loved the miracle that resulted from kindness to a frog.

nce upon a time there lived a learned and pious man and his wife. Their only son, Hanina, had grown up, married, and moved to another town.

One day, Hanina's father sent a messenger to his son, asking him to come home. Sensing that the message was of great urgency, Hanina rushed to see his parents that same day.

When Hanina arrived, he found his parents in bed, gravely ill. Embracing his son, the old man said, "My son, your mother and I are about to die. We have lived a long life and a good one together, and now we will die together. It is so ordained.

"Always remember what we have taught you: to love God, to follow God's ways, and to help others. My son, when the period of mourning is over, it will be the eve of the Passover festival. Go out to the marketplace and buy the first thing that is offered to you. Buy it, no matter what it is or what the cost may be. Take good care of it and treat it with great care and love, but do not question it. In time, it will bring you good fortune. Listen to my words, my son, and all will be well."

With tears in his eyes, Hanina promised his father to do all that he asked of him.

And things happened just as the old man predicted:

The old couple died on the same day, they were buried together, and the week of mourning ended the day before Passover. Remembering his father's words, Hanina went directly to the marketplace, wondering what adventure awaited him there.

As he entered the marketplace, Hanina saw an old man coming toward him with a silver box of an unusual ornate design.

"Purchase this, good sir, and it will bring you good fortune," the old man said.

"What does it contain?" asked Hanina.

"I do not know the answer to that question," the old merchant replied. "Only the person who owns this box and opens it at the Passover feast this evening can know what is inside."

Naturally, Hanina was intrigued by these words. "What is the price for this silver box?" he asked.

"A thousand gold pieces," the merchant answered.

That was an enormous sum for Hanina, nearly all the money he owned. But Hanina remembered his promise, paid the money, and took the silver box home. He placed the box on the seder table and, during the Passover feast, opened the box.

Inside, there was a smaller silver box of the same design.

When he opened the second box, out sprang a frog, jumping and hopping around the table gleefully.

Surprised, and disappointed, Hanina's wife gave food to the frog, which devoured everything greedily. The creature ate so much during the eight days of the Passover holiday that it grew to an enormous size. Hanina built a large cabinet for this strange possession, but the frog soon outgrew it.

The frog kept eating so much, and with such a ravenous appetite, that Hanina and his wife had very little food for themselves. Every day, they had to sell something they owned in order to keep the frog supplied with food. But they did not complain.

One day, they realized that there was nothing left in the house to sell, not even a feather pillow. Only then did Hanina's wife begin to cry.

To her astonishment, the frog, which was now bigger than a man, spoke to her.

"Listen to me, wife of the faithful Hanina," it said. "You have treated me well. Therefore, ask of me whatever you like, and I shall carry out your wishes."

The woman looked up, and only one thought was in her mind. "Give us food," she sobbed.

"It is there," said the frog. At that exact moment the door opened, and a huge basket of food appeared.

The frog turned to Hanina and asked him for his wish.

Hanina thought to himself, "A frog that speaks and performs wonders must be wise and learned too." He turned to the frog and said aloud, "I wish to know all you can teach me—the entire Torah and the seventy known languages of the world."

The frog agreed, and his method of teaching was exceedingly strange. He wrote out a few words on strips of paper. Then he ordered Hanina to swallow the papers. When he had done this, Hanina knew everything he had wished to learn, including the languages of the beasts and birds.

Soon, Hanina became known as a learned and respected sage.

One day, the frog spoke again.

"The day has come," said he, "when I must repay you fully for all the kindness you have shown me. Your reward will be great. Come with me to the woods and you shall see marvels performed. Bring a wagon with you."

Hanina and his wife followed the giant frog to the woods very early one morning. The frog looked comical as he hobbled along.

Arriving at a clearing in the woods, the frog cried out in its croaking voice, "Come to me, all the inhabitants of the trees, the caves, and the streams, and do what I ask of you. Bring precious stones from the depths of the earth and bring roots and herbs."

Then began the strangest procession: Hundreds upon hundreds of birds came twittering and flying through the trees; thousands upon thousands of insects came crawling from holes in the ground; and all the animals in the woods, from the tiniest to the largest, came in answer to the call of the frog. Each group brought some gift and placed it before Hanina and his wife, who stood in shocked silence watching it all. Soon, a great pile of precious stones and herbs and roots was heaped before them.

"All these belong to you," said the frog, pointing to the jewels. "Of equal worth are the herbs and roots—with them you can cure all diseases." The frog then taught Hanina's wife how to use them as remedies for all kinds of disease.

"Because you obeyed the wishes of your dying parents and did not question me, you are now rewarded," the frog explained.

Hanina and his wife thanked the frog and then asked hesitantly, "May we know now who you really are?"

"Yes," replied the frog. "I am the son of Adam and Lilith. God has given me the power to assume any form I desire. I must leave you now. Farewell, *farewell, farewell.*"

With these words, the frog began to grow smaller and smaller until it was the size of an ordinary frog. Then it hopped into a stream and disappeared. At that moment, all the creatures of the forest returned to their homes.

Hanina and his wife piled all of their treasures into the wagon and pulled it home.

They became known for their wisdom and their charity, as well as their wealth, and they lived happily and at peace with all their neighbors for many, many years.

Kindness Returned

The theme of grateful animals repaying someone who helped them is common in the folklore of many nations: Chinese, Indian, Greek, Tibetan, German, and is classified as A-T 560. Such stories as "The Fisherman and His Wife" and "The Grateful Animals and the Ungrateful Man" are well-known tales and can be found in many story books. There are a number of Jewish versions in the IFA, all of which use the central motif of falling in love through the sight of a hair of an unknown princess (TMI 11.4.1) and that of the identification of a hair dropped by a bird (TMI H75.2). The connection of this tale with the preceding tale, "Kindness Rewarded," is not only through the commonality of names, but with the shared features of the folktales' delight in having humans interact with animals. Many such animal tales in Jewish lore are indexed in Noy (1976).

In some books, this story, "Kindness Returned," is a continuation of the Hanina and the Frog story ("Kindness Rewarded"). However, the second half can stand by itself, so I have chosen to treat the two as independent stories. Whereas in other versions, Hanina marries the princess after his wife dies, my retelling led me to create an ending which, at least to me, is more just, especially to his wife. So be it. That is the way of folklore, and I do not doubt that stories have changed in the oral and written transmissions in a similar way.

The sources for this story are the same as for "Kindness Rewarded" (see introduction). Louis Ginzberg (1909–1938) referred to similar stories in the *Arabian Nights* concerning the gratitude of three animals (the fish, the dog, and the raven) towards human beings who have been kind to them. Those tales, in turn, are based on an animal fable found in *Pantchatantra*. And so it goes. Stories are often retold and embroidered with the different threads of a specific culture. That is how such a story found its way into Jewish legend.

nce, the Land of Israel was ruled by a foreign King who was a mean-hearted man. He was not only a cruel King, but he also refused to share his power with anyone, and so he would not marry. The King's counselors often spoke about this. They kept hoping to persuade him to marry. "Perhaps," they reasoned, "he might become a kinder person if he had a good wife."

Finally, the counselors appealed to the King, and the chief advisor spoke out. "Your Majesty, it is proper for a king to be married and to leave an heir in his place. Only thus will his name be remembered and his deeds live on. Otherwise, when he dies he will soon be forgotten."

The King thought this argument made sense. "I will think it over," he said. "Return in three days' time for my answer."

When the counselors returned at the appointed time, the King greeted them in the garden. Just as he was about to give them his answer, a black raven flew overhead and dropped a long strand—a single strand—of golden hair that it had been carrying. The King caught the golden strand as it floated downward, turned to his counselors, and said, "You tell me I should marry, and indeed *I will marry.*" He paused and then continued in a challenging tone, "But *only* to the maiden from whose head this hair comes. Only she will be my Queen. If you cannot find her in one year's time, you and your families will be killed—and all the Jews in the kingdom will be severely punished."

The royal advisors were perplexed. Here the King had finally agreed to marry, but then he had set an impossible task for them: to find the woman with the golden hair. To make matters worse, if they didn't find the woman, they and their families would all be killed. They examined the golden hair carefully, but they found no clues as to the woman's identity.

Desperately, they asked, "Your Majesty, give us three days to give you an answer as to our plans." And the King agreed.

Just at that time, Hanina arrived at the palace. He was often invited by the King to offer his advice on various matters. The King held him in great esteem, as did all the people of the land. As Hanina walked through the royal gardens, the black raven flew overhead and cried out, "*May the Lord protect you from the dangers you will soon encounter.*" Hanina, who could understand the language of the birds and of all animals, heard this and asked in astonishment, "What dangers, O Raven?" But the bird had already flown away.

The royal counselors, upon hearing Hanina's voice, hastened to meet him. They surrounded him and they all began to speak with one voice, "Hanina, you are wise. Hanina, you know the language of the birds and of all animals. Hanina, you would be doing a good deed beyond all others." And they told Hanina about the task the King had set for them, and about the punishment they, along with all the Jews, would endure if the woman with the golden hair was not found in one year's time.

Hanina listened and thought to himself, "It is curious that a black raven brought this golden hair, and that a black raven gave me an unusual blessing. What is the meaning of this, I wonder?"

To the advisors he said, "I will find this golden-haired woman who is destined to be our Queen. I know the language of the birds and, perhaps with their help, I will succeed in finding this woman and saving us *all* from the King's cruel threat."

Hanina hurried home to begin preparations for his journey. He called his wife and children to him and told them the story. They wept and pleaded with Hanina not to go. "No one can accomplish this task," they said. "The world is so big, and the King has no right to demand such a search!" But Hanina hugged each of them and asked them to have faith in God. Then he blessed them and bid them farewell. When he left, he took with him three loaves of bread, some healing herbs, and twelve silver coins.

As Hanina walked through a forest, hoping to meet the frog who had once helped him, he heard a huge raven cawing and crying. "What is the matter, my friend raven?" asked Hanina.

And the raven answered, *"I have not eaten anything for three days."*

Remembering the laws of kindness to animals, Hanina took out a loaf of bread and gave it with an open hand to the raven.

The raven ate it and felt better. *"You have saved my life,"* said the bird, *"so I will bless you. May God protect you from all the dangers you will encounter. May I be able to repay you for your kindness."*

Hanina wondered at this blessing, but the raven flew away quickly, and Hanina continued on his journey.

Suddenly, a monstrous wild dog appeared, moaning and yelping. "What is the matter, friend dog, that you cry so bitterly?" asked Hanina.

"I am ill, and I am starving, for I have not been able to eat during the last six days because of my illness," complained the dog. *"A large dog like myself should be fierce and strong, but I am weak, overcome by an unseen enemy."*

Hanina healed the dog with his herbs, and gave the dog his largest loaf of bread. The dog ate hungrily and then gratefully repeated the raven's blessing.

At the edge of the forest, Hanina came to a river. As he was eating the remainder of his third loaf, the fisherman came along, threw his net into the water, and soon was pulling the net in with a heavy load. Seeing that he was having some difficulty, Hanina rushed over to help the fisherman. When the net was pulled to the river bank, they saw that it held a large beautiful fish. The fisherman was overjoyed at his catch, and Hanina merely said to him, "Sell me this fish and I will give you twelve silver coins."

The fisherman accepted this offer at once. Hanina took the fish and threw it back into the river. The fish swam away, but only after giving to Hanina the same blessing he had heard from the raven and the dog.

After traveling a long distance, Hanina came to a city. The Queen who ruled over the city was the woman with the golden hair, but Hanina did not know that.

As Hanina passed by the palace, the Queen saw him from her window. She knew he was not from her city because of the garments he wore, but she sensed that he was looking for her. She asked her servant to bring the stranger to her.

When Hanina came before the Queen, she asked him with great curiosity, "Tell me, who are you and where do you come from? And why are you here?"

Hanina told the Queen about the King and his need to find the woman with the hair to match the golden strand. He then showed the Queen the long golden hair to prove that he was telling the truth. As he unwound the long piece of hair, the Queen pulled a long golden curl from beneath her crown, and it matched perfectly the hair Hanina had brought. Hanina caught his breath and slowly released it, as he began to tremble.

"What makes you so fearful, Hanina?" asked the Queen.

"Your Majesty, I hoped these long months to find you, and I had faith that God would bring me to you. But now that I have found you, I must make a request of you, and I hope you will fulfill it.

"Dear lady, I beg you to return with me to the Land of

Israel to wed our King. He has been alone too long. Once he marries, he will surely become less cruel. Only if *you* return with me will the King's counselors and their families be saved from certain death and the Jews from great suffering. That is the King's condition."

The Queen said to herself, "I do remember sitting in the garden one day when the wind was blowing gently. I took off my crown so that I could feel the wind blow through my hair. Suddenly, a bird swooped down and pulled out a strand of my hair." Then she said to Hanina, "That you are here does not surprise me. But I see you are a wise man with faith in God. Therefore, before I grant your request to marry your King, you must fulfill two tasks for me. Only then will I accompany you to your land, marry your King, and save the Jews and the King's counselors."

"My time is short, for I must return within three months," Hanina pleaded. "The lives of our people are in danger. What are your tasks, dear Queen?"

"Take these two empty flasks," said the Queen, "and bring them back to me filled with water, one with the water of paradise and one with water from *Gehenna*."

"How is that possible?" cried Hanina in despair. "*I am only a human being!*"

The Queen replied, calmly but firmly, "When you have fulfilled the first task, I will tell you what the second one is. Only after you have successfully completed both tasks will I go with you to marry your King."

"I have no choice," replied Hanina in desperation. "I will immediately begin the search for the waters."

And so Hanina took the two flasks and left the palace. Standing in the nearby forest, Hanina began to pray. "God of the Universe, what can I do? I searched for the woman with the golden hair and found her, and there was some hope that I could save the Jews by bringing her to marry the King. But now I must first do something that is beyond my powers. What shall I do?" And Hanina shook the flasks angrily at God, and he felt like smashing them against a tree. Instead, he fell to the ground and began to weep.

Suddenly, Hanina heard the croaking sound of a raven,

the same raven he had fed when it was hungry. "*I am the raven who met you in the forest,*" said the bird. "*When I was in pain, you fed me. Tell me why you are crying, and I will now help you.*"

Hanina pointed to the two flasks and said, "O Raven, I must fill these flasks with water. Not water from the river, but from Paradise and from *Gehenna*. How can anyone help me?"

"*Do not doubt God's powers,*" answered the raven. "*Tie a flask to each of my wings and be in this place when I return,*" commanded the raven. As soon as Hanina had tied the flasks to each of its wings, the raven flew to *Gehenna* and filled one flask with the boiling black waters of the river in *Gehenna*. As it did so, its wings were singed, and blisters broke out all over its body.

But the raven did not stop—it flew on to the waters of Paradise. The raven bathed in the waters, its feathers became shining black, and its body was healed. The raven filled the other flask with the pure water and returned to meet Hanina.

Hanina joyfully brought the two flasks to the Queen. Taking the flask filled with the *Gehenna* water, she poured a drop on her palm. Instantly, her flesh was burned. But when she poured onto her palm a drop of the cool, pure water from Paradise, her palm was healed. She knew then that Hanina had successfully accomplished the first task.

"Now Hanina, since you have brought what I asked for, you must help me find something I lost many years ago," said the Queen. "When I was a young girl, my father gave me a beautiful gold ring with a pearl mounted in a setting of the most exquisite design. I loved this ring very much. But one day I went swimming in the river and forgot to take off my ring. When I returned home, I realized I had lost it in the river. Find this ring for me, and I will keep my promise to return with you and save the Jewish people."

Once more, Hanina prayed for God's help. He felt so alone and helpless. How could he find a tiny object lost so many years ago amongst the billions of grains of sand at the bottom of the river? It was a hopeless task, and all his efforts had been wasted. Hanina walked along the bank of the river, praying for God to help him find the ring.

As he was staring at the water, a fish, the very one he had saved, came to the surface and said, *"Hanina, you who saved my life, tell me how I can help you now?"* And Hanina told the fish what the Queen's request was—to find the ring that she had lost many years before.

Without hesitation, the fish dived deep into the river and found Leviathan, the king of all fish, and told him the story and of the debt it owed Hanina in return for saving its life. Leviathan immediately ordered all the fish near him to gather and to send messages to all the fish in the river that this ring must be found as a reward for a man's good deed.

The fish responded by searching and sifting through all the sand until a fish found the golden ring buried deep in the sand and brought it to Leviathan. Leviathan gave it to the big fish saved by Hanina, who then threw the ring up on the river bank.

Just as the ring landed on the ground, a large boar came running up to swallow it, but the monster dog who had been healed and fed by Hanina ran out of the forest and scared off the boar. So the dog, too, repaid its debt of gratitude.

Thanking the fish and the dog, Hanina quickly picked up the treasured ring and returned to the Queen's palace.

The Queen was amazed, and she was very happy to have the ring. As she put it on her finger, she said to Hanina,"I promised to come with you if you completed these tasks. I shall make my preparations and be ready in three days."

Taking along her counselors, the Queen accompanied Hanina back to the Land of Israel.

When the King heard that Hanina and the Queen were coming, he rode out to greet them on his royal stallion. He was very pleased when he saw the majestic golden-haired woman. He liked her very much, and so he commanded that preparations for the royal wedding begin.

The King now held Hanina in even greater esteem. He gave Hanina the royal signet ring and made him his chief counselor. The other counselors, whose lives Hanina had saved, grew very jealous and they began to hate Hanina.

"Can they not see how Hanina saved their lives?" Hanina's wife often asked. "How hard would it be to return kindness with kindness?" She was shocked and saddened by the counselors' envy and hatred. Only a few months after Hanina's return, she died, as though she had been stabbed by their daggers, so cruelly did their vicious words and deeds cut at her heart.

Hanina grieved bitterly for his wife. When the Queen heard the news, she went to the place where the body was being prepared for burial. She stood beside the body and touched the heart of Hanina's wife with the pearl of the ring. Then she carefully poured some of the water of Paradise on the body. As she did so, she prayed to the Holy One, Blessed Be He, to restore life to this good woman.

Slowly, Hanina's wife opened her eyes, and she was restored to life. Hanina was overjoyed to see his beloved wife alive again and thanked God over and over again.

When the King learned of this, he commanded the Queen, "Kill me and restore me to life. I have always wanted to know what death would be like—just for a moment."

"Your Majesty, I will not kill you, for life is sacred and you must not think of death as a game. Besides, this water can only restore life to a good and pure person, not to one who has done cruel and wicked deeds. You would need to repent for much that you have done."

But the King would not listen, thinking only of what he wanted to do. After all, *he* was King. So he turned to his servant, handed him his sword, and ordered, "Kill me, or else I will kill you!"

The servant slew the King on the spot.

The Queen then took the flask containing the waters of *Gehenna* and poured it over the King's body, which was instantly burned up and turned into a pile of ashes.

The Queen turned to the witnesses and said, "Dear people, every person, even a king, must take life seriously. I could only bring a person back to life who was holy and good. But as your King was wicked, he was not restored to life. I can do no more."

After the King was buried, the Queen decided to return to her land. Before she left, she turned to the counselors and said, "If you choose Hanina to rule over you, you will have a ruler who is kind and just." The counselors listened and saw the wisdom in her words.

They selected Hanina as their King, and there was peace and justice in the land.

Laughter

Castor oil, cod liver oil, and olive oil were remedies my mother recommended for every ailment. She was a great advice-giver and wanted to help everyone who came to her for guidance. If someone mentioned a medical problem in the course of a conversation, she would offer her fail-proof medical advice, which was likely to be one of the three oils. Since my mother was from Russia, this was, no doubt, an old-world or "old-fashioned" remedy.

The "miracle" treatment in this story, from Cahan (1931), is another fail-proof cure that Jews have found necessary, as well as effective, for centuries—namely, laughter. Humor is the clearest mirror of a people, and for the Jews it has also been a natural healer. A-T Type 571 contains the central motif in its third section, TMI H341.3 Foolish action by hero, princess made to laugh, but this telling is unique.

A recent study by Black (1984) concludes that laughter has great therapeutic value. The more people laugh voluntarily, the better they feel because, Black points out, physiological changes occur during laughter that have not been sufficiently explored. Norman Cousins, who discovered the healing power of laughter in his own life, wrote about it in *An Anatomy of an Illness*.

Sholom Aleichem certainly understood the tremendous benefits of laughter and advocated it through his philosophy and his stories. And so have Jews throughout the centuries, because humor has helped them learn ("Before beginning a lesson, tell a humorous story," says the Talmud), cope, and heal naturally, especially when they have experienced so much grim reality. Jews add irony to their laughter, in order to see reality from a different perspective—as they have done even in the darkest of times.

Jews have a great repertoire of humorous stories, tall tales, anecdotes, and jokes, many filled with self-disparaging humor, but many with the joy of discovering an incongruity, a sense of relief, a saved situation. And sometimes Jews will tell a story simply for the joy of sharing a social laugh to make them feel close to one another. Jewish literature offers a marvelous collection of humorous characters: fools from Chelm, the tricksters such as Hershele Ostropolier, *shnorrers*, and *badhanim* or marriage jesters, to name a few.

I was introduced to this story by Ruth Rubin, who read it to me in Yiddish. She had taped it years before, and we sat together, listening and laughing. And our delicious and contagious laughter and enjoyment ring in my ears as I tell it to you.

How does caster oil cause laughter? Here is the story. And I wish for you hearty laughter always.

A word about the rhyme at the story's end: In many cultures there are ritual closings when the storyteller finishes his tale. There are also rhyme endings to some Jewish East European and Middle Eastern tales. In this case, there is the Yiddish rhyme that ends the tale:

A shtekele arein	Throw the twig in
A shtekele arois	Throw the twig out
Die meise is ois	It's the end no doubt.
A shtekele arois	Throw the twig out
A shtekele arein	Throw the twig in
Die meise is gor fein.	How nice the story's been.

 doctor and a cobbler once lived together in the same house. The doctor worked on one side of the house and the cobbler on the other. The doctor healed sick people who came to him, and the cobbler made shoes for them.

Whenever the cobbler had a little time, he would go over to the doctor's side of the house and silently watch him at his work. He never said anything, because he didn't really understand what the doctor was doing. Still, when the doctor prescribed castor oil for a patient, well . . . that was something he did understand.

When the doctor died, the cobbler began to practice in his place. Well, he practiced in a way, you see, for no matter who came, no matter what the ailment, he gave them all the same advice: "Drink a spoonful of castor oil."

If someone came with a headache, his advice was, "Drink a spoonful of castor oil." Whether the patient had a toothache or a broken finger, the cobbler would recommend a spoonful of castor oil. That was his sole treatment—castor oil. And it always seemed to heal the patient.

One day, the King's daughter fell ill. A swelling grew in her throat. The King called in the best doctors in the kingdom, but no one was able to heal the princess. Time passed—the boil kept getting bigger, and still no cure could be found. Finally, the news of the princess' ailment reached the distant town where the cobbler lived.

As soon as the cobbler heard about the princess' illness, he packed a bottle of castor oil, together with his cobbler's tools, and set out for the King's palace.

When the cobbler arrived at the palace, the guard asked him, "What do you wish here?"

The cobbler answered, "I want to enter the palace."

The guard questioned him further. "And what will *you* do here, in the palace?"

The cobbler replied, "I heard about the princess' illness, that she has a bubble in her throat. Since no doctor has been able to help her, I have come to heal her."

The guard took a good, long look at the little cobbler with the long beard, at the castor oil and the cobbler's tools—and he burst into laughter.

"The greatest physicians weren't able to heal her. Who are you to think you can do what they couldn't?" And the guard laughed even harder. "No, I won't let you in."

"What does it matter to you how I look or what I carry?" argued the cobbler. "If I say I'll heal the princess, I will heal her."

The guard could not get rid of this cobbler. So, after a while, he went to see the King about the cobbler. "There is this Jew at the gate, and he keeps insisting that he can heal the princess."

The King had lost all hope, but when he heard this, he ordered the guard to let the stranger in. The guard brought the cobbler before the King, and the King said to him, "Listen, whoever-you-are, I will give you a chance to heal the princess. But if you don't heal my daughter, then I will have your head cut off. What do you say to that?"

"Agreed," answered the cobbler. "I accept the challenge."

Then the cobbler was led to the princess' chamber. She was lying on the bed, poor thing, and it was sad to see her with her throat wrapped in bandages and her breathing slowed and difficult. It was a pity to see her suffering so. The cobbler went to work. He took the bottle of castor oil and the hammer and began to hammer at the bottle cap.

But the bottle broke, and the castor oil spilled all over the floor. When the cobbler took one step with the new leather shoes he had made for himself, he slipped and fell, spinning around and around and around and, with his beard, wiping up the entire bottle of castor oil.

The princess started to laugh, loud and strong. The bubble in her throat burst, and instantly she was healed. Well, there was great rejoicing throughout the palace.

When the King realized what had happened, he approached the cobbler and announced, "Since you have healed my daughter as you promised, I give her to you as a wife and half my kingdom as well. A gift for a gift."

> Throw the twig in
> Throw the twig out
> It's the end no doubt.
> Throw the twig out
> Throw the twig in
> How nice the story's been.

Miracles All Around

Sometimes people become known by a certain characteristic or a phrase associated with them. Whatever it is then becomes attached to their names. For example, there were two cousins named Irving in my family. Because of a slight age difference, or more likely a difference in physical size, one was known as *Big* Irving and the other as *Little* Irving—even into their adult years.

A friend told me that the color of his hair made him known as "Yankl-the-red-haired" (*Yankl-der-roiter*). I remember a woman who was known for saying "no" to any suggestion or request, or so it seemed to her family. Her husband referred to her, with a touch of affectionate humor, as "Dvore the nay-sayer" (*Dvore di neinzogerke*). He would sometimes close his letters with "*Di neinzogerke* sends you regards." That was as much her name as was her given name.

In our story, which comes from the Babylonian Talmud, *Taanit*, and is also found in Ibn Shahin (1557), Nahum is called Nahum *Gam zu Letova* (Nahum This-Too-Is-For-The Best) because that was his philosophy of life. And it turned out to be for the best. This tale is known around the world in variant form, but this version (506*C in the IFA) is apparently limited to the collecting area of the workers connected with the IFA, who have garnered at least four instances of oral transmission. It is also found in a similar version in Gaster (1924) (440) and in Bin Gorion (1916–1921) (VI, 224).

here once was a man named Nahum Gam zu Letova, which means, "This, too, is for the best." People called him that because, no matter what happened to him, whether it was for good or for evil, he would always say, "*Gam zu letova.* This is also for the best." When he said those words, they sounded like a little prayer, and they would keep Nahum from becoming overly joyful or envious, upset or angry. Soon everyone began calling him Nahum Gamzu.

During the reign of the Roman emperor Caesar, the Jews decided to send a gift to him. Perhaps, they thought, the emperor would remember this gift and act more kindly toward the Jews in times of trouble. But who should be the one to deliver this gift? The rabbis decided that none other than Nahum Gamzu should be the one to present the gift.

The Jews, poor though they were, gathered together precious jewels, wrapped them in fine handwoven cloths, and put them in a chest. Then Nahum started on his journey to the emperor's palace. In the evening, he stopped at an inn.

As he was sleeping, some of the townspeople stole the contents of the chest and filled it with earth so he would not notice the theft when he lifted it in the morning.

When morning came, Nahum opened the chest to make certain everything was in order. When he saw the earth in place of the precious stones, he said aloud to himself, "*Gam zu letova.* "This, too, is for the best." And Nahum took the chest, undisturbed, and continued on his way to the palace.

When he reached the palace and came before the emperor, Nahum placed the chest before him and said, "This is a gift from the Jews. Let this also be for the best."

The emperor signaled to his servants to open the chest.

When the cover was lifted, the emperor saw nothing but the earth. His advisors sifted their hands through the earth, looking for the hidden treasure. After all, who brings *only earth* to an emperor? But when the advisors found nothing of value, they said, "Your Majesty, the Jews are making a mockery of your royal dignity. Put this man to death."

At that moment, the Prophet Elijah appeared in the guise of one of the emperor's advisors, and he spoke out, "O King, this earth *may* hold great value for you. Perhaps it is part of the earth used by Abraham, the beloved of God, earth that became *transformed* into swords and arrows when it was thrown before the enemy. Remember that the Hebrews captured cities with this earth. Why not try it and test its worth *before* you kill this innocent man?"

The emperor listened and, after a while, said, "Very well, I accept your counsel. There is a city I have been unable to capture for some time now. Let us use it to find out if this earth has the magical qualities of ancient times."

The soldiers took the earth and threw some of it in the air toward the city. The earth turned into swords and spears and arrows, and the emperor was able to capture the city.

Overjoyed by his victory, the emperor ordered that the chest be filled with precious jewels as his gift to the Jews, and he gave Nahum a magnificent robe as a reward.

Nahum left the palace and, on his way home, he stopped at the same inn.

The thieves were surprised to see Nahum and *especially* to see him return with so much honor and reward. Since they were curious as to what had happened at the palace, they asked Nahum to tell them about his journey.

Nahum told them, "I brought the emperor a chest filled with earth. And he was so pleased with my gift that he gave me these jewels and a special royal robe."

On hearing this, what did those thieves do? They took several chests, filled them with the same earth they had put into Nahum's chest, and brought those chests to the emperor. "O Emperor, we bring you the same earth that the Jews sent you."

The thieves were already picturing themselves in royal robes, carrying home chests full of gold and precious jewels.

The emperor commanded, "Test this earth." But when the soldiers threw the earth into the air, it remained earth and only fell back to the ground.

Then the emperor ordered that the thieves be put to death and buried in that same earth.

As for our friend, Nahum, well, he continued to say "*Gam zu letova*" for the rest of his days.

Gam zu letova!

A Companion in the
World-To-Come

Curiosity about the world-to-come, preparing for the world-to-come, and concern about the world-to-come are themes in many Jewish stories. In Peretz's *Sholom Bayis* ("Domestic Happiness"), there is a scene in which the porter Hayim hears the rabbi discuss this topic on Shabbos afternoons in the synagogue. He listens with intensity as he is transported to *Olam Haba*. Then the porter prays fervently for a "little piece of the world-to-come for myself, for my wife, and for my little children."

In several Jewish stories, the question of who will be a certain pious man's companion in Paradise causes the pious man to begin his search. The question is resolved by finding out, usually in a dream, that the companion is a humble worker—a barber or a butcher. How can a common butcher be deemed worthy to be the heavenly companion of a scholar? That's what this story is about. The tale can be found in *Tanhuma B* (Introduction) and in other variants in Wistinetski (1538), Ibn Shahin (1557), *Yalkut Sippurim Umidrashim* (1923), and in several versions in Gaster (1924).

This version of the story also appears in the Israel Folktale Archives (IFA 9518) as collected by Tamar Agmom from Hakham Eliyahu Modgorshvili (from Soviet Georgia) in Shenhar (1974). In a parallel tale from Soviet Georgia (IFA 9314), "The Companion in Paradise" is a robber. (This variant was collected by Zalman Baharav from Semion Plagashvili in Cheichel (1973). Other variants (IFA 5804) are found in Marcus (1966). The IFA lists this tale as type 809*A; the European tale A-T 809 has a similar central theme, but the match is not a close one.

To discover the worthiness of the scholar's other-world companion, we must hear the butcher's story ourselves.

lam Haba—the world-to-come—Paradise, where each one of us will find companions of equal worth.

Once, a great scholar named Joshua, a man known as much for his humility as for his learning, was thinking about the world-to-come. And he wondered, "*Who* will be one of my companions after all, in *Olam Haba? Who* will be worthy to sit next to me?"

This question began to occupy his thoughts so much that he fasted and prayed to God to send him a sign so he might know who would receive the same reward as he.

One night, in a dream, Elijah the Prophet appeared to him and said, "Shmuel the butcher will be your companion."

Joshua awoke, disturbed and disappointed to hear that a butcher would be his companion for eternity. He fasted and prayed still harder, with greater fervor. And again at night he had a dream in which Elijah appeared. "Joshua," said Elijah, "I have told you already who your companion will be in *Olam Haba*. It is the same Shmuel the butcher."

And Joshua woke up filled with anger. "A *butcher!*" he cried. "A mere butcher. Not a sage, not a scholar, not a leader of the community, but a *butcher!*" And he began to weep bitterly.

Suddenly, Joshua heard a voice calling out from Heaven. "Joshua, if you were not a good and pious man, a

man of understanding and learning, you would be punished
for those thoughts. Why do you weep? Because a butcher
will be your companion? Do you know what *good deeds* this
certain butcher Shmuel has done? You look only at his
worldly condition and his bloodied clothes. But in the
world-to-come he will have great honor. There is *no doubt*
that he deserves to be your companion—and you should
have no doubts either."

The next morning, Joshua decided to meet this com-
panion-to-be. When he found him, Shmuel was in his shop,
working.

"*Sholem aleikhem*," offered Joshua.

"*Aleikhem sholem*," returned Shmuel.

"Tell me, if you will, what good deeds, what *mitzvot*, do
you perform?" asked Joshua.

Shmuel the butcher replied, "Good deeds? Well, I am a
butcher and work hard to make a living. I am careful about
the meat I sell, and half of my profits I give to charity. The
other half I use for myself and my family."

"Yes, yes, I see," said Joshua, "but many people perform
these *mitzvot.*" And then he quickly added, "I don't say this
to lessen the worth of these good deeds, but is there nothing
more special that you have done? Perhaps—perhaps a deed
that no one but you could have done? Something out of the
ordinary?"

The butcher remained silent for a long time, while he
thought. Finally, he said slowly, remembering in his mind's
eye, "Yes, there was something that happened a long time
ago—many years ago, in fact."

"Tell me, please, I want to hear your story," pleaded
Joshua with great interest. The butcher began.

It was a long time ago, as I have said. One day, I looked
out of my window and saw a caravan passing by. Walking
behind the caravan was a long line of people, obviously
captives or prisoners. As I watched the line of prisoners, my
eye caught something that made me want to cry: a young
girl of about twelve, walking among the captives and weep-

ing. I ran out of my shop and walked beside her. "What happened to you?" I asked. "Where are you from?" And the child replied, "I am a Jew, and I was taken captive by these peasants to be sold as a slave. I come from a town far from here. They killed my whole family. I am so afraid. I remember hearing that Jews free other Jews. I pray that a Jew will come to redeem me, too." And she wept again.

When I heard this, my heart ached for her in her misery, and I feared for her. So I said, "Remain silent. I will go to your master and redeem you." I went to the peasant who had captured her, and I bought her, paying a high price— but there was no question as to what I had to do. She was young and so forlorn, so fearful. I took her to my home, and she became part of my family.

I had an only son, and when the time came for him to marry, the young girl was also of marriageable age. One day, I called my son to me and said to him, "My son, I want to advise you, and I ask that you follow my words so that your life will be good in this world and in the next." And my son answered, "Father, whatever you ask, I will obey your wishes." So I said to him, "My son, marry this girl. She will be a good wife, and I will provide whatever you both will need for the wedding and for your own home."

My son took my advice and we all rejoiced. I prepared everything for the wedding, so that nothing would be lacking. A banquet was arranged and everyone in the town was invited—the rich and the poor, even passing strangers and visitors from other towns. The poor sat with the other townspeople, so no one should feel left out or different. The best food and wine were put on the tables, people ate and drank, the musicians played, we laughed, we sang. It was a festive meal fit for a king.

Before the wedding ceremony began, I looked around the tables to be certain everyone had had enough food and wine. It was then I noticed that the people at one table had not touched their food. I went over to them at once and asked with some concern, "Friends, why did you not eat? Is there something wrong with the food?"

"No, No!" they replied. "The food is excellent, and we

find no fault with it." Finally, one guest said, "How can we eat when here sits a man at our table who weeps as if his heart is broken?" Then another said, "We have lost our appetites. How can we eat when we see someone suffering so? When he cries, so do we."

Hearing these words, I turned to the man who was the cause of their unhappiness and asked him to step outside. Then I said, "Friend, your weeping is spoiling our *simkha*. Tell me, what is the matter? If you need money, I will lend it to you. If you are in trouble, tell me, and perhaps I can help you. No one should bear such pain alone."

The young man looked at me a moment, and then he said, "I am not in debt or in any trouble. Nevertheless, my pain is great, and I don't know what to do. The young woman who is about to marry your son is *my betrothed.* We come from the same town, and ever since we were children our parents had planned that we would marry. Our parents were good friends, living next to each other. When I was born, my parents planted a cedar in my honor. And when she was born, her parents planted a cypress nearby. They hoped that eventually the branches of the two trees would be intertwined and form a *huppa* for our wedding. But then tragedy came upon us; we were both taken captive, and we lost track of each other. At long last, I was redeemed, and I have been searching for her everywhere. That is how I came to this town. Since everyone was invited to your wedding, I came, too. But when I found out who the bride was, I could not keep from crying."

I didn't know what to say, but then I asked, "Can you prove what you say?"

"Yes," answered the young man. "I have the written agreement of our betrothal."

"What else can you tell me so that I can be certain that this is really the girl you seek?" I asked. "Does she have any identifying marks you can describe?"

"Yes, my beloved has a heart-shaped mark on her right hand," he answered.

I myself had seen that unusual mark on her right hand, and I knew that he spoke the truth. So I said, "Do not depart. I must speak to my son, and you will have your heart's desire. I will return in a few moments."

I went immediately to see my son and, with an aching heart, I said to him, "My son, when I asked you to follow my advice in the first place, you obeyed without question. Now I ask you to take my word once more. Remember, I want your happiness above all.

"This young woman is betrothed to someone else, and her *basherter* is here. I have examined the betrothal document he has with him, and there is no doubt about it. So I ask that you give back everything I have given you—the bedding, clothing, and jewelry—so that this young couple can have something to begin their life together. For your marriage, which I will arrange soon, my son, I will *double* what I did today, so that you will have a full share of happiness. This I *promise* you."

Without hesitation, my son agreed to my request. So I brought the young woman, like my own child, to the *huppa*, and she was married to her *basherter*. The two of them lived in my home for a while until they decided to return to their home town.

With an open heart, I gave them gifts and accompanied them part of the way because they had become very dear to me. Soon after, my son married a young woman from our town, and now they live happily together. God has been good to me, and I have lived to see my grandchildren brought to the *huppa*, too.

The scholar Joshua listened and wept when he heard the butcher's story.

Then he quietly said, "Now I understand better than before how highly I am esteemed by God in Heaven. My friend, my companion, I am honored and rejoice that I will be one of *your* companions in the world-to-come."

The Promised Robe

This is a story of devotion, of a wife's loyalty to her husband. It is a love story of faith in God and of trust between a man and a woman. It is also a story of sacrifice. Above all, it is a love story.

The tale comes from Farhi (1870) and Gaster (1924). It can also be found in *Yalkut Sippurim Umidrashim* (1923) and in Rosen (1858). This tale is allied to A-T 888, but with a reversal of roles of the wife and the husband.

The story is also centered on *Olam Haba*—the world-to-come. The desire to know who will wear the promised robe in the world-to-come sets the two scholars off on a search for Joseph the gardener. As in other tales, the choice is surprising at first. Why should not a scholar wear such a magnificent robe? Or a generous rich man? Why only a poor gardener?

More than just a "search-and-a-reason" narrative, the *real* story-behind-the-story deals with Joseph's faithful wife—a woman of courage and action.

t was the eve of the Day of Atonement, and two sages were walking in the courtyard of the Temple in Jerusalem. Suddenly an angel appeared carrying a robe of great brilliance and beauty, but the garment was incomplete because there was no collar on it.

Each of the sages said to himself, "This robe is surely meant for me in the world-to-come." And they asked the angel, "Tell us, we beg you, *who* will wear this wonderful robe?"

And the angel replied, "This robe is for Joseph the gardener, who lives in Ashkelon."

After the Sukkot festival was over, the two sages left Jerusalem and decided to meet this remarkable gardener, Joseph. They were curious about the man who deserved such a magnificent robe.

When the sages arrived in Ashkelon, the noblest and richest people of the town came to greet them and invited them to be their guests. But they refused all offers, asking only to meet Joseph the gardener. The people brought the two sages to the small house outside the town where Joseph and his wife lived. They found Joseph in the garden, tending his herbs.

When Joseph saw his visitors, he was greatly surprised. "Welcome to my home," he said as he bowed to them respectfully, "but I am puzzled to find such honored guests coming here rather than accepting finer offers of hospitality in town. I have only two loaves of bread to offer you."

The guests happily accepted the bread, and together they pronounced the blessing and ate.

After saying grace, the two sages turned to Joseph and said, "We were eager to find you and to ask you about yourself: How do you earn a living, and may we know where you come from?"

"My dear guests," began Joseph, "as you can see I have no occupation other than planting and selling the herbs on this small plot of land. My father, who was a learned and wealthy man, lived in Ashkelon for many, many years. When he died he left a great deal of money but, somehow, I was not able to manage his affairs well enough, and soon nothing of his wealth remained. The people of the town turned against us, since we were no longer prosperous and could not pay our debts.

"We left Ashkelon and came to this small plot of land on the outskirts, which had been owned by my father, and here I planted herbs to sell. Whatever I earn, I give half to charity and keep half for ourselves to live on. Life has sometimes been hard, but God has been good to us and sustained us.

"People knew we had very little to eat. Sometimes for Shabbat we did not even have flour to bake bread. But my wife was ashamed to let the neighbors know that she had nothing to bake. She would burn twigs in the oven so that there would be smoke in the chimney.

"One Friday some neighbors came to the house, thinking to expose my wife's trick. When no one was in the kitchen, they opened the oven. And a miracle happened, because the oven was filled with delicious *hallas*. They called out to my wife with great excitement, 'Come quickly, the loaves of bread are done! It's a good thing we came and opened the oven in time, or your bread would be burned!'"

"My wife, who had hidden in the back when she first heard the neighbors come in, came out slowly, afraid they were making a fool of her. And then she saw the wonderful *hallas*. It was a miracle from God. The neighbors never again came to shame us."

The sages listened, and then said, "Joseph, your faith in God will be repaid. When we were in Jerusalem, we saw an angel holding a robe that shone like the sun, but, strange as it may seem, it has no collar. However, the angel told us the robe is destined to be yours. We have come to meet you and to learn how you came to be worthy of such a wonderful robe. Praised be God, for He has prepared much good for you in the world-to-come."

Joseph thanked the sages for the news they brought, and blessed them.

When the sages had left, Joseph's wife came into the room and said, "My husband, I heard what the two sages told you about the robe. Do as I tell you, and your robe will be made perfect. Go and give a certain amount to charity. I know you do not have that much money, so I have a plan. Take my advice, and all will be well."

"What is your advice, my good wife?" asked Joseph. "I will listen and heed your wise words."

"Sell me in the marketplace as a servant," said the wife. "Then take the full amount and give it to the poor. In that way, your robe will be completed and you will indeed be worthy of wearing it."

"Sell you?" cried Joseph. "No, no, I cannot listen to this advice. Besides, how can I sell you to another man who might desire you? Then I would have committed a much greater sin, so that the robe would be lost to me completely. I will not even consider this suggestion of yours."

"Husband mine," insisted the wife, "I swear that I will never allow any other man to touch me, even if it means my life."

So Joseph was finally persuaded to take his wife to the marketplace and to sell her as a servant. He then gave the money he received to the poor.

The man who bought Joseph's wife was a wealthy merchant who was used to having his way with his servants.

But this woman refused all his gifts and fought him with all her strength. He offered her gold and jewels and beautiful clothes—even offering to set her free—but she rejected his offers and would not allow him to come close.

Finally, the merchant became angry with her, since he could not have his way with her, and he gave her to his overseer. The overseer also tried to seduce her, but she resisted his advances, too. Because of this, she was treated cruelly, and life became very hard for her. But she bore it all patiently.

One day, she was in the marketplace when her husband, Joseph, saw her. He was about to go over to her, when he noticed a man approach her, while the overseer was not looking, and say to her, "I will buy you from your master if you will marry me." And she replied, "No, I cannot marry you, for I am already married."

The man offered her money, and still she refused. When Joseph heard this, he knew she was true to her oath. He went up to her and wept at what had become of their life together. But she said, "Have faith, Joseph." And then the overseer called her away.

That night, Joseph could not sleep. Suddenly he heard a voice from deep inside him—and yet from far away.

"Joseph, your robe is complete, and it is a fine robe. But the robe of your wife is even more splendid, because it is due to *her* that your robe is completed. Now, because of your faith in God, and your faithfulness to each other, you will be rewarded. Go to the center of your garden and you will find a treasure hidden there by your father."

Joseph rose from his bed, took a shovel, measured to the center of the garden, and indeed found a treasure of gold and jewels.

He hastened to redeem his wife from her master, and he brought her home.

Together, they performed many good deeds of charity and lived in comfort and happiness all their days.

The Leopard and the Fox

Fables are short, didactic, and simple. As a relatively modern development, fables have a clearly stated moral (although they also contain multilayered values) and use animals and plants, men and gods as characters. In earlier Jewish fables, many of them probably translated and adapted from Indian, Roman, and Greek sources, the animals were not only endowed with human personalities, but also spoke wisely about Torah. The greatest collector and teller of Jewish fables was without doubt Rabbi Meir, a student of Akiva, who lived in Hellenic Asia Minor during the second century B.C.E. According to the Talmud, he collected 300 fables, some of which are found in the Talmud and *midrash*.

During the Middle Ages, three other Jewish scholars contributed to the body of Jewish fables:

1. Berechiah Hanakdan (about 1190 C.E.) was born in France but, while living in Oxford, he wrote 107 "fox fables" (*Mishlei Shualim*). While many of his fables can be traced to *Aesop*, and some to *Romulus* collections, others are similar to the work of *Marie de France*. Confusion over their respective birth dates makes it unclear who influenced whom. Berechiah Hanakdan's foxes, though, echo talmudic discussion and quote biblical sources. Though his fables include a great deal of quoted Scripture in the *nimshal* (the commentary that supplies the moral of the fable), his goal was not to teach religion. Rather, he sought to give lessons in social behavior. He opens each fable with an aphorism or *pitgam* and closes it with a mini-sermon. He made sure to write his tales, rather than entrusting them to the oral tradition.

2. Jacob ben Eleazar (1195–1250) and later Rabbi Joel in 1250 translated *Kalila and Dimna*, a well-known collection of fables, from Arabic into Hebrew. Originally written in Sanskrit, *Kalila and Dimna* was first translated into Persian, and then, in 750 C.E., into Arabic. These wondrous tales, presented in a frame-story by two jackals named Kalila and Dimna, served as a treatise on human nature for the princes of India, a sort of handbook for rulers. Interwoven with ethical sayings and proverbs, the fables and parables explore

universal questions of truth and deceit, ambition and loyalty, fear and power.

Containing many maxims from the Talmud and stressing Jewish values, the book was popular among the Jews of that time.

It was, however, Rabbi Joel's Hebrew version of *Kalila and Dimna* that served as the text for John of Capua's Latin translation in the 13th century. This Latin version, called *Directorium Vitae Humanae*, became the source of the European versions, which became known throughout the continent and were soon transformed into popular European folktales.

3. In the 13th century, the Hebrew poet Joseph ibn Zabara collected fables from ancient Hebrew, Greek, Arabic, and Indian sources for his *Sefer Shaashuim* (*Book of Delights*). Influenced by the Arabic pattern of such books as *Kalila and Dimna* and by the Indian Bidpai fables, the author weaves several shorter tales into one major frame-story. The book has a "chain" structure with various tales serving as links.

"The Leopard and the Fox" comes from Ibn Zabara's *Book of Delights*. There are four didactic stories found within the frame of the leopard and fox tales, in the pattern of *Kalila and Dimna*. The first of these, the miracle remedy, and the second, the cutting off of the Goldsmith's hand, are found in similar stories throughout the Near East and have close affinities to materials from India. The King Solomon tale comes from the *Legends of Solomon*. The last of the stories is one of the most famous of all fables: the "Widow of Ephesus," A-T 1510 and Perry, *Aesopica*, number 543. It is found as an independent story in *Tosafot* (*Kiddushin* 80b). The fable is also very much a part of Jewish traditional storytelling and is found in numerous fable collections (Hanakdan 1921) and other traditional material sources. It is found in Gaster (1924) (447) and in Bin Gorion (1916–1921) (III, 239).

Here, then, is a fable for all time.

 t one time, many wild animals lived together comfortably in a land of plenty. In this place was a leopard with his mate and cubs. For a time all continued well with them, according to the patterns of nature.

Nearby lived a fox. And though the leopard and the fox were neighbors, and even friends, the fox kept thinking, "I am safe so long as the leopard feeds on other animals. But why should I always live in fear and uncertainty? Who knows when he will become hungry and angry and pounce on *me*?" So the fox talked around and around, acting according to the sage advice of the rabbis, "Before evil comes, seek a good solution and act upon it."

Finally, the fox hit upon a plan to get the leopard and his family to leave their home for a place where they would not survive. Thus the fox would be rid of the leopards without fighting or bloodshed, because actually, in any battle with the leopard, the only blood that would be shed would be the blood of the fox. And the fox was too shrewd to let that happen. And again he drew his advice from the rabbis, who said: "If someone comes to kill you, kill him first."

The next day, the fox visited the leopard. They greeted each other warmly.

"*Sholom aleikhem,*" said the fox.

"*Aleikhem sholom,*" replied the leopard.

And as they were talking, the fox said, "There is a

beautiful countryside I found not far from here—a land of flowers and food—which would delight you. It is a paradise to behold."

The fox painted such a glowing picture of this paradise that the leopard was indeed eager to see it. And yes, the leopard found it to be as the fox had described it and began to consider the move, but. . . .

"Well," said the fox, "what's the matter? If you like the place, bring your family there *today*. Why do you hesitate? Remember what the sages say, 'He who hesitates is lost.'"

"True, true," replied the leopard. "But such a decision must not be made alone. I always consult my wife first. She is my wise partner in life. And her wisdom is beyond the price of rubies."

The fox's spirits fell, for he knew how wise the leopard's wife was.

"You ask your *wife* before you make a decision?" cried the fox suddenly in outrage. He was not about to let *her* foil *his* plan. Then he changed his tone and spoke softly to the leopard, as if they were conspirators. "A woman's advice is *foolish*," he said, "and sometimes even evil. Ask her advice, by all means, but then do the *opposite* and *that* will show you what to do." And the fox worked very hard to convince the leopard not to trust his wife's counsel.

Fired up by the fox's words, the leopard returned home and said to his wife, "*Wife*, we are leaving this place to go to a paradise. I have seen it and it is so."

"Who brought you to that place? What made you decide on this sudden change of residence when we have been happy and content right here?" asked the leopardess.

When the leopard explained that it was the fox's idea, his wife simply said, "Beware of the fox!"

And then she continued, "The two craftiest creatures in God's creation are the snake and the fox. So, before you follow the fox's advice, you should know how the fox defeated the lion."

"How did he do that?" the leopard asked.

This is the story the leopardess told her husband:

There once was a lion who was a friend to the fox. But the fox kept thinking of ways to cause the lion's death. He knew he could not fight the lion and win. So the crafty fox thought of a plan. He came to the lion, pretending to have a pain in his head. Oh, he could go on the stage, he was such a good actor.

"What can I do to help you feel better?" asked the lion, his friend.

And the fox cried out, "OOooooh, my head hurts so. OH, I remember an old remedy that my grandmother always used for such a pain. But I will need your help to bind up my feet and hands—for that is the remedy."

The lion agreed and tied up the fox according to his directions.

A moment later, the fox began to smile, and he shouted "Yes! Yes! YES! It is indeed a remedy for pain—my head hurts no longer. It's a miracle remedy."

So then the lion untied the fox. But one day the lion's head began to ache. He ran to the fox's den and cried, "Brother fox, tie me up, for my head hurts me terribly."

And, of course, the fox tied the lion with long flexible twigs. Then taking some heavy stones, he crushed the lion's head.

"So much for the fox's friendship, my husband," concluded the leopardess. "It is false and evil. Tell him to go to this paradise himself. *We* will stay *here*."

"O wife," replied the leopard impatiently. "They are right when they say women are foolish and have no head for decisions. The fox is my *friend*. I have confidence in him." And the leopard went to find the fox.

By the time the leopard located the fox, he had calmed down and realized that the story his wife had told him had disturbed him, after all. So he told the fox about his doubts.

The fox replied, without taking a breath, "Well then, if you follow your wife's warning, you might end up like the gold-smith."

"What do you mean?" asked the leopard.

And the fox replied with the following tale:

Once a goldsmith was working when his wife came into his shop and said, "Listen, husband, we can be rich if you follow my advice. The King has one daughter whom he loves more than anything else, even more than his life. Make a gold statue of the princess as a gift. It will please him beyond measure, and surely he will reward you greatly and we will be rich."

The goldsmith took the suggestion, and his wife brought the statue to the King. When the monarch saw it, he became enraged. "It is written," he declared, "that no idols should be created. Who-ever made this statue, let his right hand be cut off."

And so it was done. The poor goldsmith never again fashioned anything out of gold. Instead, he cried out, "O husbands, look at me and learn a lesson! Never heed your wife's advice, for it will cause you suffering in the end."

The fox watched the leopard's reaction, and he con-tinued, "If this hasn't convinced you, then remember what King Solomon often said, 'One good man among a thousand have I found; but a virtuous woman among all those have I not found.'

"Listen, and I will tell you how the great King proved the truth of what he said."

Everyone knows about King Solomon's great wisdom and understanding of people. One day, he proclaimed that women are selfish and love not their husbands more than themselves. His advi-sors disagreed. So he decided to test his statement and prove he was right. He sent his attendants to find a married couple who were known for their virtue and deep love for each other.

When such a couple was found, the husband was brought to the King, who said to him: "We have searched the entire city for a man worthy to marry my beautiful daughter and love her as befits a person of high rank. You have been chosen as that man. After your marriage, I will appoint you my chief advisor. But since you are now a married man, go home and slay your wife so that you will be free to marry my daughter and enjoy the new position I offer you."

At first the man protested, but the King insisted.

"How shall I do this deed?" asked the man finally. And the King gave him a sword, but it was made of lead and in fact would not hurt or kill anything. *Remember*, the king was only testing the man's love for his wife, and did not mean to do her bodily harm.

The man returned home, his heart heavy with the thought of what he now had to do. When he saw his wife, he was overcome with love and emotion. "No, I cannot do this terrible deed when she is awake," he thought. "I will wait until she is asleep."

But when she was asleep, he leaned over her— and then sprang back. "No," he cried, "not even for the entire Kingdom will I kill my wife, the woman who has brought such joy to my life. What joy would I have from marriage to the King's daughter but a bitter joy?" And he went to Solomon and told him he could not accept his offer.

A while later, the handsome Solomon sent for this man's wife in secret, declaring his passion and love for her. "Since I cannot marry you while your husband lives," he declared, "you must slay your husband tonight, and tomorrow you will be my queen." And as he said these words, he handed

her the sword which looked like steel but was
made of lead.

The woman returned home with the sword.
That night she fed her husband well and gave him
plenty of wine to drink. And in the middle of the
night she took the sword and struck him while he
slept. Of course, the sword did not hurt him, but it
did wake him up. And she had to confess what she
had planned to do.

They went together to King Solomon, and Solomon turned to his scoffers and said, "Now no one
can ever tell me that a woman is to be trusted."

Then the fox again waited a moment before he added,
"More than that. Not only can a woman not be depended on
to advise you while you live. She will betray you even in
death."

"How is that?" asked the leopard.

"Listen and I'll tell you," replied the fox.

There was a custom in ancient Rome that
whenever a criminal was hanged, the body remained on the gallows for ten days as a warning to
everyone. To make sure that no relatives came to
cut down the body and bury it before the tenth day,
an officer of the King stood on guard at the gallows. If the body of the condemned man was stolen,
the officer on guard was hanged in its place.

One night, as an officer was guarding the body
of an executed criminal, he heard shrieks that
pierced his soul, and cries that went directly to his
heart. He ran toward the cries and found himself in
a nearby cemetery. There on the ground, lying
across a fresh grave, was a young woman, weeping,
lamenting the death of her beloved husband.

"My good woman," said the officer, "what terrible thing has happened to make you weep with
such pain?"

"My lord," answered the woman, between sobs, "my husband, whom I loved more than life itself, has died and my grief is too great for me to bear. So I weep and pray for my death to come quickly now." The officer calmed her, persuaded her to return home, and accompanied her to the city gates. Then he went back to his post at the gallows.

But the next night, and the next, the grieving widow returned to her husband's grave and would not be consoled. The officer meanwhile had begun to embrace and kiss the woman, and before long their love was kindled and they lay together.

Returning to the gallows together with the woman, the officer discovered that the body he had been guarding was gone. He was suddenly terrified and whispered to the widow standing next to him, "Go home quickly. I must run away or I will be hanged for neglecting my duty."

But the widow replied, "Do not run, my love. We can dig up the body of my husband and hang him in place of the stolen body. Your life will be saved."

"I cannot dig up a body from its grave," protested the officer.

"Then I will do it for you," said the widow, who only hours before had wept over her husband's grave. "Helping a live person is more important than worrying over a dead one."

When the body of the woman's husband was dug up, the officer took one look and cried, "Alas! All your efforts are useless. They will know this is a different man, because the criminal they hanged was bald and your husband was not."

"Oh, that should not cause you any concern," said the woman. "I will make him bald, too." And saying that, the widow plucked out all her husband's hair and hung him on the gallows. As for the officer and the widow, they got married.

That's the end of the tale.

The fox did not have to say anything more. With fire in his eyes, the leopard ran to his wife and commanded, "Woman! Take our children and *follow me* to our *new home.*" And so the leopard family arrived at their new home, with the happy fox accompanying them most of the way. Then they waved farewell to each other, and the fox skipped joyfully to the leopard's abandoned home.

"Good," chortled the fox. "Now I can take over their spacious, comfortable home. They will certainly not return and threaten my freedom ever again." And he stretched out and went to sleep.

Just as the leopards settled into their new home, in paradise, the season of rains and floods began.

In the middle of the night, the rains poured down, the river rose over its banks, and the leopards were carried out of their home over the raging waters.

And the leopard cried out, "Woe to me, and woe to the man who does not listen to his wife's good counsel."

And a cold angry wave swept over the leopard.

The Artist's Search

When I first heard an outline of this story, which was related to me by friends, it caught my imagination. My friend Rachayl Davis had telephoned to tell me a story that her husband Hillel had remembered hearing from his father, Rabbi Herman Davis of Chicago. Rabbi Davis had been a superb storyteller who often integrated stories into his sermons. Though Hillel had his father's notes, he found no reference to this story among them. He simply remembered it. We searched for the tale's sources but could not find its origin.

The search for something extraordinary—the most beautiful melody, the bravest man, the most important gift, and so on—has been a key element in many folktales. The search in this story is for something that touches the *neshome*, the soul.

My thanks to Rachayl and Hillel Davis for telling me this tale, which I have adapted with their permission.

The love song I have chosen for a scene in this story, *"Papir iz dokh vais,"* is one of the most beautiful Yiddish love songs. It was translated by Roslyn Bresnick-Perry. (For more on Jewish love and courtship songs, see Rubin (1979, pp. 69–96)).

here once was an artist who was restless. Why was he so restless? Because every time he began to paint a scene, he discarded the unfinished painting, saying always, "No, this is not beautiful enough. This does not *touch* my soul."

He kept searching for what would be the most beautiful subject to paint. He walked by the water, the Nemen River, which ran near his home, and painted the flowing water. But still dissatisfied, he put a new canvas on his easel and started over.

He walked all around the village.

He looked up at the sky and down at the earth.

He looked at the animals in the fields and at the workers in their workplaces—the carpenter, the shoemaker, the tailor, the butcher.

He would start to paint what he saw and then stop, just as quickly as he had begun. Nothing pleased him completely. Nothing seemed to be beautiful enough, satisfying both his senses and his soul.

One morning, as the sun was rising in the sky and the light spread a rosy glow across the village, the artist awoke and thought to himself, "I must find the most beautiful thing to paint. Since it is not here in my village, I will go out into the world and search."

With that thought, he quietly said his morning prayers and dressed as quickly as he could. Gathering up his artist's tools, he left his home, while his wife and family were still asleep.

Months later, the artist found himself in a beautiful park, sitting under a tree. He heard music, a beautiful melody, played on a violin. Looking around, he saw a young man and a young woman sitting at a table under a nearby tree, singing a love song to each other.

Papir iz dokh vais
   un tint iz dokh shvartz
Tsu dir main zis leben
   tzit doch main hartz.
Ikh volt shtendig gezesn
   drai teg nokh anand
Tzu kishn dain shein ponim
   un tzu haltn dain hant.

As paper is white,
   and ink surely black
My heart yearns for you, sweet life,
   you're all that I lack.
I'd sit three whole days,
   all time I'd withstand
To kiss your sweet face,
   and to hold your dear hand.

Quickly, the artist began to draw the scene, capturing the love he saw in the lovers' faces and heard in the words they sang to one another. What could be more beautiful in the world? He felt happy that he had found what he had long been looking for.

He then started for home.

On the way home, he came to a bridge, where he was stopped by a guard in order to allow some soldiers to cross the bridge first. As the soldiers came closer, the artist asked one of them where they were going. "Home!" cried the soldier. "The war has ended, and the fighting is over. We are at peace, at peace!" Tears filled his eyes, and as he added "Blessed be God, the God of *Shalom*," a look came over his face such as the artist had never seen before.

"*Peace!* Yes, the feeling of peace, the look of peace—that too is a most beautiful thing in the world." And the artist began to paint, to capture on his canvas this feeling and the look he had seen on the soldier's face.

The artist continued on his way home, feeling satisfied that he had captured a second most beautiful thing in the world. But the story is not over yet.

One morning the artist got up especially early in order to start out for home. He was not far from it now. He left the inn where he had stayed and was walking along a country road, when he saw in the window of a small cottage an old man putting on his *tefillin*. The artist stopped to watch as the old man prayed, pulling his *tallis* around him, completely immersed in his prayers. His face was beautiful to look upon, radiant in prayer.

Standing in the road, the artist worked quickly to paint the expression of faith that he was witnessing. "Yes, yet a third most beautiful thing in the world," said the artist aloud to himself, as if committing it to memory.

It was just before the beginning of the Sabbath when our artist approached his home. Through the open door he saw his wife sitting with the children around the table. She was reading a letter she had received from him before they were married. And he heard her read, "And so, *mein tiere, tzu dir main zis lebn tzit dokh main hartz. Tiere*, dear one, write to me on Friday, so I will have something to read on Shabbos. Your friend, Moshe."

There was such love in the way she read the letter, holding on to the sweetness of their courtship days. The peace of the Sabbath and the joy of the blessing filled the house as he saw his wife rise from the table, take the children to her, and, placing her hands on their heads, bless each one in turn. Then she lit the candles to welcome the Sabbath bride.

The words of the psalmist came to the artist's lips: "Thy wife shall be as a fruitful vine . . . thy children like olive plants, round about thy table" (Psalm 128:3).

The artist could no longer restrain himself. He opened the door wider and called out, "*A gut Shabbos,* my wife, my children. I went searching throughout the wide world for beauty, only to discover that the three most beautiful things in the world—love, peace, and faith—are here in my own home. I did not recognize them before."

And the artist extended his hand for his wife's forgiveness. She took his hand and, together with their children, all in a close circle, recited a prayer of thanksgiving.

So the artist and his family were reunited, and from that day on they celebrated the Sabbath, and every day, with even deeper feelings of love, peace, and faith.

The First Shabbat

I have always been fascinated by the Creation story, as have millions of people for three thousand years. It is all the more enchanting when we first hear it in childhood. "In the beginning" are three of the most famous words in the world, but in Hebrew they are one word, "*bereshit.*" *Bereshit* is also the name of the first book of the Bible, which is known in English as "Genesis," from the Greek word meaning "origin."

Dr. Joseph H. Hertz has written in his commentary in *The Pentateuch and Haftoras*: "Like summer and the starry skies, like joy and childhood, these stories (of Genesis) touch and enthrall the human soul with their sublime simplicity, high seriousness and marvelous beauty. And they are absolutely irreplaceable in the moral and religious training of our children" (p. 141).

Although there are many stories and *midrashim* about the Creation, I was drawn to thinking about the first Shabbat. What a celebration it must have been! Ginzberg (1909–1938) has collected a great number of *midrashim* on the Bible. I used this source for my story of "The First Shabbat."

There is one segment in the story that is not fully elaborated: the moment each letter of the Hebrew alphabet presents itself before God in the hope that the Almighty will choose it to begin the creation of the world. This "contest" has been fleshed out by many writers. See especially Ben Shahn's superb *The Alphabet of Creation*. It is a story in itself.

long time ago, before there was a Beginning, 2000 years before God created this world, God created seven things:

God created the Torah written with black fire on white fire;

God built the Divine Throne in heaven, which later was placed over the heads of the Holy *Hayyot*;

God created Paradise on His right side,

and *Gehenna* on His left;

and in front of God there was the Celestial Sanctuary. On the altar, God placed a stone on which the Messiah's Name was engraved.

And God's Voice calls out,

calls out and says, "Return to me, O my children, *shuvu banai*, return to Me, O My children, return, My builders."

Then God lifted up His Torah, and spoke. "I say I am King, but I do not feel like one."

The Torah, whose advice is always wise, replied, "You say You are King, but over whom? A leader cannot be a leader unless he has someone to lead. You will be King *only* when You have others surrounding You who will listen to You and obey your commands."

And God thought to Himself, "How true! How true!" And

so God created a world, but He was not pleased with it and destroyed it.

And then God created more worlds, and still He was not pleased with them, and destroyed, in turn, each world that He had created.

Finally, God decided to create another world, *our* world, in a different way—through the *word*.

When God decided to create our world, He turned to the twenty-two letters of the Hebrew alphabet, which He had engraved with a pen of flaming fire on His crown. "I will create this world through my word," He announced. "Come before me, and present your case. State why I should create the world through you." All the letters descended, one by one, from His crown and stood before God, each petitioning God to create the world through it. Each letter, beginning with the last letter, *Tav*, pleaded with God, saying: "The positive words formed by me are surely an indication that You should create the world through me."

And each letter gave God some examples to prove its case. But God in turn rejected each letter by showing that some negative words were formed by it, too.

Finally, the letter standing next to the first letter, *Bet*, came forward and said: "*Rebono Shel Olam*, O, Lord of the World! May it be Your will to create Your world through me, for all the people in the world will praise You daily by saying, '*Barukh*, Blessed be the Lord forever.'" God found this to be good, and He decided to create the world through the letter *Bet*, starting with the word "*Bereshit*."

Only *Alef*, the first letter, remained in a corner. When God saw *Alef* standing apart, He realized that *Alef* was too modest to come forward. After all, *Bet* had already been chosen. "Have patience, *Alef*; you will have a reward, too," said the Lord. And God rewarded *Alef* by putting it at the head of the Ten Commandments.

And God created the world through His word.

Bereshit bara Elohim et hashamayim ve'et haaretz. In the beginning, God created Heaven and Earth. *Bereshit*, in the beginning; *bara Elohim*, God created; *et hasha-*

mayim ve'et haaretz, Heaven and Earth. In the beginning
God created three things on each day of creation. On the
first day, God created Heaven
> and Earth,
> and light—a light so luminous that one could see from
> one end of the world to the other.

And God saw that it was good. And it was evening, and it
was morning, a *first* day.

On the second day, God created the sky which separated the earth from the heavens,
> God created fire
> and God created the angels.

And it was evening and it was morning, a *second* day.

On the third day, God created the dry land which God
called earth and the waters, which God called seas, and God
saw that this was good.
> Then God created the trees and herbs of all kinds, fruit
> trees, and vegetables, giant trees—the cedars of Le-
> banon and the cypress trees—the willow and the palm,
> the grasses and flowers and tiny plants.
> And God also created, on this day, Paradise.

And God saw that this was good. And it was evening and it
was morning, a *third* day.

On the fourth day, God created the sun,
> the moon
> and the millions, and *millions,* and *millions* and
> *millions* of stars in the sky to shine upon the earth—
> and He made the comets, too.

And God saw how good this was. And it was evening and it
was morning, a *fourth* day.

On the fifth day, God brought forth the fishes that
swim in the seas,
> and the birds that fly in the air
> and God also created Leviathan, King of the fish.

And God saw that it was good. And it was evening and it
was morning, a *fifth* day.

On the sixth day, God created twice as much, because
He knew that the seventh day was for rest. So on the sixth
day of creation, God created the cattle,

and the reptiles,
the beasts of the fields,
and *Ish*, Man, whom God called Adam,
and *Isha*, Woman, his partner, whose name became
Hava, mother of all, *after* she left the Garden of Eden.
And God also created demons, but because the Shabbat
was coming very soon, God became rushed and so had
no time to finish the demons' bodies, and so they remain spirits *only*, to this day.

In the twilight, between the sixth day and the Shabbat,
when darkness was beginning to blend in with the light,
God quickly created eleven more things because God knew
they would be needed later on in our world:

the rainbow, which remained invisible until the time of
Noah;

the manna that the Israelites would eat when they
crossed the desert;

the water springs which would provide the Israelites
with water in the desert;

the writing upon the two stone tablets which God gave
to Moses at Mt. Sinai;

the instrument with which the writing was done;

the two stone tablets;

the mouth of Balaam's she-ass;

the grave of Moses;

the cave in which Moses and Elijah would dwell;

the rod of Aaron, with its blossoms and its ripe almonds

and, oh yes,

the *shamir*, the wondrous worm about as big as a grain
of barley, which would cut through rocks so that King
Solomon could build the Temple in Jerusalem without
using iron tools.

And God saw all that He had made and found it *very
good*! And it was evening and it was morning, the *sixth* day.

The Torah had told God that He could be King only if
there were creatures to obey Him and to praise Him. So God

had created all the angels and the Holy *Hayyot*, the various animals and birds, the fish and people, too. God had been very busy during the first six days of creation.

But now, on seventh day, the Shabbat, all of God's creations rested—and the Source of Life rested, too. Now everything on earth and in the heavens found the time to praise God. As God ascended His throne, His throne of Joy, all creation burst into song.

God was pleased! And He looked at all the faces surrounding the throne. He looked for a very long time.

"I like to look at you; it gives me great pleasure," God said.

Then God asked that all the angels walk by Him so that He could see them and greet them.

And all the angels did as He asked: There was the angel of the water, the angel of the rivers, the angel of the mountains, and the angel of the valleys, the angel of the deserts and the angel of the trees, and of the shrubs, and of the flowers, and an angel for each blade of grass, and each leaf, the angel of the sun, the angel of the moon and the angel of the stars, the angel of Paradise, the angel of *Gehenna*, the angel of the wild beasts, and the angel of mercy, the angel of dreams, the angel of love, the angel of hate, the angel of life, the angel of death, the angel of praise, the angel of smiles, the angel of tears, the angel of the rainbow, the angel of song, the angel of wind, and the angel of stories, the angel of the ants, the angel of the grasshopper, and so many many many more angels.

There were also the angels of each heaven, the chief angel of the angels, the angel of each division of the heavenly hosts, the chief angel of the Holy *Hayyot*, the chief angel of the cherubim, the chief angel of *ofanim*, and all the other splendid, terrible, and mighty angels. They all appeared before God and sang and danced. They rejoiced as they played the timbrel, the harp, other stringed instruments, and the flute and sang: "Let the Glory of God endure forever! Let God rejoice in His works."

In the midst of all the celebration, God invited the angel of the Shabbat to sit upon the throne of glory. And God turned to all the angels and proclaimed: "Shabbat it is unto God!" and all of heaven responded: "Unto God it is Shabbat!" And God said: "Shabbat is a sign between Me and the children of Israel forever."

And it is said that *Ish* and *Isha*, the partners that God had created, were allowed to ascend to the highest heaven, *Arabot*, the seventh heaven, to join in the rejoicing over the first Shabbat.

Ish and *Isha* turned to God and said: "Every day we will bless You, and we will praise Your name for ever and ever."

And all the angels sang: "All Your works shall praise You, O God, and Your faithful ones shall bless You."

And together they proclaimed: "The Lord is King; the Lord was King; the Lord will be King forever and ever. *Hallelujah!*"

In this way, by sharing the Shabbat joy with all of God's creatures, God dedicated His creation.

This was the celebration of the first Shabbat in heaven by God, by all the angels, and by the first people in *our* world.

The Scroll of Bereshit

The story of Creation imparts an extraordinary sense of wonder and beauty. Yet, when a child begins Hebrew lessons, it is traditional to begin with the book of Leviticus. Why? Doesn't it make sense to start at the beginning of time with the magnificent descriptions of our world's creation? Wouldn't the language and images stir the imagination and create a greater desire to learn? Rashi certainly thought it would, as perhaps others have. Certainly, the parents in our story believe in the power of *Bereshit*. It is through the scroll of Genesis that, in this tale, a child is reunited with this parents.

There are versions of this story in many sources, including *Hibbur Maasiyot* (1647), Jellinek (1853–1877), Eisenstein (1915), Ibn Shahin (1557), *Lukkutei Hamaasim* (1648), *Yalkut Sippurim Umidrashim* (1923), Gaster (1924), and Bin Gorion (1976).

One of the most beautiful versions, written by Haim Nahman Bialik, is called "In the Beginning." As a talmudic tale, the lesson of Bialik's tale is: If teaching a child one book, namely Genesis, brings so great a reward, how much greater would be the reward for teaching the child the whole Bible and all of the Talmud.

There are other levels to be uncovered in this wonderful story, which has fascinated me since I first discovered it. As a storyteller, I agree with the parents in this tale that stories, like honey, can draw a person to the excitement of learning, and that they can be healing, especially stories like those in *Bereshit*.

 man and his wife had an only child, a son, whom they loved more than anything else in the world. He was the apple of their eye. And when the child reached the age when he could begin the study of Torah, the father brought him to the teacher in the synagogue, and said, "When my child was born, I hired a scribe to write the Book of *Bereshit,* Genesis, so my son could hear the beautiful story of God's creation before he learns anything else." And he handed the scroll of *Bereshit* to the teacher.

But the teacher gave the scroll back to the father, saying, "This is a beautifully written scroll, and *Bereshit,* the story that tells of God's creation, must be studied. But not during the first lessons. Our lessons must begin with the Book of Leviticus. Why? Because a child is pure and he must busy himself with pure things. So he must learn first the Priestly code, about the offering of the sacrifices and the laws for atonement. Leave your son's study to me."

But the father did not agree. "Why begin a story in the middle and not at the beginning?" he asked. "True, it is a custom to begin with Leviticus, but I want my child to learn *first* of the wonders of creation from the *beginning.*" But the teacher would not be persuaded to begin with *Bereshit.*

The father thanked the teacher for his time, and took his son home. "I will teach you myself," he said to the lad. The child's mother agreed, too.

On the first day, the father took the scroll and unrolled it, spread a bit of honey on the first words, and told his son to lick the honey off the parchment. As the child did so, the father said, "As honey is sweet, so shall be the Torah and learning." And the mother and father kissed him. So began the boy's study of Torah.

Each day, father and son sat and learned, the boy repeating the words after his father. "*Bereshit bara Elohim et hashamayim ve'et haaretz.* In the beginning God created the heaven and the earth."

And each day the boy knew more and more, asked more and more questions, and grew to love the words and the world.

One day, the son was sitting in the garden near his home, reading his scroll. Suddenly some soldiers from a foreign land came into the city and seized the child. He managed to grab his scroll, and he soon found himself in a wagon on his way to another country.

When the boy did not return home for the evening meal, his parents were afraid that something had happened to him. They began to search everywhere, until a stranger told them he had seen the invading army take a group of children away. Then the parents understood what must have happened. "Our child, our only child," they cried, and their cry was terrible to hear. The husband tried to console his wife. Then they ran to the rabbi.

The rabbi spoke gently and asked them, "If someone left a deposit with me, but came back and asked that the deposit be returned, should I keep it or return it?" The couple were puzzled by this question, but the husband answered, "Of course, you must give it back. God forbid that you hold onto it if it does not belong to you."

"Your child was a loan from God," said the rabbi. "He has demanded the deposit back. We cannot do anything more. It is now in God's hands."

"But rabbi," said the couple, "our son is not dead. He

has been kidnapped, no doubt to be trained for their army. We cannot believe they have killed him."

And the man and woman wept and called out, "O God who is so great, God-Most-High, we will continue to have faith that our son may return to us alive and well." And they found some consolation in their faith and in prayers.

When the prisoners, many of them children, arrived in the distant land, they were thrown into prison, and all their possessions, including the scroll, were taken from them.

One night the King, who lived in the city to which the captives had been brought, could not sleep. He became depressed, then angry. His counselors did not know what to do for him. But as long as the King could not sleep, neither could they. The potionmakers made special sleep potions, but they did not help. The singer with his harp came, and still the King did not become calm. In desperation, one of the advisors suggested, "Read to the King. Perhaps the laws of the kingdom or a scroll of stories. Anything to make the King listen and rest."

One of the advisors went to the King's library of scrolls. Taking a scroll from the top of a pile, he brought it to the King's chamber. The scroll that the advisor had taken happened to be the boy's scroll of the Book of *Bereshit.* When he unrolled it, the advisor saw the strange alphabet and could not read it. When he showed it to the other advisors, one of them said, "Perhaps this is the language of the Jews. There is a Jewish captive in the King's prisons. Bring him here to read this scroll."

So the boy was brought before the King. And when he saw the scroll, his beloved scroll, he began to cry with great sobs. The King looked up and asked, "Do you know what this is and how to read it?"

"Yes," answered the boy.

"Then read it to me," commanded the King.

"*Bereshit bara Elohim et hashamayim ve'et haaretz,* In the beginning, God created the heaven and the earth."

And he continued telling the beautiful story of each day, and of the wonders of God's creation, leading to the celebration of the first Shabbat. The King grew calm and listened with amazement. When the reading ended, he nodded and fell asleep. The boy remained nearby, holding the scroll close to him.

In the morning the King awoke, rested and happy. He saw the young boy still sitting in the chair, hugging the scroll. "Tell me," he asked, "and do not be afraid, my child—who are you, and where do you come from?"

The boy replied in a quiet voice, "O King, I am an only child of parents who live in another land. I was taken captive by your soldiers one day as I was reading my scroll in the garden. My parents cannot know where I am, and they surely must be filled with worry and unhappiness."

The King stood up and said, "Blessed be God, Creator of the heaven and the earth, who sent you here to help me. To show my gratitude, you will be returned to your parents immediately."

The King then ordered that the boy be clothed in royal robes, given a chest filled with gold, and delivered safely to his parents.

And when their only child came running into the house, the grieving parents could not believe their eyes. They were overjoyed to see their son, and together they thanked God for bringing them together again.

When they had finished their prayer of thanksgiving, the boy told them all that had happened. "And thanks to the scroll, I was saved and was able to come home to you, my dear parents," he concluded happily.

Then the father and mother and their son laughed with joy, and together they began to read, "*Bereshit bara Elohim et hashamayim ve'et haaretz. . . .*"

A Tall Tale

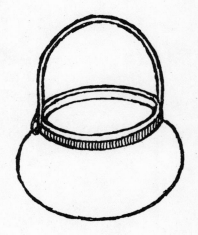

It's fun to tell tall tales with a "Can you top this?" spirit. The delightful mechanism of this tale and others of its type (A-T 1920F) of forcing the victim into an impossible situation so as to elicit the admission "It's a lie!" is known from our oldest stories, including some from Europe, Japan, and Turkey. One such tale, from Denmark, comes to mind, "The Princess Who Always Believed What She Heard." The test of telling a skillful lie is also found in the Sefardic repertoire of Jewish tales.

A variant of this tale (IFA 342, from Iraq, recorded by Naim Daniel) is in Noy (1963). The IFA has at least seven versions of this tale, and it has analogues in many folktale traditions. It has a close relative type in A-T 852, which is represented in this work by "The Seven Lies."

Three brothers figure in this tale. It seems that whenever there is a contest, the youngest always wins, whether it be for the hand of a princess or the "It's a lie" contest. How he does it, poor soul—well, let's see if *you* can top this!

n a certain kingdom, there was a King who loved contests. He often staged riddle contests, joke contests, juggling contests, singing contests, dancing contests, clapping contests, whistling contests, shouting contests, talking contests, walking and running contests, smiling and frowning contests. If you could think of any other contest, no doubt he would have thought of it, too.

One day, the King overheard his advisers talking among themselves, and he heard one of them say, "His Majesty is always so agreeable to everything we advisers present to him. It seems as though he relies on us more and more. Not that we would take advantage of his good nature. But he *is* always more interested in his contests than in listening and weighing our judgments."

"That's it! That's it!" shouted the King. The advisers looked up and saw the King running around in circles in great excitement. "We'll have a contest."

"Another contest? What sort this time, Your Majesty?" asked the advisers without much enthusiasm.

"A contest to find someone who can make me say, 'It's a lie.' Whoever makes me say, 'It's a lie,' will become my chief adviser."

Well, the royal advisers were delighted with that idea, because each was sure he would become the chief adviser.

They all tried to get the King to say, "It's a lie." After all, they were used to embroidering the truth. But they all failed.

The princes and the merchants all tried, each thinking he would succeed by stretching the truth, as he had so often done before. The King remained silent or answered with an even more outrageous response, but he did *not* call out, "It's a lie."

In the kingdom lived three brothers. The oldest was a circle-maker, a natural good-for-nothing; the second was a tailor, actually more of a rag-patcher, a sewer of *lottes*; and the third was a fool, poor soul, a real simpleton.

When the two older brothers heard about the King's latest contest, they decided to try their luck. After all, who doesn't want to become chief adviser to a King? When the youngest brother heard that they were going to the King, he said, "I want to go, too." So, since they pitied the young fool, poor soul, they took him along.

When the three arrived at the palace, they were brought before the King. The oldest brother began, "O King, I am a circle-maker, but that's because my father was a circle-maker with a stick. His stick was soooooo long that it would reach up to the sky, and he could draw a full circle around the moon even on a dark night, and push the stars into circles and . . . "

And the King smiled and replied: "Really! My father, the King, had a tobacco pipe, and the pipe was so long that when he wanted to smoke it, he turned it towards the sun and lit it there."

The good-for-nothing brother hung his head and moved aside.

Then the tailor brother stepped forward. "O King, I am a tailor, but really a patcher. Yesterday there was a terrible storm. The thunder and lightening were so violent that the heavens were torn to shreds. So what did I do? I threaded my needle and patched the sky, placing a *lotte* here and a *lotte* there."

The King again smiled and said, "Oh, you are some

patcher! Your needle made such holes that it poured from the heavens the whole night through."

The second brother hung his head and moved aside.

Then the youngest brother, the fool, poor soul, shuffled over to the King. He carried a large heavy pot. He stood looking up at the King. The King looked back at him and laughed: "Well, well, so what do you have to say? And this pot, why are you carrying it?"

The youngest brother replied: "My King, I came with this empty pot, so that when you give me back the 500 gold coins you owe me, I'll have something to carry them in."

"IT'S A LIE!" shouted the King as he jumped up from his throne. "I don't owe you a single gold coin!"

"It doesn't matter whether you owe me any gold or not, O King; what matters is that you said, 'It's a lie,' and I have won the contest," replied the fool, poor soul.

And the youngest brother remained in the King's palace.

The Dream and
the Treasure

Dreams are stories we tell ourselves when we sleep. The dream world is one of the greatest of human mysteries. Who can ever explain dreams completely? Perhaps their mysterious nature is one reason for our continued fascination with dreams, as well as with stories involving them.

Some of the most wonderful Jewish stories involve dreams. In addition to biblical stories dealing with dreams (e.g., Joseph and his brothers, Jacob and the ladder, and so on), there are many folktales. (See "The Dream Interpreter.") But how many of us heed the voices in our dreams? King Solomon was wise enough to take the good advice of the voice in his dreams. And so does our hero in this story—but only after the third time.

The origin of this cosmopolitan story is a bit of a mystery in itself, since there are similar stories in the cultures of many European countries including England, Ireland, and Holland, in addition to the Hasidic East European versions. The story occurs in the *Masnávi* of the Persian poet Jalaluddin Rumi, written about 1260 C.E. (Cowell). In this source, a young spendthrift of Baghdad is warned in a dream to go to Cairo, but when he reaches that city, he is told about a treasure back in his own place. A variant of this story is found in the de la Pryme (1699).

"The Dream and the Treasure" is truly an international tale type. Although no tale type is actually universal in being literally found all over the world and in all cultures, this type (A-T 1645) might well qualify for the record of having the greatest distances between its collected versions. It is known among the Native Americans, well known in European oral versions, and has an exact parallel to the Jewish forms in a series of tales collected in Japan and generally listed under "Misokai Bridge." These tales tell of a "pious, honest charcoal maker named Chōkichi," who dreams of a treasure at Misokai bridge, or is told in a dream that if he stands at that bridge, he would hear something good. When he finally goes to the bridge, he tells his dream to a Tofu maker, who tells him in turn that he ought to pay no attention to such dreams, and that he had just had one in which he was told about a charcoal maker named Chōkichi and of a treasure buried near his house. The charcoal maker hurries home and finds the treasure. The tale and its versions are to be found in Mayer (1985), number 66. The Jewish versions in the IFA range from Iraq to Afghanistan.

In every variant the names of the places and of the main character and his occupation change. In one Dutch version, the main character is a shoemaker who lives in the village of Oosterlittens and travels to Amsterdam as directed in his dream, and in another Dutch version he is a peasant of Dort. In the English version he is "The Pedlar of Swaffham," traveling to London; in the Irish version, he is "The Peddler of Ballaghadereen" who goes to Dublin to seek his fortune.

Sawyer (1962) thinks the original source of the Irish tale and its variants is "a Hebrew legend from one of the lost books of the Apocrypha." She continues: "Mr. M. R. James gives an excellent version of it in his *Old Testament Legends.*"

I. L. Peretz wrote a story using a similar theme. So did Simha Bunem of Pshiskhe, as well as Nahman of Bratzlav, two Hasidic master storytellers. Another source in which this tale appears is Nachman (1896).

I mention all these sources to illustrate how a tale has traveled, probably from East to West, and has been kept alive by different peoples and cultures, with varied interpretations—but always with meaning for the folk. One Hasidic interpretation might be very different even from another Hasidic interpretation, and again different from the Irish interpretation. But that's why telling our stories, in their many variants, can help us understand each other better.

It was a Hasidic version that I first heard years ago, told by Elie Wiesel (1972). I loved the story immediately. Here is my version of "The Dream and the Treasure."

 long time ago, in the Polish city of Cracow, there lived a man called Avrom son of Berl. Avrom had a wife and many children. In their small cottage, there were only two rooms: a kitchen and a bedroom. The bedroom was divided into two parts by a sheet in the place of a wall. On one side of the improvised wall was the bedroom for Avrom and his wife. On the other side, all the children slept. The kitchen had an earthen floor that was covered daily with fresh straw. Everyone loved to stay in the kitchen because of the black, pot-bellied stove that warmed them through the long, cold snowy winters.

Avrom was a hard-working man. But no matter how much he worked, he earned barely enough for the family's daily needs—food, candles for Shabbos, material for clothing, lessons for the children. When a dress became too short for one of the daughters, a pretty, embroidered ribbon would be added to the skirt to make it longer. And when a pair of pants became too small for one of the boys, some patches were sewn on the worn spots and the pants would be given to a younger son.

Avrom tried his best. He tried hard not to think of all the money he owed to shopkeepers and to teachers. So while he worked, he would often hum to himself or make up stories about faraway places—and even about his own life in Cracow.

Of all his daydreams, Avrom was particularly fond of one: He would sit and think about having the finest meals for Shabbos, and thus be able to invite many guests to share the Shabbos with him and his family.

"Ah," he would say to himself, "come my friends, we have plenty of room and plenty of food for everyone." Avrom would then picture how it would be to return from the synagogue with all his guests and find the house brightly lit and the table beautifully prepared for Shabbos with wine, two large *hallas*, and all kinds of delicious foods. He would think to himself that being able to have guests—and also an extra piece of fish—would give him the greatest pleasure.

Just as these thoughts came to Avrom during the day, dreams came to him also at night when he slept.

One night, he had an unusual dream. Avrom saw himself standing under a bridge. All around him were magnificent buildings, and one building looked like a palace. Suddenly a voice spoke to him and said: "*Avrom, this is the great city of Prague. There is the bridge leading to the King's palace. Dig a hole right where you are standing under the bridge and you will find a treasure.*"

Avrom suddenly awoke and saw that it was morning. "Prague? How can I go to Prague? I don't even have enough money for my family's needs," he muttered to himself as he proceeded to get up, wash, and say his morning prayers. After a few moments, Avrom realized that it had been only a dream, nothing more. Dreams are nice, he thought to himself, but he had to get to the synagogue and then to work. The family depended on him.

But all day long, the words of the voice in his dream remained in his mind.

On the next night, Avrom had the same dream, and again he heard the same voice. Only this time the voice teased him. "*Avrom, what are you waiting for? Are you enjoying your poverty?*"

The following morning, Avrom told his wife about his dream. She listened and smiled in an understanding way. "Oh Avrom," she said, "you are such a dreamer! You talk and think of faraway places all day, so why shouldn't you dream about them at night, too? It's getting late now. Better get to *shul* quickly or you'll be late for morning prayers."

That night, the dream came to Avrom for the third time, but this time the voice in the dream was more insistent. "*Avrom! The treasure is there waiting for you. What can you lose by seeing for yourself? Go and take it! It will solve all your problems!*"

After the third time, Avrom decided to go to Prague to see if the dream really would come true. Since he had no money to spend on traveling by coach for this foolishness, he would have to go on foot. His wife put some bread and cheese in a sack and filled a bottle with water for the journey.

At dawn, just as the sun was rising and immediately after saying his morning prayers, Avrom began to walk the long miles to Prague. During his journey, whenever he was tired, hungry, or discouraged, he would sing psalms praising God. He knew in his heart that God would protect him. Avrom had deep faith in God, no matter how hard his life was. Sometimes the tunes he sang had no words, just "*Bim bam bim bam, biddi biddi bam,*" but they were joyous tunes that made him feel light and happy—and close to God. Often he danced little steps along the way, and that made his feet seem less tired, too.

Finally, weeks later, in the middle of one afternoon, Avrom arrived in Prague. To his amazement, he saw everything just as it had been in his dream. In fact, he had the feeling that he had been there before, but that was impossible. There, in front of him, was the palace of the King, and here was the bridge leading to the palace. It was not a big bridge. Avrom was somewhat disappointed at seeing that it was really so small. But he knew the exact spot where he had stood in the dream, so he went and stood there. Then he noticed that there were palace guards everywhere, and he knew that he had to be careful or they would become suspicious of him.

As Avrom stood there, thinking what to do next, the captain of the guards approached him and demanded in a commanding voice, "Are you waiting for someone or perhaps looking for something you lost?" Avrom was bewildered for a moment. Should he tell the guard a lie? No, he would not do that, he thought to himself. Hesitantly, and feeling somewhat foolish, he told the guard about his dream and why he had come all the way to Prague, half expecting the guard to call him a liar and have him arrested.

Instead the guard started to laugh, and replied, "If I had such faith in dreams, I would not be *here* right now. I, too, had a dream in which a voice spoke to me. It told me to go to the house of a Jew named Avrom son of Berl in Cracow. If I looked under the stove in his kitchen, I would find a treasure, the voice told me. I have heard that half the Jews in Cracow are named Avrom and the other half are named Beril—and they *all* have stoves. So how would I ever find the right one? Do I look like a fool who would spend his time searching under stoves? No, I'm afraid, my foolish man, that you have believed your dream for nothing. Instead of finding a treasure here, you have only worn out a pair of your shoes by making this journey."

Avrom listened in amazement as the captain spoke, describing Avrom's *own* house. Is it possible that there was a treasure in his own home, hidden where he could not see it?

With an eager heart, Avrom hurried back to Cracow.

When he finally arrived home, he dug under his stove right there in the kitchen and yes, there he discovered the promised treasure.

Avrom was so happy that he first said a prayer of thanksgiving to God. With some of the treasure he built a House of Prayer, which was called "Reb Avrom's *shul.*"

Of course, he kept some of the treasure for his family, and he was able to pay all his debts. But whenever anyone needed help, Avrom remembered his own poverty and offered help from his treasure with an open heart.

The Rooster Who
Would Be King

"The Rooster Who Would Be King" is based on a Nahman of Bratzlav story. I was first introduced to this extraordinary tale in 1978, during my second CAJE (Coalition for Alternatives in Jewish Education) Conference, held that August in Irvine, California. I had the great pleasure of meeting Arthur Kurzweil while standing on the lunch line during one of the conference days. We talked, I remember, about our role models, and we discovered that we both shared the same "mentor," Elie Wiesel. (I remember saying that, besides Elie Wiesel, my other role model was Ruth Rubin, the Yiddish ethnomusicologist and singer.) We shared more "who we are" conversation and then resumed the busy teaching/learning schedule of the conference. When we arrived at the airport to fly back to New York, we discovered that we had been booked on the same flight, so we continued our discussion. Arthur mentioned a book of stories he would like to give me, which included "The Chicken Prince." Although Nahman of Bratzlav originally spoke of the prince as a rooster, the tale has gone through all the fowls. I loved this story on a *sod* (secret) level, a level that transcends explanation. I also knew I had to tell it some day.

It was a long time before I began to tell this story, and now, whenever I do, teachers, parents, and mental health professionals respond by telling me parallel stories dealing with their children as well as their patients.

One could call this story a "how-to-educate-a-person" tale. Nahman, no doubt, had in mind the relationship of a *rebbe* to his pupils, namely, how to turn them into *talmidei hakhomim*. But before that could happen, he had to make *mentshen* of them. There is a great deal of time-tested wisdom in this "rooster" tale that we can apply to any learning situation—between parent and child, teacher and student, or therapist and patient. It is a story that can be understood on many levels. I call it the quintessential teaching story.

 long time ago, there lived a King and Queen
and their son the Prince. They considered this
prince to be their jewel, their greatest treasure—the apple of their eye. The King made
certain that the Prince had the most learned
teachers and the wisest soothsayers to instruct him in all
that a prince would need to know in order to be a great king,
when the time came for him to rule the kingdom.

One day, a strange illness overcame the Prince, and he
began to act like a rooster. He took off his clothes and
roamed all around the palace, flapping his arms like a rooster and crowing loud and long. He also stopped speaking the
language of the King and Queen. He ate only corn from the
floor, like a rooster, and refused to sit at the table with
others, eating only *under* the table *alone*.

The King and Queen became very upset and called for
the best doctors in the kingdom to treat the Prince, in hopes
of curing him of his illness. But nothing that the doctors
and the soothsayers and the other healers tried seemed to
make any difference, and the Rooster Prince continued happily crowing and flapping his arms, and hopping around in
the palace, wherever he wanted to go.

One day, a wise old man came to the palace. "Your
Majesty, I would like to try to cure the Prince," he said to the
King.

"Where are your medicines?" asked the surprised King,

because all the doctors carried at least one bag filled with bottles of potions and oils.

"I have my own ways, Your Majesty," answered the wise man. "Allow me seven days *alone* with the Prince."

The King reluctantly agreed, since there was no other hope.

The wise man was brought to the Prince. The first thing he did was to take off all *his* clothing, jump under the table, and sit opposite the Rooster Prince. The Prince stared at the stranger for a very long time.

"Who are you, and what are you doing here?" crowed the Rooster Prince curiously.

"I am a rooster. Can't you see that?" answered the wise man matter-of-factly but patiently.

"Oh, I am a rooster, too. Welcome!" replied the Prince, happy to have found a friend.

Time passed with the two companions crowing and flapping their arms.

One day, the stranger got out from under the table and began to walk around—a little straighter each day. The Rooster Prince had grown so fond of his friend that he began to follow him wherever he went. And the two roosters hopped around the palace together.

On another day, the wise man put on a shirt and a pair of trousers. "What are you wearing, my friend?" asked the Rooster Prince. "Roosters don't wear clothes!"

"You're right, dear Prince, but I was a bit chilled. However, I assure you, you can still be a good rooster even with clothes on. Try it," challenged the wise man.

The Rooster Prince put some clothes on, too—and continued crowing and flapping his arms.

The next day, the wise man sat at the table and ate some corn from a golden platter. The Rooster Prince sat next to his friend. The wise man signaled to the servants and soon the table was set with silverware, goblets, and golden plates. Slowly, the wise man began to eat all the delicious foods—in a proper manner—and the Prince began to imitate him. Soon a whole meal was eaten, and the Rooster Prince crowed most happily.

The following night, the wise man began to sleep on a bed. He again assured the Prince. "Don't worry, my Prince, you can be a good rooster just the same, even sleeping on a bed." And so the Rooster Prince resumed sleeping on his royal bed and no longer slept under the table.

Soon after, the wise man began to discuss the philosophy of life with the Prince. "Wait a minute, roosters don't have to think, and they certainly don't debate the merits of a way of life," declared the Prince. "Roosters just exist, being fed and cared for without any worries."

"You may be right," answered his wise old friend, "but on the other hand, it doesn't mean you can't be a good rooster if you do engage in discussion. After all, *you* will know that you are a rooster, just the same."

The Prince thought this over, and began to discuss philosophical ideas with the wise man.

On the seventh day, the wise man bid farewell to the Prince. As he was about to leave, he said, "My friend, remember—roosters are fair game for the hunter. So always try to pretend you are a human prince. Act wisely and help others. Farewell!"

From that day on, the Prince walked, ate, and talked like the prince he was.

And when, in time, he became a great King ruling over that entire kingdom, no one besides himself knew that he was still a rooster.

The Woodcutter's
Riddles

When King Solomon met the Queen of Sheba, they challenged and entertained one another with riddles. These can be found in some of the Solomon legends. There are many such stories in Jewish lore based on riddles. It may be that Jews have an interest in riddles because, when we were in danger throughout the centuries, we have had to communicate through cryptic messages.

What are riddles anyway? The dictionary defines a riddle as "a question or statement so framed as to exercise one's ingenuity in answering it or discovering its meaning." Riddles have mysterious hidden meaning and require us to analyze them, in order to gain a new perspective, to make new connections in our minds. Sometimes we get locked into set meanings of words and phrases, but riddles can cause us to understand them in more interesting ways. Riddles stretch the mind and they are also challenging and entertaining, as Solomon knew.

This Yemenite story comes from Gamlieli (1978). A similar story, also filled with riddles, is "The Plucked Pigeon" (Cahan 1931). This variant shows the Arabic influence, seen especially in the exchange of the popular ingenious riddles.

Beside the riddles, I love this story, because of the two characters in the tale—a wise old man and a parent-king who set out to teach the young prince a lesson about life. The older people in our lives, whether they are parents, rulers, or simple woodcutters, have the wisdom, experience, and understanding that young people often need.

n days of old, there lived a King who was as kind as he was wise. In his skill at solving riddles, he was second only to King Solomon. One day, as he was walking in the woods, he saw a very old man cutting wood. The King went over to him and gently asked, "How are you feeling? Are you well enough to cut the wood? Perhaps you will rest awhile and share some of my food?"

The old man greeted the King respectfully and answered politely, "Thank you, Your Majesty, I am very well. And now I will continue my work."

The King said, "Nevertheless?"

The old man answered, "If there were, there isn't."

The King understood immediately that here was a clever old man. So the King again asked him, "How are the two?"

The old man answered, "The third among them."

"And how are the friends?" asked the King.

And the old man replied, "The parcel came undone."

The King continued to ask, "And how are the brothers?"

"The distant one is near," was the old man's reply.

The King's wonder grew with each answer, so he decided that he would help this wise old man. The King said to him, "I see that you are indeed wise in understanding riddles. Therefore, heed me well: Do not sell cheaply."

The old man smiled and answered, "There is no need to teach a wise old man."

When the King heard this reply, he smiled and, with a hearty handshake, bid the old man farewell.

Now the King had a son who was spoiled, a young man who loved jewels and gold too much. He was impetuous, as young men can be, impatient and unwilling to listen to anyone else's advice or suggestions because, after all, *he* was the Prince, and wisdom should come naturally to a prince, a member of the royal family. Was not his father the wisest of men? So too, he thought, would he become the wisest of Kings.

The King was often disturbed by his son's arrogance, and decided to teach him a lesson.

One day, he called the Prince to him and said, "My son, I will tell you four riddles. If you can find the solutions in thirty days, I will know that, in time, you will be worthy of taking my place, and can begin the royal training. But, if you fail, you will be sent far from here, to live there in a distant place for the rest of your life."

The Prince began to tremble and, with a quavering voice, he said, "Riddles! You know I am not good at solving riddles." Waiting for a change of heart, he fell silent. But when he saw his father's mind was set, he continued, "Very well, my respected father. I am listening."

The King then told him the four riddles: "The first riddle is, 'Nevertheless?' and the answer is, 'If there was, there isn't.'

"The second one is, 'How are the two?' The answer is, 'The third among them.'

"The third is, 'How are the friends?' and the answer is, 'The parcel came undone.'

"And the fourth is, 'How are the brothers?' The answer is, 'The distant one is near.'"

When the Prince left the King's palace, he walked in the royal gardens and tried to find the solutions to the riddles, but he could not discover their meanings no matter how hard and long he thought about them. After a few days, he went to all the fortune-tellers and soothsayers in the kingdom, even to the King's advisors, but no one could tell him the meaning of the riddles.

Toward the end of the thirty-day period, the Prince was in despair. He knew he would have to leave the kingdom. On the thirtieth day, he took leave of his friends and family, and went for a walk in the woods he had loved as a child.

As he was walking down a path, he came across an old woodcutter. The old woodcutter greeted him and said, "Why are you so sad, sire?"

"Chop your wood and leave me alone," replied the Prince curtly.

"The old have wisdom and understanding above all others," said the old man patiently.

The Prince thought to himself, "I have told those riddles to so many and yet no one could help me. Maybe, just maybe, this old man can interpret them. It's worth a try." Aloud, he said, "Very well, old man. Perhaps there really is wisdom in your head, for I see you have lived many years in this world. I will see if it is the kind of wisdom I have need of. I will ask you four riddles. Can you tell me what they mean?"

"Let me hear," said the old man.

The Prince began, "The first riddle is 'Nevertheless?' and the answer is . . ."

"If there was, there isn't," said the old man, completing the first riddle.

When the Prince heard this, his spirits rose and with excitement he continued, "How are the two?" and the old man replied, "The third among them."

"And how are the friends?" asked the Prince. "The parcel came undone," said the old man.

Finally, the Prince asked, "And how are the brothers?" And the old man replied, "The distant one is near."

The Prince went over to the old man, kissed him, and asked, "Please, *please*, tell me what these riddles mean?"

"The solution will cost you dearly," answered the old man.

"I will pay you fifty silver pieces."

"Oh no, young sire, even hundreds and thousands of silver pieces would not equal the value of the solution," said the old man.

"I will pay you ten thousand. . . ."

"There is better trade than silver," interrupted the old man.

"Then gold. I'll bring you gold pieces," the Prince pleaded.

But the old man did not accept the offer. "To remain in his home and kingdom, a man would give everything he owns," The Prince thought to himself. He turned to the old man and said, "Wait here a while. I will go home and return with a fitting payment."

Soon, the Prince returned with two porters carrying a chest full of precious stones and jewels.

"These are my most valuable possessions, the things I love most in the world. Please take them and solve the riddles," said the Prince in desperation.

When the old man saw the chest and its contents, he agreed to help the Prince.

"On a certain holiday," began the old man, "the King went for a walk in the woods and saw me cutting wood. He asked me, 'Nevertheless?' meaning, despite your age you still work so hard, and despite the holiday you do not rest? And I replied, 'If there was, there isn't'; meaning, if I had money I would not be a woodcutter, but I don't have any. Since the King understood, he asked, 'How are the two?' meaning, 'How are your legs?'; to which I replied, 'the third among them,' explaining to the King that I am aided by a third leg, my walking stick.

"The King asked me, 'How are the friends?' meaning my teeth, which are always together. And I replied, 'The parcel came undone'; that is, I am left with only a few scattered teeth in my mouth.

"The last question was, 'How are your brothers?' The King meant my eyes, and I answered, 'The distant one is near,' meaning the eyes that used to see so well from afar have become nearsighted.

"So that is the source of the riddles and their meanings."

The Prince immediately returned to the palace and, with great relief, told the King about his talk with the old man.

The King called the old man to the palace and said: "Old man, I told you not to sell so cheaply."

The old man replied, "That is why I assured you that you do not have to teach a wise man." And he showed the King the chest full of jewels.

"Definitely a fair price for a lesson well learned," said the King as he smiled triumphantly.

The King Who Wanted to Know the Fisherman's Daughter's Story

In this story, too, a poor fisherman has a daughter who helps him fish. But it differs from "The Fisherman's Daughter" in that the daughter finds another kind of treasure that she uses in a very Jewish way. She is an active heroine, like the other fisherman's daughter.

This tale includes several stories-within-a-story, in the Mideastern fashion, creating a type of "chain" story. It comes from Afghanistan (IFA 8294, collected by Zeruhin Kort from Yitzhak Simantov) and may be found in Cheichel (1970). This tale contains a number of well-known motifs including TMI D1451, Inexhaustible purse furnishes money.

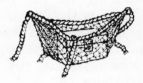

O nce upon a time, there was a fisherman who was very poor. He went fishing every day, but much of the time he returned home without catching anything.

This fisherman had a daughter whom he loved very much. In the evening he would often cry out to her: "My daughter, my daughter, today, as I do every day, I threw the net out but the fish swam away. How shall we live? There is no food in the house for supper, and you do not have proper clothes to wear. What shall I do?"

One evening, his daughter replied: "Father, let me go with you tomorrow and throw the net—*just one time.* Maybe *mazel* will be with me. Maybe I'll be able to catch two or three fish, and then we can buy food and I will be able to buy clothes for myself."

"*Mazel? Mazel* deserted us long ago," answered the father. "If I can't bring fish home, how can you?"

But the daughter asked every day until finally the father agreed.

So they both went down to the sea and, with her father's help, the daughter threw out the net. When they gathered it back in, they felt that they had caught not two or three fish, but perhaps *hundreds*. They pulled and pulled and, with great difficulty, managed to bring it in. And what did they find in the net? A box.

They carried the box home, and when they opened it, they found the most exquisite jewels—a treasure rescued from the depths of the ocean.

With great joy the daughter hastened to sell some of the jewels and buy the fine food and clothes she had dreamed about. Then, with some of the money, she bought a piece of land far outside the city walls. There she had an inn built.

And she said to her servants, "When you see any travelers approaching this city, rich or poor, bring them to this inn; feed them well, and see that they have *all* their needs for *three days*. On the *fourth day*, when they are about to leave, give them each five coins and food for their journey. And should anyone ask who owns this inn, or why you give hospitality without any questions or payment, *do not answer.* Say only, 'That is the way of this inn.'"

One day the King heard about this inn and its custom of welcoming guests. He could not believe anyone would be so generous. So he decided to see for himself. Disguised as an ordinary citizen, he set out to find the inn. When he arrived, the servants welcomed him, as was their way. After three days of gracious hospitality, the servants gave the King-in-disguise the customary five coins and food for his journey. The King was amazed that what he had heard about the inn was true.

"Who owns this inn?" asked the King. The servants refused to answer, as they had been instructed. When the King identified himself by showing them his ring-seal, the servants realized who their guest really was. How could they refuse to answer the King? They told him who owned the inn.

"A fisherman's daughter!" exclaimed the King in astonishment. "How does she have so much money to spend *this* way? If I were to give away such amounts, the King's treasury would soon be empty! Bring me to this fisherman's daughter," commanded the King.

When the King met the young woman, he said, "I thank you for your kind hospitality." Then he immediately asked, "But where does this wealth come from? And why have you chosen to distribute the money in this way? It is indeed puzzling to me."

The fisherman's daughter smiled and replied, "Your Majesty, in a land that is several days' journey from here, there lives a wealthy man who owns many buildings. Every morning, he gets up on the roof of his mansion, calls the believers to prayer, and climbs down afterward. Then, when he walks in the marketplace, all the merchants flee from their stores. Ask this man why *he* behaves this way. If this crazy rich man will tell you *his* secret, *I* will tell you mine."

The King left that same day, and after several days reached that city where the rich man lived. And yes, in the morning the rich man climbed up on the roof to call the believers to prayer. After he had come down from the roof, he walked in the marketplace. Wherever he walked, the merchants ran away. The King, still in disguise, approached and asked him, "*Why* do you behave this way? And *why* do the traders run away when you enter the marketplace?"

The rich man replied, "That is no business of yours."

The King then showed the ring-seal and the rich man knew who was standing before him.

"Your Majesty," said the rich man, "in a land a few days' journey from here, there is a city. At a certain crossroads, there sits a blind man who gives money to everyone that passes him and hits him in the face. In fact, he gives more money to those who hit him harder, and only a few pennies to those who merely tap him. The King should ask this blind man why *he* behaves this way. If Your Majesty can discover *his* secret, *I* will tell you mine."

The King journeyed to that city, and found the crossroads where the blind man sat. He approached the blind man and tapped him on the cheek. The blind man gave the King several pennies. But along came a man who struck the blind man with a heavy ringing blow, and the blind man gave him a fistful of money. All day the King stood and observed that whoever passed struck the blind man, and those who hit harder received more coins.

When evening came, the King saw that the blind man

was about to leave, so he said: "I am a stranger here and I have no place to sleep. May I be a guest in your house?"

The blind man replied, "Every guest is a gift of God. Come with me to my home." At his home, the blind man prepared a meal, and they sat at the table and talked.

Finally, the King asked, "*Why* do you sit at the cross-roads and wait for people to hit you? And then, *why* do you give more to those who hit you harder? Please explain this strange behavior to me."

Answered the blind man, "You are my guest. Eat and drink as much as you please, but do *not* get involved in my affairs. And do not throw salt on my wounds!"

The King then touched the blind man's hand with his ring-seal, and the blind man understood that this was the King. And then the King offered, "Perhaps I can help you."

The blind man slowly replied, "Whether you can help me or not, listen to my tale. When I was young and strong, I used to carry cargo on camels, and I owned twenty camels. Well, one day a man came to me and hired me to transport merchandise from a certain place. So we went to this place far outside the city, and there, in a hole in the ground, were many pitchers of gold and silver and jewels. It looked as though the man had found a treasure trove. Well, we put the treasure on the twenty camels and started on our way.

"Suddenly, a thought struck me: 'Why is this treasure *only for him* and not some of it for *me*?' So I told the man what I was thinking, and he agreed to share it. 'Fine, the load on one of the camels will be yours,' he said.

"We continued on our travels. After a while, I turned to the man and said, 'Why do *you* deserve nineteen full loads and *I* only one?' And the man answered: 'Another load belongs to you.'

"Then once again I said, 'Why do *you* have eighteen loads, while *I* have only two?' And the man gave me another load. This went on, the man giving me more and more, until at last he said, 'I give up everything, except for one pitcher, which I will take with me.'

"'Oh no,' I replied hastily. 'That pitcher remains on the camel, too.' The man became angry and hit me so hard on my face that I saw sparks and flashes of color, and I lost my eyesight. The man took the pitcher and went away. Since then, I have sat at this crossroads hoping that I will know that man by the way he strikes me, and that maybe his blow will return my eyesight to me."

After the King had heard the blind man's story, he thanked him, wished him good health, hoped that his sight would be restored, and left.

The King then returned to the city of the rich man, and told him the blind man's story.

"Now I will tell you my story," replied the rich man. "All the houses and mansions here once belonged to my father. As a young man, I would go up to the roof every day and wake all the believers for prayer. One morning, when I was on the roof, a big eagle swooped down, grabbed me by the hair, and carried me off to a distant country. I was a stranger in that land and wandered through the streets looking for work.

"I found a job in the home of a rich family that liked me very much, and I worked hard for them. They had a daughter and we fell in love. The parents were delighted that we wanted to be married, and made a very big wedding, inviting all the important people of the town.

"My wife and I loved each other very much. We had two children, and our family lived happily together. The only thing that disturbed my peace of mind was that I lived so far from my parents and my city.

"One day, as I was walking in the garden, the eagle came again, caught me by the hair and brought me back here. My father had died in the meantime and left all his wealth to me. Now all the townspeople run away when they see me, because they are ashamed of me. I have no friends now that I am away from my wife and children. So every morning I go up to the roof to wake up the people for the morning prayers. But I also pray and hope that the eagle will come again and return me to my wife and children."

The King listened and blessed the man, and wished him luck. Then he returned to his own city and went to the fisherman's daughter. He told her the rich man's story.

When he had finished he said, "Now it is *your* turn to tell me where your wealth comes from."

The young woman told the King all that had happened—how she and her father had been poor, often without food and without decent clothes to wear. "And so I wished to try out my luck," she related. "What we caught in the net was a box of treasure, and no matter how much money I spend, the box keeps on being refilled. Since this was a gift from the depths of the ocean, gathered from everywhere, it should be given to people from all parts of the world who come here, to help them make their journeys easier."

The King was happy to hear the story of the fisherman's daughter. The story of her good heart touched his heart. He asked her to marry him, and she accepted. They invited everyone to their wedding, including all the travelers who had stayed at the inn, and everyone celebrated for seven days and seven nights.

I was there, too, saw their happiness, and drank a *lehayim.*

The Great Debate

Some great questions that are perhaps impossible to answer may be best answered by stories, especially cumulative ones. We have some examples in this book: "The Golden Watch," which asks, "Who brought the father back to life?" and "The Magic Pomegranate," which asks, "Who healed the princess, and deserves to marry her?" This story raises the question, "Which part of the body is superior?"

The answer to that question lies in Psalm 34:13–14, "Who is the man that desireth life, loveth days; that he may see good therein? Keep thy tongue from evil, and thy lips from speaking guile"; and Psalm 39:2,

> I said, I will take heed to my ways,
> That I sin not with my tongue;
> I will keep a curb upon my mouth,
> While the wicked is before me.

The prohibition against *loshen hora*, the speaking of evil, is strong within Judaism. Jews, as the People of the Word, understand the power of the tongue, which can be used for good and, alas, for evil. We have choices.

This is a midrashic tale that can be found in Makiri, Proverbs 18:3a, and in *Orehot Zaddikim*, 25, Shu'aib, Shelah, 83d-84a. There is also a variant in the legends of King Solomon. This midrashic story contains one of the most famous fables in the Aesopic canon, A-T 293, and Perry (1952), number 130, the famous debate between the stomach and the feet (or the "Belly and the Members"), which usually ends with none of the separate organs able to prove supremacy. This tale, however, allows the tongue to win and includes the "impossible task" motif of milking a lioness. The tale in this form has a parallel telling in Bin Gorion (1916–1921) (III, 71). More recently, Singer (1967) took the core of this talmudic story and wove it into his wonderful story, "Mazel and Schlimazel."

here once was a great debate between the different parts of the body—hands, feet, ears, eyes, and tongue—as to which part had the most power.

"We have the most strength because we are double," said the hands.

"So are we, so are we," shouted the feet, and the ears and the eyes, echoing each other.

"That is so much more in my favor," cried the tongue. "I am alone, and I am convinced I have more power than all of you twins."

Every day, the arguments between them continued, and each member of the body claimed superiority over the others as the fastest, the most important, the most useful, which could do the most harm and which the most good. Whatever claim one presented, the others rejected just as quickly, countering with another claim.

Once, the King of Persia was stricken with a mysterious disease. His physicians examined him and announced: "Your Majesty, the only thing that will heal you is impossible to obtain: It is the milk of a lioness." And they despaired of ever obtaining this necessary medicine. For what human can get close enough to a lioness to milk her?

As a result, the King expected to die. But as a last resort he announced, "Whoever obtains a lioness' milk will be greatly rewarded."

In the Persian kingdom there lived a young man, a brave young man, who loved his King and would do anything possible to save his life. He determined that he would get the milk of a lioness.

When the parts of the human body heard about this adventure, they agreed that it would serve as a test of which was the most powerful in helping this young man with his impossible task—to deliver the milk of a lioness to the ailing King.

The young man knew that he would never be able to approach a lioness directly, for a lioness who is nursing her young would feel threatened and attack immediately. So what did he do? When he found a lioness, he threw her some goat meat. He repeated this for several days. After a while, she became used to him and he managed to get close to her and finally he was able to milk her. This accomplished, he returned to the palace with the jug of precious milk.

On the way to the palace, the body's organs and limbs began to argue over who had contributed most to the success of the young man's feat.

"I could see where to find the lion's den, and where to throw the meat," claimed the eyes.

"I could hear by the lion's purr or roar when it would be safe to approach," argued the ears.

"It was we who got us there and brought us safely back to the palace," insisted the feet.

"Thanks to us," cried the hands, "we were able to draw the milk from the lioness and carry it back to the King without spilling any of it."

In all this discussion, the tongue was ignored. "Wait, just wait," the tongue said under his breath. And aloud he said, "This episode is not over yet. What would you do without me?" But the others scorned him.

When the young man came before the King, the tongue took over: "Your Majesty, I have brought you what you asked for and what I set out to get *especially* for you—the prized milk of a *dog*."

"*What?*" cried the King angrily. "How dare you come before me with such insolence. Hang him, and let his tongue hang out."

And the tongue turned to the other parts and laughingly said, "*See*, or don't you see, that without me you have no power. *I* can *undo* with *one* word and in *one* second what all of you have worked so hard to do for days. Admit that I am *superior* to you all, and I'll save us all from death."

The eyes, ears, hands, and feet agreed, and quickly, too.

Then the young man spoke again, "O Majesty, in my haste I stumbled over my words. The milk is that of a *lioness*. Drink it, Your Majesty, it will truly heal you. My life is at your mercy."

There was something in the voice of the young man that moved the King to believe him. He drank the milk of the lioness and, as predicted, recovered from his illness.

Great was the reward to the young man from a thankful King. But greater still was the tongue's reward when all the members of the body admitted, "Yes, you, O tongue, hold the greatest power for good *and* evil."

May we all use the power of our tongues wisely.

A Question of Balance

Before the High Holy days, one story that always comes to mind is "A Question of Balance." First of all, it deals with God's judgment of our goodness and worthiness. The Holy Days occur in the Hebrew month of Tishrei, whose symbol is a balance or scales—God will weigh our deeds, the good and the bad, a strong metaphor for our lives.

This type of story, of an innocent and unlearned man asked to pray for rain, is a special kind of Jewish tale that appears in no other culture. There are many variants, but the four essential elements in the story are always the same: there is a drought; the community's fasts and special prayers do not bring rain; someone in the community who is not a scholar, or who may even be illiterate, must pray for rain; God answers his prayer alone, and sends rain.

In Jewish life, especially in the Land of Israel, rain is precious: It helps the crops grow, produces a rainbow (the original sign of the Covenant between God and the Jewish people), fills the rivers and streams. Jews have special prayers for dew (*tal*) and for rain, special blessings on seeing a rainbow and for eating the first fruits.

Water is an important element in many biblical stories: Noah and the flood; Rebecca at the well; Moses, who was drawn from the water and who miraculously obtained water from the rock; Miriam's well; the crossing of the Red Sea; and so on.

One of the most famous characters in Jewish legends is Honi Hameaggel, a teacher of the first century B.C.E. Honi the Circle Maker (*hameaggel*), as he was known, could also perform miracles, such as bringing rain by drawing a magic circle and standing in it while praying to God.

In many Mideastern countries, Jews were regarded as rainmakers. Thus, if there was a drought, it was thought that the Jews perhaps had not prayed for rain. (See IFA 719, recorded by Moshe Wigiser from Moshe Marad of Iraq in Noy (1963).

There is a Yiddish saying that rain brings good luck.

When it rained on my wedding day, my mother reminded me, *"Regn iz mazeldik"* ("Rain is lucky"). Whenever I tell this story about rainmaking, I recall the time I was telling a Yemenite variant in Lincoln, Nebraska, in 1986.

I was on the *bima* in the sanctuary of the synagogue, and directly overhead were two skylight windows. A light rain had been falling during the day. I started the story, and just as I spoke the words, "And the sky grew dark, and suddenly a heavy rain began to fall," the heavens opened up and large heavy raindrops pounded on the glass skylights. Everyone looked up upon hearing the rhythmic beat of the rain, and we laughed together in the joy of nature. After the story, a young boy in the front row said in a voice tinged with wonder, "Hey, it started to rain just as you said so in the story." And we all laughed again. No doubt he will remember that moment as I do.

Such is the power of a story and of prayer.

Water is a metaphor for Torah. Just as water nourishes us, so does Torah. A Jew cannot live without Torah, a lesson we learn from the famous parable of Rabbi Akiva, "The Fox and the Fish."

I have always been drawn, in these tales, to the earnest feelings of the simple person's prayer for rain. His statement becomes then a matter of heart-over-learning.

This wonderful tale is typed 752*D in the IFA with twenty versions, making it one of the most common tales in that extensive collection. There is, in addition, another tale with the same central motif of a simpleton (*tam*) or non-believer praying in a strange, but ultimately acceptable manner (by using the wrong words, or by standing on his head, etc.) and having his prayer accepted by God, teaching all that that method too reaches the proper ears. There are numerous versions of that form as well (A-T 827*A). Both of these forms are found in Gaster (1924, 1934) (421 and 422) and in Bin Gorion (1916–1921) (V, 71 and 230 and VI, 144), as well as in Farhi (1870) and Bin Gorion (1976). They all have as their motif "Simpleton's Prayer Brings Down Rain." A variant from Syria (IFA 9229), entitled "The Gates of Tears

Are Never Closed," appears in Noy (1972). Two others (IFA 3815 and 3820) may be found in Baharav (1964). What differs is often the method of the simple man in bringing rain. They are heartwarming and inspiring tales. I have set my version in Eastern Europe.

n a certain town, there once was a terrible drought. No rains fell for many weeks, and the ground became very dry and hard. Plants could not grow, and the food supply grew scarce. The wells were dry, and the people became more and more thirsty.

The rabbi prayed for rain. When there was no response from Heaven, he ordered a fast on the weekdays when the Torah is read in the synagogue—Mondays and Thursdays—but still no rain fell. Finally, the rabbi gathered the people together and, with their voices raised in chanting and praying, the whole community offered up special penitential prayers to send rain, precious rain.

That night, the rabbi had a dream. In the dream, a voice said to him, "*All the prayers the community offers will not bring rain. Only one man's prayers will succeed. And that man is Moishe the shopkeeper. He, and he alone, must be the messenger of the community and lead the congregation in prayer.*"

When the rabbi awoke, he was troubled by the message in the dream. "Moishe the shopkeeper!" the rabbi said aloud, but only to himself. "An ignorant man, God forgive me, a man who knows nothing of prayer and ritual. *He* should *daven* at the *bima*?" The rabbi shrugged his shoulders, put the dream out of his mind, and dismissed the whole thing as pure nonsense.

The following night, the rabbi had the same dream and heard the same message: "*Send Moishe the shopkeeper to lead the prayers, and rain will fall. Otherwise, there will be no response to any of your prayers.*"

Again the rabbi woke up with a sense of the unusual, a disturbed feeling; but again he refused to believe the dream. Only when he was visited by the same dream on the third night, did he finally listen and obey the voice.

In the morning, the rabbi called the entire community to prayer. And when everyone had gathered, they waited in silence for the rabbi or one of the leaders in the community to lead them in the prayers. To their surprise the rabbi called out, "Today Moishe the shopkeeper will lead us in prayer."

All eyes turned to Moishe, who was sitting in the back. Moishe didn't move.

"You, Moishe ben Yitzhak, come to the *bima* to lead us," repeated the rabbi.

Moishe shook his head, "No, no, rabbi. I can't, rabbi. I. . . . I. . . ." and his voice could barely be heard. But the people could see by the shake of his head and the way he almost disappeared into his *tallis*, that he was not going to do what the rabbi asked of him.

The rabbi walked through the synagogue and stood next to Moishe, and again said, "Moishe, *you* and *only you* must lead us in prayer. Then rain will fall and end our drought. I plead with you, Moishe, go up to the *bima* and begin the prayers." And the rabbi stood there with his arms open, with tears in his eyes.

"Rabbi," whispered Moishe, "I'm so ashamed. I don't even know how to read properly. I barely know the *aleph beis*. I don't know the order of prayers, and I can repeat only a few words of the *Shema Yisroel*. How can *I* go up on the *bima*?"

"It doesn't matter that you don't know the prayers," said the rabbi. "Say whatever is in your heart, Moishe. Whatever you know. God will accept it."

Moishe hesitantly stood up from his place, removed his *tallis*, and left the synagogue.

Everyone was bewildered. "What will happen now?" they asked.

But the rabbi returned to the *bima* and waited.

No one spoke.

No one dared to move. After all, if the rabbi waited, they would wait too. The synagogue was filled with silence, a silence of waiting.

In a few moments, Moishe returned, and in his hands he carried the balance scales from his shop. As he rushed up to the *bima*, the tension broke and the people began to speak with amusement in their voices. What, they wondered, was Moishe going to do with the scales—in the synagogue?

Moishe turned to the congregation, held up the scales, and began, "*Ribono Shel Olam*, Lord of the Universe, I have only my good name to show You. I am not a learned man. I cannot read Your holy words. I cannot pray in the proper way. But, *Tatele*, dear little Father in Heaven, hear me and take my words for good and not for evil. I brought my scales with me to remind You that I have always had honest scales. I never cheated anyone. I have never lied. And if I have fulfilled the commandment to be honest and to keep my scales clean, then hear my words and have mercy on us all and bring us rain." And then Moishe was silent.

The people waited.

Suddenly, the heavens grew dark and, after a few moments, heavy rains began to fall. The people, grateful for the water from Heaven, thanked God for causing the blessed rain to fall.

And then the people understood the true meaning of Moishe's words. When the merchants in the community returned to their stores later that day, they all made a small, sometimes almost imperceptible, adjustment in their scales.

From that time on, the rains continued to fall according to their seasons.

And the people prospered.

The Seven Lies

Lies? Lies are not ethical. So how can we have a Jewish story filled with lies? Judaism does *not*, of course, condone lying. In certain cases, however, lies, or rather "playing with the truth," may save a life as, for example, when Abram tells his wife Sarai to tell the Egyptians that she is his sister (Genesis 12:13). Although telling this "lie" was a sin, it saved Abram's life; for in those days kings would kill the husbands of beautiful wives and seize the women.

Some lies, however, are harmful, and they are great sins. For example, Joseph's brothers lied to their father Jacob about Joseph's "accidental death," and Joseph "delayed" the truth when his brothers came to Egypt to buy grain.

But what of "lies" that distort the truth but harm no one and often entertain those who hear them? Often we confuse lies with stories. We say things like, "Oh, that's some story!" or "Are you telling stories again!"—referring to made-up tales and, therefore, actual lies. But are "lies" always the opposite of truth? And if something is "true," must it necessarily have happened?

I think of "lies," in the context of stories, as stretching the imagination, thinking *beyond* the tight realm of reality or the merely possible. Only through the creative imagination—dreaming the impossible—can we uncover new options, new solutions, new perspectives. It's an exciting process!

While clever wordplay is a favorite element in Jewish stories from every country, the tall tale that involves a lying contest to win a princess is found mostly in the Middle Eastern regions of Persian Kurdistan, Iraq, and Turkey. (The general European versions of such liars' contests come from France, Spain, England, and Denmark, while two tall-tale stories are from Japan.)

Dov Noy included two stories of this genre in "The Tall Tale of the Merchant's Son" (IFA 7) and "The Great Lie" (IFA 342) (Noy 1963). The tale type is AT 852, a variation of the

"It's a Lie!" tale (compare Tale Type A-T 1920F; see "A Tall Tale").

This story of the seven lies (IFA 7421) is from Persian Kurdistan and may be found in Itakhimzade (1967). One incident is taken from IFA 3858 in Marcus (1966).

nce an old woman had an only son who was not very handsome. In fact, he was ugly—*but* he was witty and full of spirit. He worked only occasionally; not that he was lazy, but that's the way it was. And whatever money he earned he always gave to his mother.

One day, the old woman heard in the marketplace that the King would marry his beautiful daughter to the man that could tell him seven lies successfully. The lies must be imaginative and convincing or amusing. The old woman told her son what she'd heard.

The son became excited and said to his mother, "Go and tell the King *I* want to seek his daughter's hand in marriage."

"Oh, my son," said the old woman, "you are a *poor* young man, *neither* handsome nor tall. Besides, the King will kill you if you are not successful. So many others have already failed the test of telling the King seven lies. Don't even think of trying."

The son, who was known for his stubbornness, grew angry and said, "If you don't go, I'll go myself, and I may be hanged before I even get to see the King."

What could the mother do? She arrived at the King's palace and went into the courtyard, but she was *afraid* to go *inside*. Instead, she returned home and told her son, "Oh, there were *so many* people there, I couldn't even get to see the King."

After seven days of the same response, the son became angrier and more impatient, and he cried, "If you don't go and see the face of the King, dark and bitter will be your fate."

The next day, the mother arrived at the King's palace. The guards greeted her, having seen her every day for seven days, and asked her, "Why don't you enter?"

When she told them why she had come, they immediately informed the King, who invited her in.

"Your Majesty, I have come on behalf of my son. He is ugly and poor, but he is witty and ingenious and prefers a clever play of words to money."

"Bring him here tomorrow," said the King. "If he tells me seven lies successfully on seven days, then he will marry my daughter and can spend his whole time with word-play instead of work."

The next day, the son was brought to the King, and he immediately began to speak. "A few years ago, when my father was alive, he bought a cow. As he was leading her home, milk dripped from her udders. And those udders were *so big* and *so much milk* came from them that all the dust on the road became wet and, as a result, *the mud* was a *foot deep*."

The King and his ministers laughed and the King announced, "You have succeeded in your first lie. Return tomorrow for the second try."

The next day at the palace, the son began, "My mother milked the cow twelve times a day, and she would cook a wonderful milk and rice dish. One day, we were ready to eat this rice cereal and warm milk, but my father hadn't arrived home yet so we waited a while, then we ate. Actually, my father was on a trip to another country, and he returned only after two years' time. We had *saved* his dinner and served that *same dish* to him when he returned. The rice had flowered leaves two feet high. And the milk underneath was still *so hot* that my father burned his mouth."

The King and his royal advisors laughed, and the King announced, "You have succeeded in your second lie. Come back tomorrow."

On the third day, the son said, "When my father was a merchant, he bought a large sack of sesame seeds. On the way home, he came to a river. How could he cross the river without getting the sesame seeds wet? My father was a clever man, so what did he do? He took a long rope and many rocks, and he tied *each* sesame seed to a rock and threw it to the other side of the river. He did this until he had thrown across every grain. Then he swam across and counted all his merchandise. *Not a single sesame seed was missing.*"

Once again, the royal audience laughed, and the King invited the son back again.

On the fourth day, the son told the royal audience, "One day my father bought many, many hens. But he ran over one of them with his cart and made a big hole in her back. Nevertheless, he left the hen in the chicken house. Then what do you think happened to her? A *big tree* grew out of her back and blocked the entrance to the chicken house so that it was impossible to go inside."

On the fifth day, the son returned once again to the palace and said to the King, "You remember that sack of sesame seeds? Well, my father planted them and they grew into trees. He collected the fruit into two large sacks. He didn't have a donkey, so he took the sacks and piled them onto one of his hens—he picked the largest hen he had— and so they went to the market. But on the way they came to a river. The hen didn't hesitate: She plunged into the river and swam across with the two sacks on her back. And not a drop of water touched the sesame fruit."

The King and the ministers laughed even harder than before.

On the sixth day, the son began, "My father once had a piece of land in another place and he bought wheat to sow. But then he realized that he didn't have enough money to pay for the planting, and he had to resell the wheat kernels. So that he wouldn't look like a pauper, he brought dust from the road and scattered it in the fields, as if he were sowing. Then he went home. After the rains, people came from the far-away place to tell him that the wheat had flowered in his fields—as high as the trees—and it was the *best* stand of wheat ever seen thereabouts."

The King invited the son to return for the seventh day.

And when the son told his mother about his successes, she became more worried than ever, fearful that he would fail on the seventh trial. The son said to her, "Mother, do not worry. But I will need whatever money you have left."

His mother gave him the money. He went to the marketplace and bought seven enormous jugs and brought them to the palace courtyard.

When the King came into the courtyard, the son said, "Your Majesty, your father and my father were brothers. Our grandfather had fourteen jugs filled with gold and silver. At his death, he gave the jugs to your father to divide between the two brothers. Your father, being older and more selfish, killed my father so he wouldn't have to divide the silver and gold."

The King stood there, shocked.

But the ministers were laughing.

"I have finished, Your Majesty. If you think it a lie, then I have met your requirements and you must give me your daughter's hand in marriage. But if it is not a lie, then fill my seven jugs with silver and gold."

The King looked at the seven jugs. They were so huge that he wouldn't have enough in his treasury to fill them. He quickly turned to his ministers for counsel.

The ministers liked the young man who had entertained them, and they said: "Your Majesty, you have no choice. He has won the contest and told *seven successful lies*. Give him your daughter for a wife."

Turning to the young man, the King decreed, "It's a lie."

The young man was taken to the baths, dressed in royal clothing, and married to the princess. Together they lived a rich and happy life, and the young husband stopped telling lies.

But one day. . . .

Well, that's a story for another time.

The Demon in
the House of Study

This story, from the Babylonian Talmud (*Kiddushin* 29b) resembles the common medieval tales of conquests over dragons. In our tale, however, the dragon is a form taken by a demon, a more commonly found character in Jewish literature.

There are a few other references to dragons in our literature. One is in the story of Daniel's defeat of the dragon in the apocryphal additions to the Book of Daniel. There is also a parallel legend about the Baal Shem Tov in Dov Baer (1811), the earliest collection of tales about the Baal Shem Tov. Dragons, therefore, are not entirely unknown to the Jews in our literature.

In our story, we meet Rabbi Abbaye, whose fear of demons is well-documented in several talmudic legends, such as the one in *Berakhot* 62a. In the Talmud, the man who defeats the demon is Rabbi Aha.

It was a pleasure to work on this story with Howard Schwartz, the author of many wonderful collections of folktales. This is our retelling of "The Demon in the House of Study."

ne day, strange things began to happen in Rabbi Abbaye's House of Study. Chairs began to squeak. Not the chairs the students were sitting in, but the empty chairs.

Also, books began to disappear. Sometimes when a student was reading a book, it would fly out of his hands and vanish. And when would the book reappear? Only when he didn't need it any more.

Now, it is bad enough to be bothered while studying, but it is much worse to be distracted during prayer. And that is exactly what began to happen. Everyone's prayer shawl began to slip off and, at the same time, many of them had the feeling that something was tickling their noses, making them want to sneeze. And sometimes they did sneeze. Then everyone suddenly lost his place.

At first, Rabbi Abbaye did not worry about these annoyances too much. But when he saw how these strange happenings began to interfere with both the prayer and study of all his students, even the best ones, he became worried. And then, something much worse happened:

Strange noises were heard to come from the House of Study at night, noises that sounded like pots being banged together, and screechings like a thousand untuned violins all playing at the same time.

Rabbi Abbaye tried to ignore those noises for a long time. But finally he realized that he would have to do something. So he decided to sleep that night in the House of Study to see if he could discover the cause of the disturbances. He stretched out on a wooden bench in one corner, the one closest to the door. And at last he fell asleep.

At midnight, Rabbi Abbaye was awakened by strange, eerie noises and invisible shuffling sounds. He was so frightened that he ran out of the place as fast as his legs could carry him. He now realized that the House of Study was haunted.

It seems that even as a child Rabbi Abbaye had been afraid of spirits and demons. Nonetheless, whatever was haunting the House of Study *had* to be expelled. Who was going to do it?

"*I'm* surely not going back in there at night," said Abbaye, "and it's far too dangerous a task for any of my students."

Then a letter arrived from Rabbi Aha, the father of one of his former students. Rabbi Aha asked if he could come and study with Abbaye. Now Rabbi Aha happened to be a very devout man who never left a problem unresolved. And Rabbi Abbaye thought, "*He* may be just the one to help us."

But the more he thought about it, the more Abbaye was afraid that Rabbi Aha would refuse to confront the demon, or whatever was disturbing them. So he decided, "When Aha comes, we will not tell him about it." Instead, he cautioned the students, "When Rabbi Aha arrives, tell him he will have to sleep in the House of Study, for there is no room anywhere else." And that is what they did.

At midnight, a terrible noise awakened Rabbi Aha. He jumped up and saw a nightmarish monster looming over him, a seven-headed dragon, for that is the shape the demon had taken.

Rabbi Aha was terrified. He pinched himself, hoping that he was dreaming. But the pinch hurt, so he knew that he was awake. His heart was beating wildly and he stood frozen in place.

Suddenly the dragon roared and the ground shook for miles around, and poor Rabbi Aha was frightened out of his wits.

In his terror, Rabbi Aha began to pray out loud. He prayed with the greatest intensity, for he was afraid that his life was as good as lost.

But when he pronounced God's Name for the first time, a miracle took place: one of the dragon's seven heads flew off, crashed into the far corner of the room, and disappeared in a puff of smoke.

When Rabbi Aha saw this, he had his first glimmer of hope. He finished the prayer and then started to recite it all over again, even louder. And lo and behold, as he pronounced God's Name a second time, another of the dragon's heads went flying off and vanished in a puff of smoke.

Five more times Rabbi Aha repeated the prayer, pronouncing every word with all his heart. And each time he repeated God's Name, the dragon lost another head, and its roar diminished, until it could barely be heard.

And the *seventh time* the dragon lost its last head and vanished completely.

At first, Rabbi Aha was afraid to believe the monster was gone, but when the silence was unbroken for several minutes, he took a candlestick in his hand and searched the room and saw that it was empty. Then he gave thanks to God for saving him in his hour of danger, and hurried to leave the place.

When he opened the door, Rabbi Aha found Rabbi Abbaye and all his students crouched outside it, trembling with fear. Assuming they had heard the terrible noise and had come to help him, he told them what had happened. And when they heard the good news—that the evil spirit had been expelled—they all recited the prayer thanking God for protecting them from evil, and they celebrated.

After that, Rabbi Aha spent many years studying with Rabbi Abbaye.

Only much later did Abbaye finally confess that he had known of the evil spirit haunting them. Rabbi Aha gladly forgave his beloved teacher. And together they gave thanks to God for expelling the demon from the House of Study.

The Mirror

One day a colleague, Rabbi Alter Metzger, stopped me in the lobby of Stern College and handed me a Hebrew copy of "The Mirror." "Read this story," he said enthusiastically. "You will want to tell it." He was right for many reasons. The story contains the exciting elements of a good story: intrigue, loyalties and disloyalties, suspense, jealousy, and resourcefulness—especially when applied by a Jew when Jews are falsely accused of a crime.

This is a story that fascinated me when I first read about Rabbi Hayim Ibn Attar, author of *Or HaHayim*, his commentary on the Pentateuch. The renowned Rabbi Ibn Attar (1696–1743) was a wonder-worker who came from Sale in Morocco, but who traveled as a preacher from town to town throughout Morocco and Italy. Ibn Attar is the hero of many Moroccan legends.

There are 200 IFA versions of such a Jewish tale, with the central idea of the miraculous rescue of a Jewish community. One of these is "The Stargazing King and the Rabbi" (IFA 10086) (Attias 1976). "The Mirror" is A-T 325** with versions known from all over the IFA collecting area. Another outstanding version is found in Noy (1967), number 47 (listed there as Type 730*A). The story is found also in *Likkutei Hamaasim* (1648) and Bin Gorion (1976).

The stars have played an important role in Jewish life and lore. When we wish someone "good luck" in Hebrew or Yiddish, we say *"Mazel tov,"* which really means, "May you have a lucky constellation of stars." This comes from the idea of fate, which was identified with the formations of the stars, specifically the Zodiac, in medieval times.

Another widespread belief was that the future could be "read" in the stars and a certain time be confirmed as propitious for decisions or actions. While a number of Jewish stories concern a rabbi seeking to learn whether his companion in Paradise is as worthy as he (see "A Companion in the World-To-Come"), in this story a King wants to know whether a man born under the same sign as he is his "equal," in other words, his "mirror" image.

A mirror, or magic glass, is an important symbol in folklore (see "The Magic Pomegranate"). Many world tales focus on a mirror, which may serve as a springboard for the story's action. An example is the famous scene from "Snow White," of "Mirror, Mirror, on the wall. . . ." In a Japanese variant of "Cinderella," called "The Mirror of Matsuyama," the young daughter inherits a mirror with the magical power to bring back the image of her departed mother to comfort her. There is also a folktale from Buczacz, "The Pious and the Mirror" (IFA 8179), where a wife seeing herself for the first time in a mirror, hidden by her pious husband in the attic, thinks that her reflection is her husband's ugly mistress hidden by him there.

Mirrors, little understood at first, and rarities for some time, would allow for imaginative and creative happenings.

Here, then, is the story of Rabbi Hayim Ibn Attar, called "The Mirror."

n a certain land in the Middle East, there was a King who knew how to read the stars. He always consulted the constellations before making a decision, and even before planning a celebration.

One day, as the King was sitting in his palace, a thought crossed his mind. "What other person has been born under my sign?" he pondered. "I wonder if there is such a person, whether he is my equal? I must find out."

As his curiosity grew, he became more and more impatient for nightfall. Looking at the stars that night, the King saw that the man born under his very sign was Rabbi Hayim ben Moshe ibn Attar.

"Can this rabbi be as worthy as I?" he wondered. He was so curious that he decided to find out for himself. So he made plans to visit Rabbi Ibn Attar, who lived far from the King's palace.

After he had made all the necessary arrangements, the King bade farewell to the Queen and set out on the journey, taking with him his favorite servants. While the King would be away, his Viceroy, who was second in command, would rule.

One morning, after two months of travel, the King saw that his party was approaching the town where the rabbi lived. He asked one of his servants to lend him some of his clothing and, thus disguised, approached the home of Rabbi Ibn Attar.

The rabbi's wife greeted the King at the door. "Where is your husband?" he asked her. "My husband is in the forest, but he will return at midday," she answered.

The King decided to wait, and the rabbi's wife made him welcome.

As he waited, the King noticed how poor the house was, the furnishings so plain. "Is he really my counterpart?" the King asked himself, hardly believing it could be so.

At midday the rabbi returned, carrying a pack on his shoulders. When he saw his guest, he called out, "Oh, Your Majesty," and bowed low.

The King was astonished. "How did you know me?" he asked. "I am wearing a servant's clothing. *How* could you know who I was?"

Ibn Attar answered, "Every person has a spirit that accompanies him. When I saw you, I sensed a special spirit, and I knew that you were a person to whom homage was due, Your Majesty. But why have you come here, to *my* home?"

"I have come to meet you because you were born under exactly the same sign I was," answered the King. "I was curious about you. Could you really be my equal, I wondered? However, when I arrived. . . ." and the King hesitated a moment, "I must tell you the truth. I was shocked to find that you are so *poor*."

Ibn Attar responded, "Actually, my King, poor though I may be, I am *greater* than you."

"What?" the King cried. "How do you dare to say that to me?"

"I will prove it to you," the rabbi answered simply.

He brought a mirror to the table and said, "Your Majesty, look into this mirror and tell me what you see."

The King looked into the mirror and exclaimed, "I see the entire world! How is that possible?"

"Now tell me," continued the rabbi, "Where is your kingdom?" The King pointed to the borders of his kingdom.

"Turn the mirror around and look into it again," instructed the rabbi.

When the King had turned the mirror, he gasped. "Where is my kingdom?" he cried. "There is the whole world—but *not* my kingdom."

"Now, listen carefully," said the rabbi. "Turn the mirror again, and look into it, and show me the city where you reign. But don't turn away from the mirror."

The King did as instructed, and there he saw his city in the glass.

"Show me where your palace is in this city," the rabbi said.

As the King pointed to the palace, he saw his wife in the royal bed.

At that moment the door to the bedchamber opened, and the Viceroy entered and approached the Queen in a brazen manner.

"What are *you* doing here?" asked the Queen. "You must not be here, for my husband is on a journey, and he would think very ill of your crude behavior."

The Viceroy laughed, "Your husband will no longer be King, dear lady. If you refuse me, I will do with you what I wish, and I will not save you."

"Are you rebelling against the King?" cried the Queen.

"With me, you will have more glory than you have had with the King," declared the Viceroy. "If you refuse me, I will kill you. But *together* we will take *all* the wealth and *all* the power." The Queen did not want to turn against the King, but she could not fight off the Viceroy.

Rabbi Ibn Attar said to the King, "You are seeing what is happening now, at *this* moment."

The King began to shake with anger. "What can I do?" he raged. "I see how my wife is suffering."

"Take this dagger and throw it in the direction of the Viceroy," Ibn Attar advised.

The King hesitated, "What if I miss him and I injure the Queen?"

Ibn Attar assured him that if he aimed straight at the Viceroy's heart, he would not miss. He threw the dagger, and the Viceroy fell dead.

The Queen, more frightened than ever, looked in all directions. "Where did the knife come from?" she wondered. "Who killed the Viceroy? What strange mystery is this?" Frightened, she summoned her astrologer. "Look into the stars to see how this happened," she ordered. "Find out what this means."

The astrologer, a jealous man, quickly took command and replied: "Do not fear, my Queen. *I* will take charge, and everything will soon be in order, I assure you. But it would be wise to say *nothing* about this to anyone."

Then the astrologer called certain servants and instructed them, "Wrap up the body and take it to a secret place in the palace that I will show you. You must swear that, when the King returns, you will tell him only that the Viceroy has disappeared. Then we will get two witnesses to say they saw the Viceroy go into the front door of a Jewish home and that he never came out. It will seem certain that the *Jews* killed him and hid his body."

All this time, the King and Rabbi Ibn Attar were watching and listening. In amazement, the King wrote down everything he had witnessed in his journal—the date, the time, the events. As the King was about to leave, the rabbi turned to him and pleaded, "You yourself saw, Your Majesty, that the Jews are innocent. *Save them* from this accusation, I beg of you. Otherwise, they will be blamed and sentenced to death."

And the King answered, "On my return, if I find that these events have happened as I saw them, and the accusations are made, I will bestow upon you the greatest honors in my kingdom, dear rabbi."

When the King had returned to the palace, the astrologer, along with two witnesses, came to him.

"The Jews have killed the Viceroy and hidden his body,"

declared the astrologer. "I have witnesses, Your Majesty. Kill the Jews and throw them out of your lands. Then we can take possession of their land *and* wealth."

The King pretended to be angry. "If this is true," he declared, "I will kill them. However, we must have judges from every nation in order to be certain that our judgments are correct, and we will not be proved wrong afterwards."

And so, invitations were sent to judges of all the nations, and an invitation to Rabbi Ibn Attar also.

In the kingdom, all the Jews wept and prayed, hoping that the trial would be a fair one, and that they would not be condemned unjustly.

That night, the King asked the Queen if *she* knew anything about what had happened to the Viceroy.

"No," she answered.

"Do not be afraid to tell me the truth; nothing will happen to you," he reassured her.

But she still insisted, "I know nothing."

A third time, the King commanded in anger, "Tell me what you know, or I will kill you."

The Queen then began to weep, and she told him all that had taken place in her bedchamber. The King listened, and as she spoke, he saw in his mind's eye the events as they had happened in the mirror, and he knew she spoke the truth. He now understood, too, that the Jew who was born under his sign, Rabbi Ibn Attar, indeed was on a higher level than he. And the King praised God in the heavens above for His wisdom.

On the day that all the judges and all the court and all the Jews were assembled, the King invited everyone to a grand reception. He served the finest wine, which can best open up the heart and loosen the tongue. As everyone was drinking and enjoying the superb wine, the King announced, "Come, everyone, to a secret place in the underground passages of my palace. There, in the coolness of the ground, I have stored some rare wine for just such an occasion as this."

When the astrologer heard the King's order, he became

frightened that the Viceroy's body would be discovered. He quickly went down another passageway.

Rabbi Ibn Attar noticed this, and he motioned to the King. The King then followed the astrologer and the assembled guests followed the King. When they had almost reached the bottom of the long stairway leading to the palace's underground chambers, the King said, "What foul air I smell. Could it be only from a lack of fresh air?"

The people who had followed the King were also surprised that there was such an evil smell in the King's palace.

As they descended, the odor became stronger. When they reached the bottom, the King watched as Rabbi Ibn Attar's eyes were fixed on a specific place on the ground.

"Here, then, is my precious wine," exclaimed the King, pointing to the spot. He ordered his servants to begin digging.

In a shallow grave, they found the body of the Viceroy, wearing his royal clothing. The King became angry, and accused his servants of the crime. "Were you so jealous of the Viceroy that you killed him? *It is clear* that the Jews did not kill this man, for if they had, he would *not* be in this palace, still wearing his royal robes!"

Then the servants realized that the King knew the truth, and they in turn told what they knew. "The astrologer himself is guilty of jealousy," they said. "And because he hates the Jews, he saw a way to use the Viceroy's mysterious death to rid the kingdom of the Jews, too, and to profit from this terrible deed."

The King and all the judges who were witnesses understood that the Jews were innocent. They sentenced the astrologer and his servants, who had borne false witness against the Jews, to be killed.

The Jews in their happiness began to sing a song of praise to God.

And as for Rabbi Ibn Attar, the King bestowed upon him *great honors*, as he had promised.

The Clever Midwife

Demons are especially intriguing to Jews. Stories of demons are found in the legends of King Solomon, as when Solomon confronts the King of the Demons, Ashmedai (Asmodeus) in his search for the *Shamir*/worm. And who helps Solomon build the Temple in Jerusalem? The demons that he puts under his power. We can see from these stories, and others, that the Jews did not believe that all demons were evil and should be readily exorcised.

Other demons figured in the stories from the *midrash* and other post-biblical works, probably due to foreign influences when Jews began to live among other peoples. So we have many tales in which God confronts Satan, angels fight demons, and good struggles with evil.

Throughout the generations, ghosts and imps, *sheidim* and spirits, demons and witches, devils and she-devils have captivated the Jewish imagination in countless tales, in the Middle Ages as well as modern times. Witness the popularity of Isaac Bashevis Singer's stories today.

At times of rites of passage, specifically birth, Bar/Bat Mitzva, marriage, and death, it was believed, people are especially vulnerable, for it is then that demons try to take control over humans. However, since demons must obey the greater force of God, and are subject to justice and holy law, the same as humans (they too are part of God's creatures, having been created on the sixth day), humans have a chance to outwit the demons and save themselves. They do this in several ways: by abstaining from food or drink offered by the demons, by using certain objects—such as garlic—as a protective device, by keeping silent, and especially by doing good deeds (*mitzvot*).

The midwife, who performs the good deed of assisting at a birth, receives the demon's gratitude for helping a cat—or a human who has since become part of the demon family—to give birth. In all the versions I know of, the child born is always a boy, which is cause for great celebration, especially in Sefardic communities.

Tales like "The Clever Midwife" were told from generation to generation by women for a number of reasons, one of which was to teach young girls how to act in a time of crisis. One of the popular versions is "The Reward of a Midwife" (IFA 279, recorded by Mordecai Zahavi from a workman from Zakho, Iraqi Kurdistan), which is included in Noy (1963).

"The Clever Midwife" contains an important and widespread motif found elsewhere in this collection and nearly world-wide. TMI C242, Taboo: the eating of food of fairies or witch (demon), is a very old idea supported by a belief that having partaken of the food in the netherworld, the fairy-world, or the house of a demon traps the human there for all time. Here the motif is found together with its nearly paradoxical opposite, TMI F333, Fairy grateful to human midwife, which allows the midwife to leave and to even be rewarded so long as she does not eat there. The A-T Tale Type 476* "In the Frog's House" is the European version, found in a number of IFA versions. There are at least seven variants of "The Clever Midwife" in the Israel Folktale Archives; IFA 8902, from Morocco, the source of this tale; IFA 2789, from Iraqi Kurdistan; IFA 8140, from Bukhara, and IFA 1145, from Yemen, IFA 8997, Palestinian Sefardi; IFA 8897, from Turkey; IFA 4564, from Ashkelon. The story of "The Clever Midwife" has been told for generations and can be found in Kaidanover (1705), *Meshalim Shel Shlomo*, Farhi (1870), Bin Gorion (1916–1921), as well as folktale sources of earlier centuries.

One note regarding midwives and their roles in Jewish life: According to the Bible, Pharaoh commanded the Hebrew midwives Shifra and Pua to kill all Jewish boy babies. But the two midwives did not obey that order, for they feared God. Because of their good ways, God helped the Israelites to multiply and increased their prosperity (Exodus 1:15–21). That was the reward of the midwives Shifra and Pua, and it became our legacy.

n a village in Morocco, a midwife was returning home after helping at the birth of a child. It was the middle of the night and, since there was no moonlight, the midwife held a candle to guide her on the way home.

Suddenly, the candle went out, and the midwife could not see which way to walk in the darkness. She began to pray to God, "Help me, dear God. It is such a long way home. What shall I do?"

Suddenly she felt a cat rub against her leg and the cat spoke. "What is wrong, dear lady?"

"I've lost my way. I can't see in the darkness," replied the midwife.

"Here is a match for you to light your candle," said the cat. "Then stay behind me. I know the way." And the cat gave the midwife a match. Together they walked in the night, the midwife following the cat, until they arrived at the woman's home. The grateful midwife turned to the cat and said, "May God grant that, just as you saved me, I will save you. Farewell."

A year passed and one evening there was a knock at the midwife's door. The midwife opened the door, and there stood a tall man, out of breath. He said to her, "Come quickly, grandmother, we need your help. There's a woman about to give birth."

The midwife did not hestiate for a moment. When someone needed her services, she could get ready in a wink of the eye.

With great haste, they walked. The man led the midwife to a house outside the village. There the midwife was brought to the bedroom, where she saw a young woman about to give birth. Within a short time, the woman produced a son, and the midwife tended her with great skill.

When they were alone, the young woman called the midwife to her and said, "Do you know who I am? I am a demon, and a year ago I was in the form of a cat, and you blessed me. Now, since you have helped me, I must warn you to be careful. When my relatives invite you to eat, *refuse* and say you are fasting for seven days. If you *eat* anything, no matter how little, you'll become a demon.

"Next they will tempt you with a room full of gold, silver, and pearls. Take *nothing* of their treasures. But since you must be rewarded for your work, for that is the demon's custom, ask *only* for a small rug."

The midwife thanked the woman, and promised to remember her advice.

When the relatives came to the house to celebrate the birth of a son, they invited the midwife to eat the delicious foods they had prepared. But she refused, saying that she was fasting for seven days. Then they brought her to a room filled with gold, silver, and pearls, and they offered her whatever she wanted. But she refused this offer as well. Then when they asked her, "*What* will you accept? For we are *obliged* to give you something," the midwife replied, "I will accept a small rug," and they gave her a small rug.

As the midwife was about to leave, the newborn baby began to cry with a loud, seemingly endless wail. The relatives began to complain. "What is wrong with him? Why does he cry *so much*? Can't someone make him *stop* that *awful* crying?"

Suddenly one of the demons stood up and said, "Whenever a demon baby is born, there is a human twin born at the same time. Since the human baby boy born at the same moment is a quiet child that does not fuss, I will go and exchange the babies. That way, we'll have some peace and quiet." And so she did just what she had proposed.

The midwife, seeing this, hastily suggested, "Bring me the child and I will dress him."

After they had exchanged the two babies, they gave the human baby to the midwife. The human baby was a quiet, calm baby. The midwife thought quickly and decided on a plan. She dressed the baby and, when none of the demons was watching, stuck a pin into the sole of the child's foot. The baby began shrieking and wailing. Oh, how he cried, poor child!

All the demons began to grumble, "Oh, this child cries *louder* than our own. Quick, bring back our own child, if that's the way it is with a human baby."

So they exchanged babies once more, and the midwife quieted down the demon baby with sugar water. After a few moments, the demon baby slept. Then the man took the midwife back to her home.

In the morning, the midwife ran as fast as she could to the woman whose child had been exchanged briefly with the demon's baby. She found the baby crying frantically, and she hastened to pull the pin from his foot. That calmed him down. Then the midwife told the whole story to the mother, adding, "Never again turn your back to the child." She blessed them and went directly to the great *rav*, Reb Yehoshua ben Nun, and told him what had happened. He listened carefully, and then replied after some thought, "This is not the first time that I hear of demons taking children away or exchanging them. But this time I will make an end of it." And the great *rav* excommunicated the demons and made them outcasts.

The midwife finally returned home. Wanting to rest, she sat on the small rug given her by the demons. Suddenly, there were piles of gold coins all around her, and the trinkets she kept on the tables turned into precious stones.

From that day on, the midwife had more than she needed for herself. She gave great amounts of money to help the poor. But she especially wanted to help children. So she decided that whenever a baby was born in that community, she would put aside a certain amount so that child could have the best teachers for learning Torah. And then she put aside another amount for the child's marriage. And so it was in that community. The midwife was remembered as a generous and righteous woman who celebrated life.

And since then, the demons are down below, no longer in our world, and we do not see them, nor do they frighten us *any more*.

The Miser's Keys

As in "The Clever Midwife," this story involves the dealings of a human and a demon during a rite-of-passage ceremony—in this case, a circumcision (a *brit milah*) (see introduction to "The Clever Midwife"). The *mohel* does indeed perform a *mitzva*, especially by doing the circumcision without asking for a reward. As it says in *Pirkei Avot* 4:2 (*The Sayings of the Fathers*), "The reward for a righteous deed is the deed itself." In all other aspects of his life, however, the *mohel* in our story is a miser. Surprisingly enough, it is from the demon that he learns a valuable lesson.

This story is essentially the same tale type as "The Clever Midwife," but with the significant change of person, motive, and reward. Again the taboo against eating is observed, and the reward is given as payment. This story also shows strong affinities to A-T 503 "Gift of the Little People."

This story was adapted from many sources: Kaidanover (1705), Jellinek (1853–1877), Eisenstein (1915), Farhi (1870), Bin Gorion (1916–1921), in addition to Bin Gorion (1976). This tale was collected also in the oral tradition as part of the Israel Folktale Archives (IFA 10097), in Attias (1976). Another version can be found in Ben-Yehezkel (1957). In Noy (1972) there is still another version called, "The Stingy Circumciser and the Ghosts" (IFA 9182), collected by Hagit Matras from Rachel Albukher (Palestinian Sefardi). Actually, there are 15 IFA versions of this tale.

From all these variants, one may conclude that everyone is bent on teaching a miser how to use his keys more openly. Stories, too, hold treasures and serve as the keys with which to reach the treasures of understanding and change.

here once was a wealthy Jew who lived in a large house and owned a store. Wealthy though he was, he was a miser who never gave even a single coin to charity. When the poor came to him for money, they left empty-handed. Even when a traveling rabbi came collecting for a charity, he never contributed to the fund. In fact, on weekdays he did not go to pray in the synagogue just so he would not have to give to charity. Instead, he would pray alone at home.

Besides being a storekeeper, he was also a *mohel.* Whenever a male child was born and the *mohel* was called, then no matter how far away it was, the *mohel* always closed his store and eagerly went to perform the *mitzva* of *brit mila*, the circumcision of the child. Furthermore, he would never accept any payment. He always said, "Performing this *mitzva* is reward enough for me."

One day, a man came to his store and invited him to circumcise his newborn son. The *mohel* immediately closed his store and left with the man, walking to a far-away village. And it was a very long journey.

After walking and walking they came to a high mountain, and there on the mountaintop stood a beautiful village. They entered a magnificent home. The man excused himself to go on an errand in the village, so the *mohel* began to look around the house. Going from room to room, he noticed the fine furnishings and richly woven carpets.

As he passed by an open bedroom, he saw the woman who had recently given birth. Seeing the *mohel*, the woman motioned for him to come near her bed and spoke in a hurried whisper, "I must tell you something before my husband returns. My husband is not human; he is a *demon*. I am as human as yourself, but I can never return to your world, since the demons kidnapped me when I was very young, and now I must forever remain here with them. If you wish to return to your world, *listen carefully* and remember this: Do *not* eat *or* drink of their food and do *not* accept any gifts from them. As soon as you benefit from something of theirs, you will not be able to leave here."

The *mohel* was filled with a terrible fright at the thought that he found himself in the presence of demons. He thanked the woman and returned to the dining room, where tables were set.

Soon, the father of the child and many guests arrived to celebrate the birth. They invited the *mohel* to join them but he declined, saying he was tired and had no appetite.

The following day, they all went to the synagogue with the infant. The *mohel* circumcised him according to the Laws of Moses, and then everyone returned to the house for a festive meal.

Again the demons urged the *mohel* to eat with them, but the *mohel* refused and told them he was fasting that day.

That night, they held another reception in honor of the birth and invited the *mohel* to join them in eating the prepared delicacies. Once more the *mohel* did not eat anything, saying this time that he did not feel well.

After eating and drinking, the host invited the *mohel* to come with him to a special room. The *mohel* became frightened, thinking they would force him to eat or would even kill him. But when they came into the room, he saw splendid treasures of gold and silver.

The host said: "Take whatever you like from here as *your reward* for performing the *brit.*"

"Thank you," replied the *mohel*, "but I lack for nothing."

So the host brought him to another room. This room was filled with diamonds, pearls, and rubies.

"Choose something from among these precious stones that pleases you," offered the host.

"Thank you, but I lack for nothing," repeated the *mohel*.

Finally, the host took the *mohel* to a third room, where keys of all kinds hung on the wall. The host picked up one bunch of keys.

Upon seeing the keys, the *mohel* stared, his mouth open wide.

"You seem startled at what you see in my hand—merely some keys—more surprised and interested than when I showed you magnificent gold and diamonds."

"Well, yes, that's true," stuttered the *mohel*, "but I am more surprised because the keys you are holding seem to resemble *my* keys *exactly*."

"Exactly," said the host. "Now I will reveal a secret to you. I am the chief of all the demons, and there are several demons who are in charge only of misers. Every miser who hoards his money and does not give to charity has his keys taken by those demons, who leave the keys here. *You* are one of those misers and that is why we have your keys and you cannot use your money.

"But since you performed the *mitzva* of circumcising my son and refused to accept payment, I am telling you these secrets. And because you tasted nothing here, not even an olive, you are permitted to return to your own world of humans.

"I give back these keys to you. But when you return home, you must change your ways and give charity to the poor and to all who ask for your help. Do as I say, and you will have a good life."

The *mohel* thanked his host as he pocketed his keys and promised to follow a new path. (But then, wouldn't you do the same?)

Then the host took the *mohel* back to his home.

From that day on, the *mohel* remembered his promise and began to give charity to anyone in need. He also went to the daily prayers in the synagogue and became known for his generosity.

And from then on, his life was good.

The Nigun
(The Melody)

The Hasidic movement was founded by Rabbi Israel Baal Shem Tov (1700–1760) of Podolia. He traveled from one town to another preaching his ideas—that all are equal, that purity of heart is superior to study, that joy rather than sadness should dominate one's relationship to God. He taught these ideas through stories.

Hasidim accord music an all-important place in their lives. They continue to believe that it is through music, especially when sung by the human voice, that one can attain salvation, get rid of evil, and reach the ultimate communion with God. Thus, the Hasidim treasure the human voice—the voice that can sing and tell stories.

I would like to note two important points about Hasidic music that will help the reader understand the "truth" of this story.

First, Hasidim believe that words limit a melody. Therefore, there is an entire body of Hasidic *nigunim* (tunes) *without* words. A wordless *nigun* can be repeated endlessly. Instead of words, meaningless syllables, such as *ay-ay-ay*, *ya-ba-bim*, *bim-bam*, are used. As a matter of fact, each Hasidic group claims its own set of syllables to sing. The only one they all share in common is *"Oy vay."* (Velvel Pasternak has documented *nigunim* and their sources. It is from Velvel and from Ruth Rubin that I have learned so much about *nigunim*.)

Second, the creation of new songs was and continues to be regarded as one of the highest virtues and is the responsibility of the spiritual leaders. These songs are taught orally, memorized, and carried to the Tzadik's followers, although many are now being transcribed and recorded.

The singers in the Hasidic "courts" were always alert to new tunes, adapting, reshaping, and interpreting them. Many of these new tunes were fashioned out of "primitive and secular tunes, rhythmic marches of passing military bands, songs of the non-Jewish countryside," including shepherd love songs (see Rubin (1979)). On hearing one of these melodies, the Hasid has the responsibility of freeing it and of returning the holy spark to God by singing the melody as a holy *nigun*.

Hasidim have always sung their *nigunim*, at the Sabbath table—devotional melodies, songs of yearning and joy, dance tunes, march tunes and waltzes. The power of a *nigun* is illustrated in a story told by Rabbi Shlomo Riskin:

> A simple, uneducated Jew with no great religious learning was invited to a Hasidic *seuda shlishit* (third Sabbath meal). The Rebbe presented a brilliant discourse on the Torah portion of the week, demonstrating his depth of insight and his rare oratorical abilities.
>
> "I don't understand," exclaimed the guest, with a puzzled expression on his face.
>
> One of the Hasidim then told a story, a wondrous miracle-story.
>
> "I still don't understand," whispered the guest, tears beginning to form in his eyes.
>
> At length, the assemblage began to sing, a tune of joy and of love, a song of peace and of yearning, a Sabbath melody which captured the desire of a people for God, the rejoicing of a people in its Law. Slowly, the stranger began to lift his voice in song together with the Hasidim, to move his fingers to the rhythm of the music, to join hands with his friends as they rose together to dance. "Now I understand," he declared, with glistening eyes and an open heart.

A number of years ago, in 1978, my dear friend Ruth Rubin and I were having lunch at a coffee shop near Stern College. During our conversation, she remarked, "I remember a Hasidic story with a *nigun*. Do you want to hear it?" As I am always ready to hear a story, she told me briefly what she could remember of the tale and sang the *nigun*.

As soon as I heard the story and the *nigun*, I knew that I wanted to tell this story. I went home, wrote a draft, sent it to Ruth, and it went back and forth until we had worked out a version that integrated the narrative with the *nigun*.

This story has become one of my favorites and I include

it in my programs as often as I can. (Years later, a woman who heard me tell the story informed me that the *nigun* is similar to the tune used with a Polish folk dance. In fact, she proceeded to sing the Polish tune and dance the folk dance—and it *was* practically the same melody.)

"The Nigun" is A-T 1415 with elements from A-T 910, especially TMI J2080, wise counsels.

In October 1985, I had the pleasure of being invited as a featured storyteller at the National Storytelling Festival in Jonesborough, Tennessee (sponsored by NAPPS, the National Association for the Preservation and Perpetuation of Storytelling). On Friday evening, I told the story to the 4,000 people who came to listen to a weekend of storytelling.

It was an experience to hear people from all over the country, people of various ethnic groups and backgrounds, sing the *nigun* as though it had always been part of their lives. For the next two days, people greeted me with the *nigun*. It was wonderful!

One evening at the festival a man approached me, started singing the *nigun*, and said, "I can't get this melody out of my head." I laughingly replied, "So give me 50 rubles and I'll take it out of your head." After reading the story, you'll understand what I meant.

But the fact is, once a story or a melody enters your head via your heart, it's part of you. You own it and must tell it or sing it again and again. I think that man is still singing our *nigun*.

In the story, I have indicated when the melody is to be sung or played. The musical notes are found integrated at the appropriate places in the story. You can, of course, improvise and sing the melodies whenever you feel like it. *Warning*: It is very difficult to end a *nigun* once you enter the world of song.

 long time ago, in a small town in Russia, there lived a wealthy textile merchant. Yankev ben Moishe sold cloth to the people in this town, and it was well-known that he had the very finest cloth—silks, velvets, lace, wool, and cotton. He was a respected man who gave generous amounts of money to the synagogue. Yankev ben Moishe, however, was not a learned man, so for his only daughter Rivke he wanted a young man who would be eager to learn the textile business, but would also be a talmudic scholar and a Hasid.

One day, Yankev ben Moishe went to the yeshiva and spoke to the rabbi who headed the school.

"*Sholom Aleikhem*, Reb Yisrael," said the merchant. "I have come for a very special reason. I would like to find a good husband for my daughter Rivke—someone who will continue *to study* but will also want to work with me and learn my business."

As the rabbi listened, he stroked his gray beard. Then his face brightened and he replied, almost to himself, "Hayim—of course, Hayim." Then he turned to Yankev ben Moishe and said, "There is a young man here who comes from a nearby village. He sings *nigunim* with a sweet voice that brings light to the heavens and joy to the heart. He walks in the garden and listens to the melodies of the birds, and then he composes melodies by interweaving the songs of the birds. It is well-known that each creature has a song of its own but, as Rabbi Abraham Yaakov said, 'The Children of Israel make melodies out of all of their individual songs in order to bring them to God.' On Shabbos, when Hayim sings a *nigun*, everyone listens at first, but then the students join in. They sing for hours, and their voices are truly filled with religious fervor. But the voice that is heard above them all is that of Hayim. He often says the joy of the Shabbos is more complete with a new *nigun*. He is a poor boy, however, and he will welcome the opportunity to be a part of your family, Yankev ben Moishe."

And so, Yankev ben Moishe and the rabbi shook hands and agreed that Hayim and Yankev ben Moishe were to meet that very day. Hayim was called in, and Yankev ben Moishe looked him over—as if he were a piece of merchandise to be bought and sold. He looked at Hayim's straight black hair, his *payes*, his thin short frame, his long slender fingers, and his large black eyes.

Hayim's cheeks were flushed as he stammered a "*Sh-Sholom A-Aleikhem.*" After telling Hayim why Yankev ben Moishe had come to the yeshiva, Rabbi Israel asked if Hayim had anything to say. Hayim looked down at the floor and said nothing, but gave a nod of agreement to what he had heard.

Then Yankev ben Moishe said to Hayim, "I would like to send you on a journey to buy some cloth in the city. I will give you 100 rubles and for that money you will bring back enough good satin for the wedding coats."

Again Hayim nodded in agreement, took the 100 rubles and put the money in his pocket, feeling a little scared at the whole idea of becoming a merchant and leaving the yeshiva. But he decided that he would leave on his journey early the next morning.

Early the following day, Hayim prepared to leave. Since he had not been given money to hire a carriage and driver, he began walking to the city, which was quite distant. He took some food with him so he would not have to stop at an inn for food, especially since he had no extra money.

After walking for several hours, Hayim saw an orchard

with a stream nearby. He washed his hands and then sat down under an apple tree in the orchard to rest. When he had recited the blessings, Hayim ate some bread and cheese and drank some wine for his midday meal. As he was reciting the grace, he heard a melody that was hauntingly beautiful. Hayim could not move; he did not want to miss a single note. He held his breath and hoped the melody would not stop.

Recognizing the sound as that of a shepherd's flute, Hayim gathered his bundle and started to walk in the direction of the music. His heart beat faster, and he felt the delicious excitement of hearing a melody that touches one's soul. Hayim started to run, and then he saw, in a clearing on the other side of a stone wall—a shepherd. The shepherd sat on a rock, playing the lilting melody,

and he continued to play until the end of the melody. Then the shepherd rose and started walking in the clearing, with eyes and ears only for his flock, which obeyed his every gesture and whistle. Hayim, breathlessly running up to the shepherd, wide-eyed, gesturing wildly, and barely getting the words out in an order that made sense, begged the shepherd to teach him the melody. The shepherd agreed, but added, with a mischievous smile, "I will gladly teach you this melody for 50 rubles."

Hayim nodded his head in a wide up-and-down arc, indicating agreement, and at the same time reached into his pocket for 50 rubles. The shepherd, with a surprised expression on his face, accepted the money and taught the tune to Hayim. After that, they parted.

As he continued his journey to the city, Hayim kept singing the melody over and over so that he would not forget it.

Toward evening, Hayim grew tired and hungry. He sat down in a field to eat and to spend the night. Again he recited his blessings and started his meal of bread and cheese and wine—when he heard another melody played on a shepherd's flute.

As he listened to the lively, rhythmic melody, Hayim felt excited—full of joy and fervor. He must learn this melody, too. So he quickly recited the grace, as he ran toward the music.

When he found the shepherd, Hayim pleaded with him to teach him this melody. The shepherd gladly agreed, then added, "But I want 50 rubles as payment for the melody."

Without a moment's hesitation, Hayim reached into his pocket for the remaining 50 rubles. The shepherd taught him the melody and they parted.

"How wonderful," thought Hayim, as he sang both melodies together for the first time.

"How these melodies are both part of one tapestry. It seems as though they were woven on the same loom, as part of the same cloth! CLOTH? CLOTH?"

Suddenly, Hayim remembered that he no longer had the 100 rubles given him by his prospective father-in-law to buy cloth in the city for the wedding coats.

After a moment he said to himself, "Since I no longer have the money, I cannot buy the cloth. Since I no longer have the 100 rubles and cannot buy the cloth, I have no reason to go into the city. In that case, I can now return home."

Hayim didn't care about cloth. Instead, he felt strangely happy, for now he had *two* melodies that belonged together like *alef* and *beis*, or like a *lulav* and an *esrog*, or like *halla* and honey. He suddenly felt happier than ever, for now he had a wedding gift that was better than cloth. It was priceless and more worthy for a wedding. It was something he could share with everyone. Hayim could not wait to sing the melody to his prospective father-in-law. Surely he would see how wisely Hayim had spent the 100 rubles.

Forgetting how tired he was and how late it was, Hayim started to go home. As he walked, he sang first one melody, then the other, and together they blended into one complete melody. With each note, he danced a little and ran toward his town with joy in his heart.

It was the middle of the night when Hayim arrived in town. Instead of going to the yeshiva to sleep—for how could he sleep?—he went directly to the home of Yankev ben Moishe and knocked loudly on the door, forgetting—or rather not caring—that everyone was asleep.

A sleepy voice called out, "Who is there?"

Instead of answering, Hayim began to sing the first melody.

In a few minutes, everyone in the house had come to the windows to see who was singing. For who wakes up people in the middle of the night and sings—unless he is crazy or drunk?

When Yankev ben Moishe himself came to the window and saw it was Hayim, he understood that he had not gone to the city. But what did this strange behavior mean? Yankev ben Moishe did not open the door, but said to himself, "In the morning I shall go to the yeshiva and see the rabbi. But one thing is certain—this Hayim is *not* for *my* daughter."

After a while, Hayim realized that no one was going to open the door. He decided to return to the yeshiva instead, still singing the melody over and over. What did he care that they didn't open the door? "I will teach the *nigun* to my friends at the yeshiva and they will surely appreciate it. Besides, I have plenty of time to get married—and perhaps to a girl whose father is also a Hasid."

What was *more* important was that he, Hayim, had a new *nigun* for Shabbos.

The Nigun:
Two Variations

One of the marvelous aspects of being a storyteller is that, after a program, people come over to share some of their own stories with you. Sometimes it's a personal tale or a traditional story they remember. In the case of "The *Nigun*," people have recalled other *nigunim* they had not sung in years.

In December 1985, I told "The *Nigun*" in England at the *Limmud* Conference for Jewish Educators, where I taught storytelling. Everyone sang along with me, enjoying the *nigun*. Afterwards, two of the participants told me variants of this story.

The first was told to me by Sheila Lassman, who had heard it many times when she was a child from her father, Rubin Seiden, and with the same *nigun*. The second variant was told to me by Maurice Stone, who had heard it at Camp Habonim fifteen or more years before, but commented that any *nigun* could be interwoven into his version. The two tunes I use here are Ruth Rubin's *nigun* (used in "The Niggun (The Melody)") in the variation from England, and melody 53 from Idelsohn (1932, p. 14) used in the variation from Habonim.

I listened and rejoiced that we had given each other such gifts. I asked Sheila Lassman about her father. His life story can help us to learn a little more about the role of stories in a Jew's life. This is what Sheila told me about her father.

"Ruben Seiden was born in Zlochev, Galicia, in 1903. A fervent Zionist, he spent his time in 'the fields' with the Zionist youth movement, Hashomer Hatzair. He went on *aliya* in 1925 and worked building roads with *Gdud Haavoda*. He was penniless there, and when an uncle offered him the fare to London, he accepted in 1930. He married and stayed in London, but continued with Hashomer principles—no drinking, no smoking—and loved to sing the old songs and tell the old stories. Only one of his sisters survived World

War II and went to Israel, and he must have visited Israel from 1954 onwards almost yearly until his death in 1979.

"He always spoke Yiddish to my mother and to me (and to anyone else who understood it), although he was capable of telling stories in good English. He would tell stories, including this *nigun* story, on Shabbat and on holidays after a good meal, sitting round the table, and would encourage everyone to join in.

"Ruben was a good raconteur and loved telling jokes or using jokes to illustrate a point about human nature. He would encourage others to tell jokes. Although he ran a successful evening-dress business in London, his customers would often come into the shop primarily to tell him a new joke or to listen to his stories. That *yomtovdik* atmosphere round his table, with the candles burning and all the time in the world to tell stories, was a rare delight. Thus, in one man's lifetime, did Jewish folktales travel from Galicia, to *Eretz Yisrael*, to England, and finally to the United States."

Apparently, this *nigun* story has captured the imagination of many Jews. Since then I have found two variants that are songs in rhymed versions: One has been recorded by Hava Alberstein in Hebrew, but the English translation by Ephraim Buchwald and Moshe Sokolow, "Mushka," has been recorded on the album entitled *Ruach* and sung by the group Ruach. The second song, "An Old Melody," is from a poem by the Yiddish poet Leib Kvitko and sung in Yiddish by Emil Gorovets on the recording *I Am a Jew.*

In all the variants, what comes through is the joy of discovering such a melody and taking on the responsibility of restoring it to a holy *nigun.*

Here are my retellings of the two versions brought to England, versions heard years before. The memory of them was triggered by my telling of another variant. I retell these stories in my own way with the permission of those who told them to me.

The Nigun from England

here once was a poor family—so poor that the wife was afraid there would soon be no bread on the table if she didn't do something to save the family from starvation.* The husband had not been able to find work, and he sat in the house day after day in despair.

One day, the wife said to her husband, "Take these two *zlotys* and go to the marketplace and buy something we can sell for a profit."

The man took the two *zlotys* and went to the market. Just as he entered the marketplace he heard someone singing a *nigun* that touched him deeply. He went over and pleaded with the singer to sell him this *nigun*.

"How much money do you have?" asked the singer.

"Two *zlotys*," replied the husband. "And I'll give them to you for the *nigun*. I *must* have this *nigun*."

"Agreed," said the singer.

When the husband returned home, his wife asked, "So what did you buy? Where is the merchandise?"

Her husband answered with the *nigun*.

---

*Ruben Seiden's version.

The bewildered wife became angry and scolded her husband. But the next day, seeing even less food on the table, she said, "Husband, we have one *zloty* left. Go to the marketplace and, this time, be careful how you spend it. Buy something we can sell for a *profit*."

What was the husband to do? He took the coin and went to the market. As he entered the marketplace, he heard another *nigun*.

"Why, that's the *second* part of the *nigun* I bought yesterday," he said aloud. "I *must* buy this *nigun* too."

The husband ran joyfully to the singer and begged him to sell the tune to him for the single coin he had in his pocket.

"Agreed," sang the man, and he taught the *nigun* to the husband.

When the husband returned home, his wife and his mother-in-law were both waiting for him. But when they asked what merchandise he had purchased and what was the profit, he answered by singing the second *nigun*,

then the first one,

and again the second one.

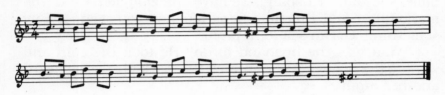

"See how they go *together*," the husband said joyously. But his wife and his mother-in-law began to shout and cry, and he ran out of the house holding his ears so as not to hear their scolding.

Soon after, the husband fell ill, and began to feel sicker each day. Soon, he could not even get out of bed. He sang the *nigun* over and over, his voice growing softer and softer as his strength left him. And one day, he died.

When his soul reached Heaven, what did it hear? The angels singing, singing joyfully, *his nigun.*

The Nigun from Habonim

 reparing for Shabbos was Moishe's greatest joy.* So on Friday mornings he always set out to the next village to buy the necessary items: wine, two *hallas*, and candles. As always, after he made these purchases, he returned home, went to the ritual bath, afterward to *shul*, and then he celebrated the Shabbos with a festive meal.

One Friday, after Moishe had spent all his money and had bought the Shabbos items, he was returning home through the woods when he heard gypsies playing a tune.

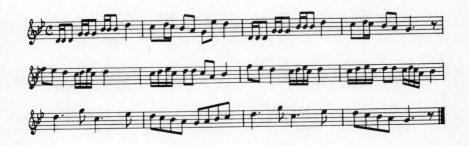

*Maurice Stone's version.

Moishe left the path and began running in the direction of the music. When he found the gypsies, he said, "Teach me this tune."

"What can you pay for the tune?" asked the gypsies.

Moishe looked in one pocket, felt deep in the other pockets and, realizing he had no coins left, suddenly said, "Wine! I have a bottle of good wine."

The gypsies accepted the wine as payment for the tune.

As Moishe happily continued on his way home, he sang the melody over and over

when suddenly, not looking where he was walking, he tripped over a low stone wall, and the melody got knocked out of his head. "*Ay, ay, ay,*" he cried. "I can't remember the *nigun.*" So back he went to the gypsies to learn the melody again.

"You must pay," shouted the gypsies. "Well, I have two *hallas,*" Moishe offered, and the gypsies took the breads and once more taught him the tune.

"I've got it in my head now for good," Moishe sang, as he turned back on the path leading to his home.

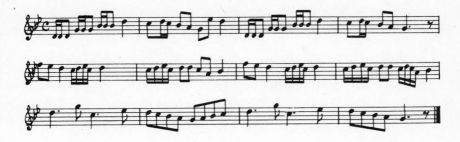

Moishe was almost all the way home, when a branch of a tree snapped and fell, hitting him on the head. When he got up, no matter how hard he tried, the *nigun* was no longer in his head.

"*Oy, oy, oy,*" Moishe moaned as he held his head. "I must go back and find the *nigun* again." And Moishe went back to the gypsies.

"You must pay," shouted the gypsies again.

"I have candles," Moishe said, and the gypsies took the candles and, for the third time, taught him the tune.

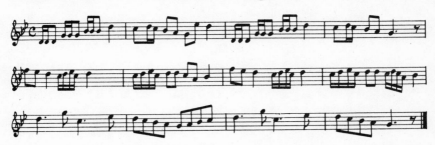

So now Moishe walked carefully, singing the melody over and over until he reached home.

Moishe's wife came out to greet him, and in a surprised tone asked, "But where is the bag with the wine for *kiddush*, the *hallas*, and the candles?"

"Wife," said Moishe with delight, "*listen* to my *nigun*." And he sang the *nigun*. That evening they made Shabbos with the *nigun*, and they sang, "*Dai dee dai, dee dee dai, dee dai dai dai dai.*"

The Nigun from Galicia

Tunes, like stories, find their way into the hearts of people, and sometimes into stories, too. Someone weaves a story together with a tune, tells-and-sings the musical story, and soon variants appear. All the variants of "The Nigun" I have found come from Eastern Europe, especially White Russia and Galicia, and were originally told in Yiddish. Even when the melody and story do not include a specifical Hasidic element, there is still the urgency to transform a secular tune into a Jewish tune and especially into a sacred song.

One variant, "The Unforgotten Tune" (IFA 5794, from White Russia), appears in Noy (1968). It tells the story of a young husband who uses part of his dowry to buy two Hasidic tunes and unites them into a single melody. Of course, when his wife and father-in-law ask him questions, he answers only with the tune, much to their frustration.

An interesting version of "The *Nigun*" is the tale called "Moshe Potato" (IFA 7811, from East Galicia), found also in Noy (1968). The story's hero is nicknamed Moshe Potato because his wife sends him to the market to buy potatoes and instead he buys a tune from an old man. When he keeps forgetting it, he returns to buy it several times, finally returning home with neither money nor potatoes. (See "The Nigun from Habonim.")

In "The Nigun from Galicia" (IFA 3229), again a trade is made for a tune, but the ending is different, and the father's reaction to his son's trading ability seems to be the opposite of the reaction we find in other versions of the tale. But that depends on how one interprets the father's words: Are they an expression of sincere understanding or a sarcastic utterance tinged with despair?

With each of these *cante* fables, the repetition of the song throughout the story allows the audience to become familiar with the tune and to sing it along with the storyteller. It creates a joyous experience, enabling everyone to participate in the storytelling.

The three-part *nigun* used in this story is taken from Idelsohn (1932, melody 13, p. 4).

here once was a businessman who had only one son, and this son never succeeded in anything he tried to do. For days this young son would sit and whistle and sing songs—songs he would hear and learn from passersby, from the melody of the wind and rain, from the sounds of the animals and the songs of the birds. His only pleasure in life was to sing and to *repeat* the songs by whistling them. And so this continued day after day.

But while nothing changed in the boy's life, two things changed in the father's: He got older and his possessions grew; that is, his fields, his gardens, and his animals all increased in size and in number.

One day, the businessman said to his son, "You, my son, are the one who will inherit all my property—and you can't even chase a stray cat off our farm."

The boy sat and answered by whistling a tune.

On another day, the father said, "What will become of you, my son? I will not live forever and, since you will inherit many riches, you *must* learn how to deal in business affairs. Listen, I have an idea. I'll give you three cows. Lead them to market in town and sell them. In that way, you will begin to understand something about business and about trading."

The son answered, "I'll try, Father."

On market day, the son got up early. With one long rope

he tied the three cows—one red, one black, one white—and he led them to the market.

On the way, the son met a wandering peddler who was sitting beside his wares and playing on a flute. He was playing a beautiful song.

"Please *teach* me the song," asked the son.

"What will you give me?" asked the wanderer, greedily.

The boy searched frantically in his pockets, "I have no money. Ah, but I have a cow." And the wanderer taught the boy the tune.

So the boy continued to the marketplace with two cows, whistling the tune over and over.

Just as he entered the marketplace, he heard a gypsy playing a soulful melody on his violin.

"Please *teach* me this tune?" pleaded the boy as he ran up to the gypsy.

"What will you give me for it?" asked the gypsy.

"I have no money—but I'll *give* you a cow," answered the boy.

The gypsy taught him the tune—and took the cow.

The son went along with one cow whistling first one tune, then the other until he reached the market. There he saw a peasant playing a joyful tune with cymbals.

"Please *teach* me *this* tune?" shouted the boy.

"What will you give me? asked the peasant, with a laugh.

"I have no money, but I do have *one cow*," replied the boy.

The son learned this tune, too, and gave the peasant his last cow.

In the evening, the happy son returned home, whistling the three tunes as he walked.

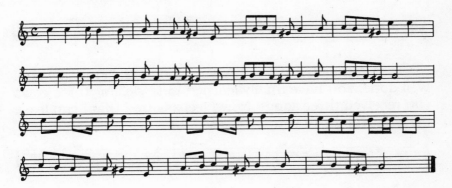

His father met him and asked, "Well, did you sell all three cows?"

"Yes, Father," answered his son.

"How much did you get for the red cow?" the father asked with curiosity.

The son whistled in his father's ear the song of the traveler.

"And how much did you get for the black cow?" the
father asked with great curiosity.

The son whistled in his father's ear the song of the
gypsy.

"And how much for the white cow?" the father asked
with even greater curiosity.

The son whistled in his father's ear the song of the
peasant.

The father turned to his son and said, "Fine, my son.
Well done. You have finally learned to trade. For three cows
you received three songs. Now I feel assured that I can leave
my inheritance to you."

Krasavitza

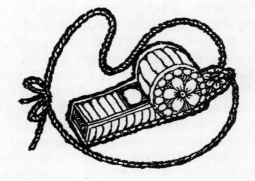

I find certain words pleasant to hear and marvelous to speak. One of those special words is *"krasavitza."* A Russian word that has become part of the Yiddish language, it means *a beautiful woman.*

Whenever I heard this word, used mostly by my mother, it sounded lovely. It evoked a picture not only of physical beauty, but of mental beauty as well—a total beauty. This is the connotation I carry with me of the word. Say the word aloud—*"krasávitza"*—and you'll understand what I am saying.

This story is adapted from a tale called "The Strong Brother and the Bad Sister" in Cahan's (1938) *Yiddisher Folklor*, a collection of Yiddish stories, anecdotes, folksongs, riddles, and superstitions from Eastern Europe.

Too many folktales refer to evil or wicked women, a trend that does not reflect the reality of women's lives or of our society—not today and not any time. Can women be evil and wicked? Yes. Have women been evil and wicked in the past? Of course. But women are no more evil than men, and they should not be depicted as such in so many of the world's folktales. Who knows who originally told the tale—was it a man or woman? And why? And to whom? And with what changes in each retelling? There are always variables in a folk story. So once again, there has been a change—to a strong sister and a bad brother. Folktales are fluid and, in order to survive, must be allowed these changes. If the reader wishes, the characters and their main attributes can be reversed, and the story told as Cahan collected it.

"Krasavitza," like "The Demon in the House of Study," contains elements from the International Tale Type A-T 300 "The Dragon-Slayer," a story known on virtually every continent. Jews everywhere were fascinated by these challenges and symbols, transformations and superstitions, and with magic objects. Adapting and incorporating them into our folk stories was not unusual. It is the stuff of folklore.

ven when Krasavitza was a young girl, she was a brave and dear child who loved adventure.

One day, her grandmother said to her, "My little Krasavitza, I see how you love to run like the wind. I also see how quick your mind is when your brother, who is not as brave as you, fights you with words. But I'm afraid that, some time, you may find yourself in trouble when neither your bravery nor your cleverness will be enough to save you. So I am giving you this whistle. It is a *magic* whistle, and when you blow it three times, it will help you when you are in need."

Krasavitza took the tiny carved whistle and was about to blow it.

"No, no, little one," warned her grandmother. "Blow it *only* when you must. Otherwise, it will be useless." The grandmother put the whistle on a ribbon, which she tied carefully and placed around Krasavitza's neck.

Years passed, and one day Krasavitza and her brother, whom she loved very much, went for a walk in the woods. After a while, they realized they were lost deep in the forest. They walked and walked, and finally came to a magnificent palace. They knocked on the door and, when no one answered, Krasavitza said, "Come, brother, let's go inside. Maybe we can find some food and can rest a while."

"I am afraid to go in," answered her brother. "You go while I wait here."

So, alone, Krasavitza walked inside. There were many rooms, but not a single person did she find anywhere. In one room there was a table filled with all kinds of delicious food.

In a second room, she saw many treasures.

A third room contained beautiful gowns made of silks and velvets, but also clothing made of wild animal skins.

In another room, chests were filled with gold and silver and jewels.

In the fifth room, Krasavitza saw weapons, including swords and knives.

And in the sixth room, there stood a golden bed.

Quickly, Krasavitza ran back to her brother and said, "There is food here and a place to rest, but *no one* is here." So both of them went into the palace, and they ate some food. The brother was so tired that no sooner did he lie down on the golden bed than he fell fast asleep.

"While he sleeps I will see if I can find a path out of these woods," Krasavitza thought. And she left, noting the direction in which she was walking.

Soon after she left, the robber princess who lived in this palace returned. When she found the handsome young man lying asleep on her golden bed, she took a knife from her boot and, keeping it behind her and ready to plunge it into the man's heart, cautiously approached the bed.

Suddenly, the young man awoke, and seeing this beautiful woman, was amazed. He smiled and asked, "Who are you?"

"Who are *you*, and how do you come to be sleeping in my bed?" the robber princess demanded.

The young man explained how he and his sister had gotten lost, and that his sister must have gone to look for a way out of the forest, since she was always taking charge of any troublesome situation.

"In that case," said the robber princess, who was now very attracted to this young man, "when she returns, tell her you must have the *milk of a lioness* to restore your health. Let's see how she takes charge of that!"

To herself the robber princess thought, "The lion will kill her. Without his sister, this charming young man will consent to be my companion."

When Krasavitza returned to the palace, the robber princess had left. Krasavitza saw that her brother was still in bed and asked, "Dear brother, are you well?"

"Not well at all, dear sister," answered the brother, who had decided to do as the mysterious woman had commanded, for he was enchanted by her ways and her beauty. "The *only* thing that will heal me is the milk of a lioness."

Krasavitza, who was prepared to do anything for her brother, immediately replied, "Very well, brother, I will get some." Taking a bowl from the palace, she left and went into the woods.

"How will I get milk from a lioness?" pondered Krasavitza. "The lion will attack if I get too close to the nursing lioness." Then she remembered the whistle her grandmother had given her years before. "Blow it three times, and it will help you whenever you are in need," her grandmother had told her.

Krasavitza blew the whistle three times. As quick as an arrow, a deer came bounding up to her and asked, "*What is your wish?*"

Surprised, Krasavitza replied, "I need the milk of a lioness for my sick brother."

A few minutes later, the deer returned with the bowl filled with a lioness's milk. Krasavitza thanked the deer, went back to the palace, and gave the milk to her brother. Then she left, saying she would soon return.

When the robber princess came into the room, she was amazed to discover that the sister had indeed brought the milk of a lioness.

"Well, I see that your sister *can* meet a challenge, even a dangerous one such as this. When she returns, tell her she must stay here with you, as you feel too ill to move. Also inform her that, as a remedy for your illness, you must tie her two thumbs together. *She* will do whatever you ask of her, and *you* must do what I ask of you," the robber princess said in an enticing voice, with an undertone of menace.

When Krasavitza returned, she asked, "How do you feel *now*, brother?"

"Worse, sister mine," her brother answered. And he told her that in order for him to get better he would try an old folk remedy: he would bind her thumbs, and she must stay with him. He was obeying the woman's instructions completely.

When the brother had tied his sister's thumbs together, the robber princess appeared in the room and, with knife in hand, she laughed as she circled Krasavitza.

"Now you are caught, little sister, and *this* time I will kill you myself. But you can choose *the place* where you will be put to death."

"In that case, put me high in a tree," answered Krasavitza without hesitation.

The robber princess summoned her guards, and they put Krasavitza high up in a tree. As soon as Krasavitza saw the guards climbing down, she reached for her whistle with her free fingers and blew it three times.

In a flash, animals of all kinds appeared. "*What do you wish?*" they asked.

"Destroy the robber princess and her guards, then unbind my thumbs and take me off this tree," Krasavitza ordered. When it had been done, Krasavitza thanked the animals for saving her life, and went directly to the bedroom of the palace.

"Oh, my brother, I did what you asked of me, but I did not know you were so wicked and false. I will leave you here, but I must go and find my way out of the forest." And with tears in her eyes, she left.

Krasavitza wandered until she came to a town. But wherever she walked, she noticed that people were crying. She went to the inn and asked why the people were so distressed.

The innkeepers told her, "The town is filled with sorrow because there is a twelve-headed snake that demands a human sacrifice every day. Today the prince must be brought to the snake."

Krasavitza made a plan. "Bring me to the King," she commanded. When she came before the King, she told him of her plan. He agreed to it. She asked that a clay figure be prepared. And when it was ready, Krasavitza approached the monster snake. She instructed the prince to stand behind her as she put the clay figure in front of her. As the snake lunged at the clay figure, Krasavitza blew three times on her whistle. In a wink, the animals appeared and asked, *"What is your wish?"*

"Destroy the snake. Then cut off its twelve heads and bring them here to me," she answered. It was over in a few moments. Krasavitza thanked the animals, and they disappeared.

The King was overjoyed that his son was saved, and indeed the entire kingdom rejoiced.

"We are grateful to you, Krasavitza, for your heroism *and* quick thinking," said the King. "If you agree, you will marry the prince and in time rule the kingdom with him."

Krasavitza answered, "Thank you, Your Majesty. I will gladly marry the prince. But first I must go on a short journey, and I promise to return very soon."

Krasavitza had been thinking about her brother. She still loved him and worried as to how he had fared alone in the palace in the woods.

The King gave her a coach and horses, and a maid and coachman to accompany her. When they arrived at the palace, Krasavitza went to the golden bedroom. Her brother was dead. She mourned for him, and with the help of the servants, she buried him in the woods and recited the *Kaddish.*

On the way back, the servants, who had been scheming against Krasavitza, stopped in the woods and said to her, "Give us your whistle or we will kill you." Krasavitza refused, but the two servants tore it from her. Then the maid quickly changed clothes with her, and the servants rode off, leaving Krasavitza alone in the woods.

When the servants arrived at the palace, the maid, now dressed in Krasavitza's clothing, presented herself to the King as Krasavitza and said, "I have returned, Your Majesty. With this whistle I have slain the snake and saved all of you. I am now ready to marry the prince."

The King did not doubt that this was Krasavitza, especially when he saw the whistle. So he ordered that preparations for the wedding should begin.

Meanwhile, Krasavitza, wearing the maid's clothes, walked toward the town. All night she walked, until at dawn she arrived at the King's palace. The guards refused to believe her story, because she looked like a madwoman. But finally she was brought to the King.

"If what you say is true, and you are not an imposter, let me see the whistle," commanded the King. The maid who was posing as Krasavitza was brought in, and she was holding the whistle in her hand.

Krasavitza spoke calmly and deliberately, "True, this woman has my whistle. But if she is truly Krasavitza, as she claims, let her produce the twelve heads of the snake that were cut off and, as you yourself witnessed, were given to Krasavitza."

The maid, of course, did not have the heads. The King then knew who Krasavitza really was, and he ordered that the imposter be hanged.

Krasavitza and the prince were married, and they live in great happiness and wisdom in that faraway kingdom until this very day.

Children of the King

Daydreaming or fantasizing "what could be" can launch many a fairy tale. Promises beyond reality—"Oh, what I would give to marry so-and-so" or "I would do anything *if only* . . ."—are also part of wishful thinking. That's where this story begins—three sisters sit at their weaving and engage in wishful thinking. . . .

In this folktale, an old man offers good advice. Could he be Elijah the Prophet? (See the introduction to "Elijah and the Three Wishes.") "Children of the King" is typed 879*G, with at least 22 versions already collected in the IFA. There are very close parallels to A-T 707 "The Three Golden Sons," especially sections I, II (a and b), III (a) and IV b. These tales are obviously related, but the Jewish versions are well established, and are found from Libya through Iran. This version is based on IFA 5752, a tale from Tunisia (Haimovits 1976). It is similar to IFA 8870 (Iraqi Kurdistan) (Noy 1976).

here once were three sisters who were skilled weavers. But while the two older sisters produced excellent cloth, the youngest wove cloth that was exquisite in design and color. Her weaving surpassed the work of her sisters.

In the evening, the three sisters would sit on the veranda of their home and talk, and even daydream.

One evening, the eldest sister said, "The King is about to choose a wife. If he were to choose *me*, I would weave huge tapestries, big enough to cover *all* the walls of the palace."

The second sister responded, "If the King chose *me* for a wife, I would weave a tent big enough to hold the King, his advisers, *and* all his soldiers."

And the third sister said, "Oh, I am tired of weaving all the time. I wish I were married to the King so I would *not* have to weave. Instead, I would become a devoted mother of two sons and a daughter, children such as the world has not seen since the days of Abraham and Sarah, Isaac and Rebecca, and Jacob, Leah, and Rachel."

It happened that the King was taking his usual evening stroll and passed the house of the sisters at that moment, and he heard everything the sisters said.

The King returned to the palace and, the following day, called the eldest sister to the palace. When she arrived, he asked her, "Can you fulfill your promise to weave tapestries so large that they would cover all the walls in my palace—if I were to marry you?"

"Oh, no, Your Majesty," replied the eldest sister in a haughty tone. "A queen should not be put to work. That was just idle chatter. If I were queen, would you want me to weave like a commoner?"

The King became angry and sent her away. "Bring me the second sister," he told his servant.

When the second sister came before the King, he asked her, "Can you fulfill your boast that, should you wed the King, you would weave a tent that could hold thousands of men?"

The second sister tossed her head and laughed, "Your Majesty, a fool believes everything. Surely you are no fool! It was said in jest, and only that."

The King became angrier and sent this sister away, too. Then he called for the youngest sister.

"Tell me," asked the King, "how do you know you will bear two sons and a daughter if you marry me?"

The young woman blushed and replied, "O King, I have seen it in a dream that I dreamt for several nights."

The answer pleased the King as much as the young woman herself and so he married her.

The two sisters were very jealous of their youngest sister, especially when she became the Queen. Then, when they found out she was pregnant and that her dream would probably come true, their jealousy turned to hatred. When it was almost time for her to give birth, the two sisters decided on a plan. They bribed the midwife so she would exchange the baby for *a cat.*

When the Queen gave birth to a son, the midwife, as planned, replaced the child with a cat. She put the infant in a basket, covered him with a piece of cloth his mother had woven, and gave the basket to the eldest sister. The sister took the basket deep into the woods and left it there.

That day, an old woman went into the woods in search of healing herbs, and she heard a baby crying. She followed the sound and found the basket. She took pity on the little child, brought him home, and adopted him.

When the midwife presented the newborn—the cat—to the King and Queen, they were shocked. The Queen wept bitterly, but the King, who loved his wife, comforted her and said, "Do not be afraid. I love you, and surely you will give birth to a normal child next time."

The following year when the Queen gave birth, once again, the treacherous midwife, at the bidding of the Queen's sister, exchanged the child—a second son—for another cat. *Still* the King felt only love for his wife, and he assured her that the next time she would give birth to a human child.

When for the third time the Queen gave birth, this time to a daughter, and the child was exchanged for another cat, the King's anger and sorrow were so great that he sent his wife away.

As for the children, each one was found by the poor old woman, and together they grew as one family and brought the old woman joy and happiness.

One day, the two sisters were riding near the woods when they saw a young girl playing near a little hut. They stopped to talk with her, and suddenly they realized she was the young daughter born to their sister.

"Do you have brothers, too?" they asked the child.

"Yes, I have two older brothers who are out hunting for food," replied the little girl.

"And do they love you?" they asked.

"Oh yes, they love me very much, more than the whole world," she answered quickly and happily.

"Well, then," said one sister, "*if* they love you, as you say they do, *why* haven't they given you *a pool*?"

" . . . and *a nightingale* that sings wonderful songs and makes life pleasant?" added the second sister. And they smiled to each other and rode off.

When the brothers returned, they found their little sister crying. "What has happened to make you cry, little sister?" they asked.

"*You don't love me!* If you did, you would make a pool for me to swim in, and you would get me a nightingale that sings beautiful songs," the sister replied.

"We *do* love you. We'll start to dig the pool this very day. Then one of us will get you a nightingale. We promise," the brothers pledged.

A few weeks later, the older brother set out to seek the nightingale. On the way in the forest he met an old man and asked him where he could find a nightingale that knew how to sing beautiful songs.

The old man replied, "My son, go straight, turn neither right nor left. After three days' walking, you will come to a large wide gate with an opening. Enter into the garden through that opening, and on the right you will see a tree on which an open cage is hanging. Hide behind the tree and when the bird returns and flies into the cage, close the door quickly, take the cage, and leave the garden. You must not linger or hestitate, not even for a moment. If you hear voices calling out that you have erred and taken the wrong bird, do not reply or your life will be in danger. Be careful and do not heed vain calls," the old man warned again.

The elder brother did exactly as the old man had told him. But as he was leaving the garden, he heard people crying out to him, "*You took the wrong bird! You mistook another bird for the nightingale!*" And the elder brother stopped and doubted himself. "Maybe I did take the wrong bird. What if I went to all this trouble for *nothing?*"

Suddenly, the elder brother found himself in a pit with others bewailing their bitter fate, for they, too, had tried to hunt for this rare bird and had failed.

Time passed and, when the elder brother did not return, the younger brother and sister were afraid he was lost. So the younger brother decided to set out to search for him. He took food with him and left. When he came to the forest, he met the same old man.

"Do you know where I can find the rare nightingale that sings such wonderful songs?" he asked the old man.

"Young man, so many young people have tried and failed," said the old man. "Why do you want to follow in their footsteps? Go home and be happy."

"Dear grandfather, I must try," insisted the younger brother.

"Well, then, hear my advice and do not take lightly what I tell you, for obedience to the old brings blessing and success." And the old man repeated the instructions he had given the older brother.

The young man listened carefully and promised to heed his advice. "No doubt my brother did not treat this advice seriously and paid a dear price for it," he thought to himself.

And so, faithful to the old man's instructions, the young man came to the garden, found the open cage, waited for the nightingale, and then took the cage with the captured bird and left. But then he heard terrible voices from all sides of the garden, mocking him with, *"That's not the real nightingale. That's an ordinary bird that can't even sing,"* and on and on.

Holding fast to his decision not to listen and not to hesitate, the second brother continued to the gate. When he reached the gate, he found it closed and guarded. He pulled out his sword and threatened to kill the guard.

The guard cried, "Spare my life. I will release all the prisoners if you give me my life." Quickly the brother agreed, and the guard led him to the pit, lowered a ladder, and the prisoners climbed up. And, of course, among them he saw his elder brother.

The brothers returned home and celebrated their reunion with great joy. The nightingale sang and brought even more happiness to the family.

Years passed, and one day the King was riding near the old woman's house. In a nearby field he saw a beautiful young woman picking wild flowers. She was so lovely that he could not take his eyes from her. He dismounted from his horse, walked over to her, and asked for some flowers. When she gave him a bouquet, he kissed her hand and asked her to marry him.

The young woman said, "I must discuss this with my mother and my brothers." When they entered the house, the King began discussing the matter with her two brothers, when suddenly the nightingale began to sing:

Has such a thing been heard worldwide,
for a father to take his daughter for a bride?

The King was astonished. "What does the nightingale mean by this?"
And the nightingale sang yet another song.

Three times the Queen gave birth
and three times did she grieve.
But each child was wrapped in the cloth she did weave.

Just then, the old woman who had found and reared the three children came into the room. In her hands were three small cloths, beautifully woven with silk threads of all the colors of the rainbow. When the King held the cloths, he recognized the designs as those made by his wife. He cried out in shock and collapsed in tears.

"I know this cloth, for your mother spent many hours weaving it with care and love," sobbed the King. "*You* are my children, my very own *children*, alive and well after all these years." He embraced them and thanked the old woman for caring so well for them.

The King at once returned to the palace, called for the midwife, and began to ask her questions, at first kindly, and when she refused to talk, with anger. "I'll order your tongue to be removed with iron pincers!" he shouted.

Then the midwife confessed to everything and told the King that the Queen's two sisters had taken the infants away to the woods, wrapped only in the cloths the Queen had woven.

The King immediately commanded that the Queen be brought back to the palace. He begged her for forgiveness, and with great joy they were reunited with their three children. He also brought the old woman back to the palace, gave her a great reward, and invited her to remain with them, since she had loved the children and they were fond of her. She lived happily with them and enjoyed great respect for the rest of her days.

As for the two sisters and the midwife, the King ordered a public trial. They received the death sentence and were hung.

Although the Queen had once said she wanted to marry the King so she could stop weaving, it was by her skillful weaving that her children were discovered and she herself was saved.

So the Queen continued to do her weaving, and so must we all.

The Red Slippers

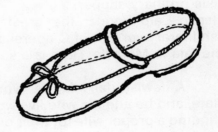

According to folklorists, there are 700 or more variants of the Cinderella tale in the folklores of the world, and it must be the best known of all stories. The Cinderella story has been traced to the earliest known version in ninth-century China. It seems that every country in the world has a Cinderella story.

It is not surprising, then, that there are at least seven versions in Jewish folklore, especially in Yiddish folklore of the nineteenth and twentieth centuries. The Jewish Cinderella story (using Yiddish names for the heroine, such as Shlumperl and Pedlerke) has been told orally in East European countries, but also in Iran. Many of these stories do not include any Jewish characters, not even a rabbi, but sometimes there is mention of a biblical character or Elijah the Prophet—and, of course, the stories are told in the language spoken by the Jews of the particular region, e.g., Yiddish in Eastern Europe, Judeo-Arabic in Morocco, Ladino in Yugoslavia. Some versions do not include the usual wicked stepmother, but there are golden slippers, or red slippers, or even fur slippers (most fitting for the cold Eastern European countries). There has been controversy as to the origin of the glass slipper in the story. Some folklorists contend that Perrault, in his famous French version of Cinderella, mistakenly substituted the word *verre* (meaning glass), for an older French word *vair* (meaning fur). But whatever shoe is in the tale, it is a magical or special shoe, made of material that outlasts ordinary slippers.

Isaac Leib Peretz, the great Yiddish writer, wrote a Jewish literary version of Cinderella called "The Match." He set the tale in Moravia. Here is a summary of the story:

A Jewish dairy farmer works on a nobleman's estate, and he and his wife live well. But they worry about finding a proper wife for their only son, since they live in an isolated place, far from a Jewish community.

One night, during a heavy snow, an old woman seeks shelter. This is their rare chance to perform the

mitzva of offering hospitality. Afterward, since they refuse payment, the old woman gives them a present for
their son's future bride, a pair of golden slippers. The
old woman, Sarah Bas Tuvim, is known for writing special prayers to be recited by mothers who wish to find a
good match for their children.

Sarah Bas Tuvim also visits a poor Jewish charcoal
maker, a widower, who has an only daughter. She gives
the daughter materials, such as velvet, gold and silver
threads, and pearls, from which to make a *tallis* bag for
her future husband. There is no lost slipper in this tale,
but somehow, through the help of the magical old
woman, the dairy farmer's son and the charcoal maker's
daughter meet, the slippers fit, and they are a match
made in Heaven.

The story of "The Red Slippers," one of the first stories I
ever heard, came from Aunt Naomi's (1921) *Jewish Fairy
Tales and Legends*, a book that has been out-of-print for
many years. This book seems to have been on my bookshelf
as far back as I can remember. How did the book get to stay
on my father's bookshelf, and years later on mine? Who
knows? The fact is that it came into my father's household
and remained there. Of all the books that ended up on my
shelf, this is the one that has meant so much to me in my life,
influencing me and sparking my imagination. I still treasure
it on my bookshelf.

Since I love this kind of Cinderella story, I have included
two variants in this book: "The Red Slippers" and "The Best
Loved."

nce there was a young girl who was as kind as she was beautiful. Her name was Rose, but everyone called her Rosy-Red because her cheeks became red as roses when she was very happy. And she was happy most of the time, even though her mother had died when she was only a baby. Her grandmother had come to live in Rosy-Red's home so she could take care of the infant.

Grandmother looked after Rosy-Red with such love and gentleness that the child thought of her as her mother. And her grandmother called her *Reizele, main goldene kepele*, with great affection. She taught the child all kinds of songs and magic rhymes that she herself had learned as a child.

All day long, Rosy-Red sang as she worked in the house, helping her grandmother, or as she walked in the woods gathering kindling wood, or planting and taking care of the flowers in the garden. Rosy-Red had a sweet-sounding, melodious voice. Whenever she sang outdoors, the birds gathered on the trees to listen to her. When she stopped singing, the birds would chirp, encouraging her to continue her song.

When Rosy-Red was one year old, her father gave her an unusual gift—a pair of red leather slippers. Rosy-Red was allowed to wear them on all the festivals and on her birthday. As she grew, the slippers also grew to fit her feet, for they were magic slippers. The grandmother knew the secret of the slippers, but Rosy-Red, who loved them better than anything else she owned, was glad that they kept fitting her. She never asked, "Why do these red slippers keep growing while none of the other shoes do?" Perhaps she was afraid to ask.

One day, Rosy-Red remembered only too sadly, she returned from the woods to find her grandmother gone and, instead, three strangers in her house. There was something disturbing about their sudden appearance there. Rosy-Red stopped singing.

"Who are you?" she asked cautiously.

"I am your new mother," answered the oldest woman in a matter-of-fact tone, "and these are my daughters, your new sisters."

"That's not true—it can't be true!" cried Rosy-Red. "Where is my *grandmother*?"

"Oh, that *old woman*?" replied the new stepmother. "Why, I ordered her to leave. There's barely enough room as it is." Instead of comforting her, Rosy-Red's two new sisters, who were as selfish and mean as they were ugly, scolded Rosy-Red for crying and would have hit her if her father had not arrived at that moment. He spoke kindly, telling her he had married again because he was lonely. He promised Rosy-Red that his wife and her daughters would be good to her.

But Rosy-Red thought to herself, "Why didn't my father tell me he wanted to marry again? Is that why he has been away so often and so busy with his own thoughts when he was home? I don't understand. He doesn't even care what happened to my dear grandmother."

Rosy-Red ran to her own little room in the back of the house and cried quietly to herself.

Suddenly, she stopped crying, rose from her bed, took the beautiful red slippers she loved so much, and hid them so that her stepsisters would not find them. She was sure they would take them away from her.

From that time on, Rosy-Red sang no more. Her cheeks

were pale as she began to feel sadder and lonelier than ever
before in her life. Her eyes were always filled with tears as
she worked all day long in silence. The chores were no
longer shared with her loving grandmother and certainly
not with her demanding stepsisters. Instead, Rosy-Red had
to do everything for them, as well as her usual chores in and
out of the house. She had to collect all the firewood, cook
and wash and clean, and draw water from the well and
struggle with the heavy buckets that made her arms and
her back ache. Sometimes, too, her slender arms were
marked with bruises, for her cruel stepsisters did not hesitate to beat her.

The stepsisters were invited out to parties and dances,
but Rosy-Red was not allowed to go with them. On these
occasions, she had to act as their maid and help them dress.

Rosy-Red did not mind doing that. In fact, she was
happy *only* when they were out of the house. Only then did
she sing softly to herself while the birds came to listen. At
other times she was too busy to notice her feathered friends,
and the birds missed hearing Rosy-Red's sweet voice.

Thus, many unhappy years passed by.

One day, when her father was away from home, Rosy-
Red's stepsisters went off to a dance. As they were about to
leave, they told her, "Rosy-Red, don't forget to draw water
from the well. We *warn you* that *if* you forget, as you did last
time, we will beat you without mercy when we return. We
will need fresh water to bathe our tired feet after all the
dancing." They laughed as they went out the door, leaving
poor Rosy-Red behind.

So Rosy-Red, tired as she was, went out in the darkness
to get the water. She lowered the bucket, but the cord broke
and the pail fell to the bottom of the well. She ran back to the
house for a long stick with a hook at the end of it to recover
the bucket. As she put the hook into the water she sang:

Almonds and raisins and pomegranates red
Smile, little imp, from your well-water bed.

Now it so happened that a sleeping water-sprite lived at the bottom of the well. He could be awakened only by a spell and, although Rosy-Red did not know it, the words she sang, which she used to hear her grandmother sing at the well whenever the cord broke, were the magic spell.

The water-sprite awoke, and he was so delighted with the sweet voice that he promptly decided to help the girl whom he saw peering down into the water. He fastened the bucket to the stick and, reaching into a treasure of which he was the guardian, he took a handful of jewels and put them inside the bucket.

When Rosy-Red discovered the jewels, she was astonished and said, "These jewels are even more beautiful than those my sisters have." Then an idea came to her: "I will give these jewels to my sisters. Perhaps they will be kinder to me."

Rosy-Red waited impatiently until the sisters returned from the dance, and she immediately gave them the jewels. For a moment they were too dazed to speak at the sight of the sparkling precious stones. Then they looked meaningfully at each other and, pretending gentleness, asked, "How did you get these jewels?"

Rosy told them what had happened at the well and repeated the song she had sung while lowering the hook into the water.

"Ah, we thought so," snapped the sisters in unison. "These jewels are *ours*. We hid them in the well for safety. You have stolen them and tried to bribe us with our own possessions."

"No, no, no, that's not true . . . " began Rosy-Red, but she protested in vain. Her sisters would not listen. They told her to get to her room quickly before they lost their tempers.

Snatching the bucket, the stepsisters hurried off to the well. They lowerd the bucket and sang the same magic words.

Almonds and raisins and pomegranates red
Smile, little imp, from your well-water bed.

But their voices were harsh. The sleeping water-sprite woke up again, but he did not like the croaking sound the sisters made.

"Ha! Ha! Ha!" he laughed. "I will teach you to disturb my sleep with hideous noises, and I shall punish such pranks played on me. Here are some croakers," and he filled the pail with slimy toads and frogs.

The stepsisters were so angry when they discovered their reward that they ran back home and dragged Rosy-Red from her room. They beat her and shouted insults at her. "You thief! You lizard! You wretched liar! You snip-nose beetle! You cheat! You cannot remain in this house another day." Then they threw Rosy-Red out of the house and bolted the door.

Rosy-Red was so shocked—and it all happened so quickly—that she couldn't say a word. It was an outrage for them to turn her out of her father's house while he was away on a journey. As she wandered away, she thought, "I can hardly be less happy living alone in the woods." This thought made her feel less afraid. Luckily for her, she had taken the red slippers from their hiding place to comfort her when the sisters had sent her to her room. She had them in the pocket of her tattered dress, and as soon as she was out of sight of the house, she put them on. They made her feel less miserable. The sun was now rising, and when its rays shone upon her, she began to sing. With her old friends, the birds, twittering all about her, she felt happy again.

On and on she walked, much farther into the woods than she had ever been before. When she grew tired, there was always a pleasant, shady place where she could rest; when she became hungry, there were plenty of fruit trees; and when she was thirsty, she always came to a spring of clear, fresh water, for the magic slippers guided her. All day long she wandered, and when toward evening she noticed her slippers were muddy, she took them off to clean.

And then darkness fell. It began to rain, and Rosy-Red grew frightened. She snuggled under a tree. When she looked up she noticed a light a short distance away. She got up and walked toward it.

When she got closer, Rosy-Red saw that the light came from a cave dwelling. "Shabbos candles! Is that possible? Here in the woods? I am dreaming," she said aloud to herself. An old woman came out to meet her. It was her grandmother, but so many years had passed that Rosy-Red did not recognize her. The grandmother, however, knew Rosy-Red at once. "*Gut Shabbos*, my child," said her grandmother gently. "*Reizele, main goldene kepele*, come in and take shelter from the rain."

Rosy-Red was only too glad to accept the invitation, and she was overjoyed to find her beloved grandmother, for only she called her Reizele.

The inside of the cave was cozy and warm. It had a feeling of Shabbos, but Rosy-Red, who was completely exhausted, quickly fell asleep.

Suddenly, Rosy-Red awoke with a start. "My pretty red slippers!" she cried. "Where are they?" She put her hand in the pocket of her dress, but could find only one slipper. "I must have lost the other one," she sobbed. "I must go out and look for it."

"No, no, Reizele, you cannot do that," insisted the grandmother. "There is a terrible storm out there."

Rosy-Red peered out through the opening of the cave and saw the lightening flash and heard the thunder roll. She drew back in fear and sobbed herself to sleep again.

Once again Rosy-Red was awakened, this time by voices. She was afraid that her stepsisters had discovered her hiding place and had come to drag her forcibly home again. So she crept into a corner of the cave and listened intently.

A man was speaking. "Do you know who might own this red slipper?" he was asking. "I found it in the woods."

Rosy-Red was about to rush out to claim her lost slipper when she heard her grandmother's voice, which was surprisingly very loud on purpose so she could overhear. The words kept her in her hiding place.

"No, no, I do not know whose slipper it is!!" the grandmother repeated over and over again.

When the man had departed on his horse, the grandmother hugged Rosy-Red and told her, "I am sorry, my dear Reizele, but I could not take any chances. That man might have been a messenger from your stepsisters, and I won't let anyone take you back to them."

The next day, the man returned with several attendants this time. Again, Rosy-Red hid in the corner and listened.

"I am a King's son," explained the man. "I *must* find the wearer of this shoe. It is such an enchanting slipper that only a graceful and beautiful girl could wear it."

The grandmother, however, still denied knowing the owner of the slipper. Rosy-Red did not know whether to be frightened or pleased when her grandmother told her afterward that the man was very handsome and of noble bearing.

Day after day he came, each day with still more attendants. Finally, he arrived one day mounted on a richly decorated horse with a hundred and one followers all mounted as richly as he was.

"The girl I seek is *here*," the man declared. "I am certain of that. My servants have searched the woods. In fact, one of my servants swears he heard a young woman singing yesterday. Where is she?"

Rosy-Red realized that she could no longer remain hidden. She liked the man's voice and felt her courage return. She stepped out of her hiding place, wearing the one red slipper.

The stranger, bowing low before her, held out the other slipper. Rosy-Red took it and put it on. It fit perfectly.

"Many girls have tried to wear that slipper," said the prince, "but all have failed. I have sworn to propose marriage to the young woman who can wear this red slipper. I am a King's son and, if you will accept my proposal of marriage, you will be my princess, and my love."

Rosy-Red's cheeks turned even redder as she looked to her grandmother for approval. The grandmother nodded her head, approving the match. Then she turned back to the prince and answered simply, "I feel the happiness in my heart and I accept gladly."

So Rosy-Red and her grandmother left the woods in a

royal carriage drawn by twenty white horses and went to their new home. Rosy-Red or Reizele, as the prince called her now, knew only happiness with her good husband and her courageous wise grandmother, who remained near her.

And she always wore her wonderful red slippers.

The Best Loved

If one were to combine the Cinderella story with Shakespeare's *King Lear*, this tale would emerge.

The motif of the "outcast child," is found in many folktales. Shakespeare, like writers throughout the ages, drew upon folklore for plots, characters, themes, and inspiration, and incorporated them into his plays. So the theme found its way into *King Lear*.

In addition to the Cinderella story, this tale draws upon another motif called "Love Like Salt," which involves a love-test by a father. The folktale's outline is something like this:

1. A King asks his three daughters to declare their love for him. (Three is a universal and common number of how many children or siblings are in a story. It's a complex number and offers us more possibilities.)
2. The third, and always the favorite, child answers that her "love is like salt."
3. The outraged King finds this an insult and banishes his youngest daughter.

Just as King Lear asks his three daughters, "Who loves me the most?", the father in this tale asks his three daughters a similar question. And while both Cordelia's and Sheindl's answers do not sound very flattering or worthy, the truth lies beyond their simple literal words.

In these folktales, the daughter is the folk heroine, whereas in *King Lear,* the literary reworking of the folktale, the King is the central figure.

Many of the Cinderella stories told by Jews were not indigenous to the Jewish people. They were borrowed from other peoples and transformed into Jewish tales or infused with Jewish meaning. The symbols have been interpreted as Jewish symbols, and the tales reflect the values and world view of those who told and retold the tales over and over again. Thus, a Jewish version of a tale becomes the carrier of Jewish values and customs.

So with this story. The answer, "I love you like salt in cooked food," becomes a Jewish answer. Salt is an important symbolic food in Judaism. It is used in the process of kashering meat and also as a preservative for meat. Therefore, salt stands as a symbol of permanence. In two places in the Bible, salt is mentioned in the context of a covenant: "And every meal-offering shalt thou season with salt; neither shalt thou suffer the salt of the covenant of thy God to be lacking from thy meal-offering; with all thine offerings thou shalt offer salt" (Leviticus 2:13) and ". . .it is an everlasting covenant of salt before the Lord unto thee and to thy seed with thee" (Numbers 18:19).

In ancient times, it was a sign of friendship to eat salt together. Even today, we salt the *halla* (or any bread) after the blessing over the bread and "break bread" together, as a reminder of this salted bond of friendship and the covenant of salt.

There is also a belief that salt on the table will drive off evil spirits. I recall that when I moved into my first home, as a married woman, my mother had brought salt, bread, and honey into the house before we arrived. In many countries, and among some Jews as well, a newborn infant is rubbed with salt or washed with salt water to protect it from the evil spirits and to strengthen the child.

Salt water is placed on the *seder* table at Passover for dipping the celery or potato or onion, depending on one's custom, to recall the bitterness and salty tears of the Jews in Egypt. But with the tears comes joy as well—the joy of freedom we celebrate at that time.

I recall an expression my mother used when she saw a young woman who lacked "a certain spark": "*Ir feilt feffer un zalts.*" ("She's lacking pepper and salt".) There's a Yiddish song that says: "*Vu nemt men a bokher far di meidel, az es feilt ir feffer un zalts?*" ("Where does one get a bridegroom for a young woman who is lacking pepper and salt?")

So salt is necessary for flavor, for friendship, for permanence, for *tam*—that special taste in any relationship, including that of a daughter and a father.

How would we answer our parents if one of them asked

us: How do you love me? Or how would we want our children to answer us if we asked that question of them? Should we even ask such a question? It's a dilemma. But then, that's how stories begin: with such a question, with such a dilemma.

This story is found in Cahan (1931) and there is a variant in Gaster (1924). The source of it is in the Babylonian Talmud, *Erubin* 53b. "Love Like Salt" is classified by Aarne-Thompson as Tale Type 923.

 rabbi and his wife had three daughters. One day the rabbi called them all together and asked, "How do you love me?"

The eldest answered first, "I love you, Father, like my life." And the father was pleased.

The second daughter replied, "My Father, I love you like all the gold in the world." And the father was pleased at this answer, too.

When the youngest daughter, Sheindl, was asked the same question, she said simply, "I love you like salt in cooked food, my Father." When the father heard this, he was so disappointed that he became angry.

"If you love salt so much," said the father, "take this bag of salt and bread and leave this house. You are no longer welcome here."

The youngest daughter left her home and began to wander through the streets of the town and finally into the woods on the outskirts, not knowing where to go.

In the distance, Sheindl saw a large house. It was an inn. There she got a job working in the kitchen and around the yard. She had to work hard from early morning until late at night, plucking goose feathers and chicken feathers, feeding the animals, milking the cows, cleaning, scrubbing, washing, and polishing. She often cried at night with her face against her straw pillow so no one would hear her.

One day there was to be a lavish wedding, for the daughter of the richest family in town was going to be married. Everyone was invited, including the innkeepers and all the guests at the inn.

Before they left, the innkeepers directed their servant Sheindl, whom they called Mieskait, to stay at the inn and to guard it carefully while they were away at the wedding, or else they would give her a beating. And then they left.

Alone in the quiet of the inn, Sheindl began to weep. Tired from the work and her crying, she began to doze. In her sleep it seemed to her that an old man appeared and said to her in a kind and soothing voice," "Why do you cry, my daughter? You, too, can go to the wedding."

"Oh no, I cannot go to the wedding. I must stay and guard the inn," sobbed Sheindl. "And besides, how can I go? I should wear my dirty old rags?" Suddenly, she opened her eyes—and there was the old man standing near her. He was real. She was not dreaming, after all.

"Here are some clothes fit for a wedding," the old man replied. "Go to the wedding. I will guard the inn while you are away. But you must leave the wedding *before* all the guests and return here *before* the innkeepers. Remember!" Then the old man handed Sheindl a beautiful gown of golden silk, some jewels, and a pair of golden shoes.

Sheindl ran into her room, quickly washed, and changed into all the new clothes. She looked so beautiful. She thanked the old man and promised to return early, and she went to the wedding. No one recognized her, of course, and all the young men there wanted to meet this lovely young woman.

The brother of the bride was a great scholar, a *Talmud hokhem*, who everyone agreed must have studied with Elijah the Prophet himself. When this young man saw Sheindl, he was impressed by the way she walked, the way she smiled, the way her face shone with such brightness and grace. But he could not get to talk to her because the rabbi's wife, and the other women, kept her away from him. Perhaps they wanted her to meet the rabbi's son or someone else's son.

Impatient, but thinking quickly of a scheme, the young scholar spread some tar on the top step of the stairway leading out of the wedding hall, so that her shoe would get stuck. Then he would be prepared to rescue her shoe from the sticky tar and thus have a chance to talk to her.

Just as he moved away from the step, Sheindl realized she had better leave immediately, as it was getting late. She quickly ran out the door and, with her right foot, stepped over the threshold and into the tar. She had no time to pry loose the stuck shoe, so she left it and ran as fast as she could to the inn. When she arrived at the inn, she quickly changed back into her work clothes, returning everything, except for the one shoe, to the old man who had waited for her as he had promised.

The scholar found the shoe stuck in the tar, but the young woman was nowhere to be seen. He carefully removed the golden slipper from the tar and announced that he would marry the young woman whose foot it would fit.

The young man began to ride everywhere, searching for his beloved. Every young woman wanted to try on the shoe, but the shoe fit no one.

Finally, the young scholar arrived at the inn where Sheindl worked as a servant. All the guests came out to greet the young man, and the innkeepers offered him a fine meal. There were some young women at the inn, and they each tried on the shoe. Sheindl watched from a corner and, as the young man was about to leave, she called out, "May I try?"

The innkeepers laughed and scolded her, "*Mieskeit,* you want to try on this delicate shoe? Return to the kitchen. You have a nerve to bother this great scholar!"

But the young man disregarded the innkeepers and approached Sheindl, offering her the shoe. Sheindl took the shoe, put it on—and of course it fit perfectly. Everyone was amazed to see that the shoe fit this servant girl.

The young scholar was very pleased to find the young woman, but he was puzzled by her appearance. Sheindl excused herself, went to the kitchen, and said a prayer. In a moment, the old man was beside her, smiling a mysterious smile and winking, as he handed her the golden gown and the other shoe. She put them on and then returned to where everyone waited for her. Now they knew that she was indeed the enchanting young woman who had been at the wedding.

The young man proposed marriage before all the inn's guests, and the young woman gave her consent.

That night, the old man appeared again and said to Sheindl, "Here is gold and silver. Prepare a great wedding feast and invite people from the neighboring towns, including your father. But be sure that all the food served to your father is without a grain of salt." She promised to do as he said.

On the wedding day, a great feast was prepared. Guests came from everywhere. All the rabbis came and Sheindl recognized her father, but he did not recognize her. The old man, who was Elijah the Prophet, performed the marriage ceremony.

The feast began and everyone drank a *lehaim* to the bride and groom and wished them well. The guests ate with great appetite. Only Sheindl's father ate very little, tasting only one mouthful from each dish.

The bride watched him for a time and then approached him and asked, "Rabbi, why aren't you eating anything?"

"Well, dear bride," said Sheindl's father, "I don't want to insult you, especially on this your wedding day; but how can I eat this food when it is without *salt*? It has no taste at all!"

The bride replied, "Do you remember how you threw out your daughter because she told you she loved you as much as *salt* in cooked food?"

"Salt in cooked food?" the man cried out. "My Sheindl!" Tears filled his eyes as he remembered his daughter Sheindl and how unjust he had been to her. "*Yes I remember,*" he said in a whisper.

"Father" said the bride, "I am that daughter. I am Sheindl." Her father embraced Sheindl and asked for her forgiveness. She forgave him, and together they celebrated the wedding and more, with their whole hearts.

The Ten Sons

What is friendship? What is friendship worth? How can one measure it? These are questions we have asked in literature and in our lives. In Jewish literature there are many stories about friendships, the most famous being that of David and Jonathan.

Another Jewish folk story that explores the nature of true friendship is about two friends who traveled to a strange land where the King, thinking one of them was a spy, was about to hang him. The suspect begged the King to allow him to return home for a month to settle his affairs. "What will you give me as security that you will return?" asked the King. The man's friend came forward and offered himself as a bond, to be hanged in his friend's place if the other did not return. Since they were true friends, you can be sure that the man returned. The King, witnessing this test of friendship, pardoned the suspect and asked both friends to be his friends as well.

In this Oriental wisdom story, one of the ten sons inherits something better than money—good friends. It reinforces the values our sages taught: "Acquire yourself a companion" (*Avot* 1:6); and, as Ben Sira advised: "There will be many who ask after your well-being, but reveal your secret only to one in a thousand."

This story can be found in *Yalkut Sippurim Umidrashim* (1923), Ibn Shahin (1557), Gaster (1924), Jellinek (1853–1878), Eisenstein (1915), Bin Gorion (1976), and other anthologies.

ho could be happier than a man who has *true* wealth: children, friends, many good deeds to his credit, and, in addition, a treasure of many gold pieces? There once was such a man. He had acquired his gold through hard work and performing good deeds, and he was proud of all that he had accomplished.

One day, he called his ten sons close to him and told them, "My children, I will one day soon distribute my wealth among you while I still live. You will each receive 100 gold pieces. You should not have to wait for my death in order to benefit from this money. Even though I remain alive, you will have full control of the money and can use it in any way you please."

Time passed. But the wheel of fortune turned, and soon the man found himself with only 950 gold pieces left to him. He again called his ten sons to him and said, "My children, a great portion of my fortune has been lost, but I want to keep the promise that I made to you some time ago. I promised to give each of you 100 gold pieces and I can still do that, but for only nine of you. From the 50 remaining gold pieces I must keep 30 for myself and my burial expenses, and that leaves only 20 gold pieces for one of you.

"I am, as you know, blessed with ten good friends, companions of my youth, and they will be friends to the son who chooses to inherit the remaining 20 gold pieces. Since

it is difficult for a parent to choose, I will ask you: Which one
of you will volunteer to become the possessor of the 20
coins?"

The father looked at his sons, one by one. Each son in
turn lowered his eyes and shook his head, indicating that
he was not willing to accept the smaller inheritance. Finally,
the father turned to his youngest son, and the one he loved
the most, the child of his old age.

"Yes, Father, I will be content with the 20 gold pieces
and I happily accept your offer," replied the youngest son as
he lovingly embraced his father.

"Good," answered the father. "But know that my
friends will be your companions, and they are worth more
than gold and silver."

Within a short time after that, the father died. The sons
observed the required seven days of mourning. Then the
nine sons, without a thought for their youngest brother,
began to spend their money in any way that pleased them.
Soon they had spent all of their inheritance.

The youngest brother remembered his father's words
about his ten friends. And so, after a time, he called on each
of the friends and said, "Before my father died, he asked me
to keep you as friends, and I want to honor my promise to
him. I am about to leave this place to seek my fortune
elsewhere. But before I leave, I would like to invite you to a
farewell dinner. Please come so that you may help me keep
my word to my father." The friends all accepted this invitation with great pleasure.

At the dinner, the friends engaged in lively conversations, each one in turn remembering a story about their
friend, the young man's father. At the end of the modest
dinner, one of the friends stood up and said: "Dear friends,
we are all recalling our old friend with such great love. And
of all his sons, only his youngest has kept his memory alive
by remembering his friends. Why should we also not respect
our friend and honor him by helping his son? Why should
this loyal young man have to go far away from our community to be with strangers in order to earn a living? Let us

each contribute a generous sum of gold and help him establish a business here in our midst."

All the other friends agreed heartily, and so it was done. The young man became a prosperous merchant and always treasured these friends as his own, often remembering his father's words, "My friends will be your companions, and they are worth more than gold and silver."

This is what he taught his own children, and his name, too, was honored through the generations.

The Clever Will

Wills left by Jewish parents usually leave the children more than a material inheritance. They also leave a legacy of moral lessons, wisdom, a right way to live. This tradition of bequeathing a spiritual legacy can be found in the Bible and the Talmud and continues in modern times.

One of the finest ethical wills ever written was left by the beloved Yiddish writer Sholom Aleichem (Shalom Rabinovich, 1859–1916). In his will, he writes (my translation):

> My wish is that my children guard their mama, enhance her older years, sweeten her bitter life, heal her broken heart. Don't cry when you remember me, but rather remember me with joy. But the main thing is to live together in harmony. Don't have enmity, one against the other; help each other in bad times; take pity on a poor person. Children, carry with honor my hard-earned Jewish name and may God in Heaven help you. Amen!

How wise he was! His will also made sure that his legacy remains a living one because he asks his children and grandchildren to gather each year, on the anniversary of his death (his *Yahrzeit*) and to read his stories, especially his humorous stories, in whatever language they understand.

This story, from the *midrash* in *Lamentations Rabba* and *Yalkut Sippurim Umidrashim* (1923) wills us to think over, in a humorous way, the intent of one parent's legacy.

"The Clever Will" contains elements of A-T 655*C "Enigmatic Will," but the central motif is a condensation of Tale Type A-T 1533 "Wise Carving of the Fowl," TMI H601, known from Northern Europe through India. This motif is also often found in the "Clever Peasant Girl" tales (A-T 875) such as "The Innkeeper's Wise Daughter" in this collection.

The segment in this tale about the carving of the chicken is found in many stories, including "The Wise Carving of the Fowl" (four variants) and "Prince into Pauper" (IFA 5692, from Iraqi Kurdistan, published in Marcus (1966)).

Another version (IFA 11,459 collected by Kenny Shuler from Mazal Yakobi of Persia) can be found in Noy (1979). The second part of this version focuses on the old man who invites to his home the companion he has met on the road, a King in disguise looking for a clever woman to wed. At the dinner table, he asks the guest to serve the fowl. The disguised King gives the head to the old man (the head of the household), the feet to the mother (who stands all day in the kitchen), the wings to the daughter (who will soon marry and fly away), and the rest to the guest. The daughter is clever enough to explain the meaning of the portions. The King appreciates her cleverness and marries her. The story is called, "He Who Has Found a Wife, Has Found a Great Good." (The first part of the story deals with riddles. See "The Dream Interpreter.")

The clever carving of a fowl has captured the folk imagination, and there are twenty other versions, including IFA 1714 "He That Diggeth a Pit Shall Fall Therein," included in *Faithful Gardens*. In this version, a Jew brings a roasted rooster to the King, who orders him to divide it. The Jew gives the head to the King, the wings to his children, and the feet to the ministers.

Would you do it any differently?

 long time ago, there lived in Jerusalem a wealthy Jewish merchant and his wife and son. This merchant often traveled to faraway lands carrying with him jewels and money, always for trade, and, whenever the opportunity presented itself, for ransoming Jews.

One time, when he had traveled to a distant land and was staying as a guest in the home of a certain Jew, the merchant fell ill. When he realized he was near death, he asked his host to send a message to his wife and son, telling them the name of the host at whose house he was staying when he became gravely ill. Furthermore, he was leaving all his jewels and gold with this host. He would instruct the host to give his inheritance only to a person who would come and perform *three clever actions* and only then. This was the Jerusalemite's will, and he signed it before three witnesses. And the host promised to send the letter and the will only if the merchant should die.

The merchant then said to his host, "After I die, spread the word that no one is to give directions to your house to any stranger who comes to the city." The host promised to obey this request also.

Soon after, the merchant died, and he was buried according to Jewish law in this strange land. The host sent the letter and kept the merchant's fortune in a safe place, waiting for someone to come and claim it. But he wondered at the merchant's unusual will.

The letter sent by the host finally reached the merchant's home in Jerusalem. His wife mourned for her husband and the son for his father.

After the seven days of mourning, the mother said to her son, "Your father has left his fortune with an honorable Jew. But in order to claim it, you must do three clever things to show your worthiness. Go, my son, do not delay. It is a long journey, and may God be with you.

After traveling on the seas and by land for many weeks, the son finally arrived at the town where his father had died. When he asked about a certain man who had been his father's host, each person he asked knew the host. When he asked for directions to the host's house, however, no one would tell him.

The young man thought to himself, "This must be part of my father's plan to see if I am clever enough to find this man's house without knowing an address." And he thought of what he might do.

So the son looked around and, near the town gate, he noticed a man selling firewood from a cart.

"I will buy all the wood you have on condition that you deliver it to a certain house," said the young man.

"Agreed," replied the wood seller.

After the son had paid the wood seller, he gave him the name of his father's host. The man carried the wood directly to the house, with the young man following. When the host answered the knock on the door, and saw the wood seller, he said, "I did not buy any wood. You must have the wrong house." But the wood seller replied, "The man who bought the wood is behind me, and he asked me to deliver it to you."

The young man from Jerusalem identified himself, and the host invited him to stay for dinner. The host thought to himself, "This young man is clever, indeed, to find me in a strange town without an address. He has shown one act of wisdom."

And the host decided to test the young man again. The host ordered his cook to prepare five pigeons for dinner. At the table, the host placed the five pigeons on the serving plate before the young man and said, "Young man, since you are our guest, do us the honor and divide the pigeons so that each of us will have an equal portion."

What could he do? The young man looked around the table and counted: There was the host and his wife, their two sons, their two daughters, and himself. There were seven people and only five pigeons. (And, as you know, pigeons are small to begin with and not easily cut up.)

With some hesitation, but at the insistence of the host, the young man served the pigeons. He gave one pigeon to the host and his wife; one pigeon to the two sons; one pigeon to the two daughters, and he kept two for himself.

The host was somewhat annoyed at this division, for after all the guest had taken two pigeons for himself, while the other pairs in the family had to share a single pigeon. "Arrogant and selfish?" the host thought. "Perhaps clever as well. We shall see."

After dinner the puzzled host asked, "Can you explain the reasoning behind the way you divided the pigeons?"

"It's very simple," replied the young man. "You told me to divide the five pigeons equally among the seven of us. Well, this is my account: You and your wife are two; add one pigeon and you have three. Your two sons plus one pigeon make three. Your two daughters and one pigeon make three. I am alone so, with two pigeons, I am also three. Thus everything is equal."

"Well done," thought the host. "This is a second act of cleverness." And aloud he said, "I invite you to come to dinner tomorrow night."

That next evening the host asked the cook to prepare one roasted chicken. At the table the host placed the dish in front of the guest and said, "Young man, I give you the honor of carving this chicken and serving it to us." This time, without any hesitation, the guest began to cut the chicken into parts.

The host watched and wondered how the young man would serve this one chicken to the seven at the table. The guest gave the head of the chicken to his host. Then he gave the inner parts to the host's wife. He gave a drumstick to each of the two sons and a wing to each of the two daughters. The young man kept the remainder of the chicken for himself.

After eating, the host, more bewildered than before, turned to the young man and said, "I do not understand the logic of your action. Once again you took the best and largest portion of the meal for yourself. Can you explain this to us?"

The young man answered, "It seems logical to me. You are the head of the family and sit at the head of the table, so to you I gave the head of the chicken. Your wife bore the children in her womb, and so it was fitting to give her the inside parts. The drumsticks are the legs of the chicken, just as your sons are the pillars of your house and will support you in your old age. And for your daughters, who will marry and fly from home one day, the wings are appropriate parts.

"As for me, I came on a boat and will return home on a boat. The body of a chicken, without the head, drumsticks, wings, and insides, resembles a boat. So this part I kept for myself."

And the host said, "You are a wise young man who has performed three clever actions, according to your father's will. You deserve to inherit your father's fortune."

Saying that, the host brought out the chest filled with jewels and gold that the young man's father had left with him and gave it to the rightful heir from Jerusalem.

Three Generations

Judaism demands respect for the elderly. "Thou shalt rise up before the hoary head, and honor the face of the old man," says the Bible (Leviticus 19:32). We must show respect for someone who has lived a long time and has thereby gained the matured wisdom of experience. Rabbi Joseph H. Hertz (1981), in his commentary on the Pentateuch, writes: "A famous rabbi would stand up even before an aged heathen peasant and say, 'What storms of fortune has this old man weathered in his lifetime?'" (p. 504).

And, of course, the injunction applies as much, if not more so, to the Fifth Commandment: "Honor your father and mother."

In Jewish literature, and especially in examples recorded in Gaster (1924), there are many stories that illustrate this commandment. One of the most famous talmudic tales is about Dama, a heathen jeweler in Ashkelon, who owned a precious stone needed to replace a stone in the High Priest's breastplate. When the buyers arrived at his shop, Dama told them the price and went to get the stone. But finding his father asleep in the chamber where the stone was kept, Dama did not enter the room. He would not disturb his father, even for a profitable deal.

When Dama came back and said he could not sell them the stone, the buyers thought he wanted more money, and they offered a higher and still a higher price. Only after his father awoke did Dama enter the room. Bringing the jewel out, he said: "I did not want to interrupt my father's sleep, so I will not take any profit from the honor I paid my father." And, much to the buyers' amazement, Dama accepted only the price originally agreed upon.

There are similar talmudic stories, such as the tale about Rabbi Tarfon, who knelt down so that his mother could use him as a footstool when she went to bed. The bed must have been very high, but the respect the rabbi showed his mother was even higher.

We know that lessons are transmitted from generation to generation, more by action and deeds than by words.

"Three Generations" is closely related to A-T 980 "Ungrateful Son Reproved by Naive Actions of Own Son" (TMI J121) and A-T 980A "The Half-Carpet," in which a man gives his father only half a carpet to keep him warm; his own child saves the other half for him when he grows old. This cautionary tale is found in Grimm (number 78) and as an exemplum all through the Middle Ages in various literary treatments. There is a very similar form to be found in Gaster (1924), (437).

This teaching story is found in many variants in Jewish folklore: IFA parallels originate from Morocco, Afghanistan, and Rumania. An Iraqi version (IFA 3969, found in Marcus (1966)) substitutes broken down furniture for a wooden plate. Other versions have the half-carpet or the more familiar half-mantle for the old grandfather.

This version (IFA 8189) comes from Buczacz, is found in Shenhar (1969).

No matter which variant you know, the lesson it teaches is the same.

nce an old man lived in his only son's house. Life was cheerful for him, since he had his own room and a place for his books and for studying. When it came time for meals, the whole family gathered at the big round dining table to eat together. The son and his wife treated him well. Soon there was a grandchild, and the old man took great pleasure in watching his grandson grow. He loved to take the child on his lap and tell him stories.

As the years went by, the old man's hands began to shake, at first only a little, and then all the time. Sometimes he would spill his tea because of his trembling hands, or he would drop a plate. And little by little his son became more and more and *more* impatient with him.

One day, as the whole family was sitting at the dinner table, the old man accidentally hit his plate with the soup spoon and the plate broke, spilling the soup on the tablecloth and onto his lap. His son threw down his spoon and jumped up angrily, shouting, "If you can't eat like a *mentsh*, eat alone. I'm tired of your spilling food on our good tablecloths and breaking our good dishes!"

The next day, the son brought home a wooden plate. He then set a table in the old man's bedroom, using an old sheet as a tablecloth, and served him his food on the wooden plate.

The old man said nothing and ate his meals alone day after day. But to be separated from his family in this way hurt him very much.

One day, when the son came home from work, he noticed his young child working at a task in the corner. "Well, my big son, what keeps you so busy today?" he asked.

"I'm making a plate, carving it from wood all by myself," answered the little boy.

His father was surprised. "A plate of wood? What will you use that for? We have such beautiful dishes."

And the little boy answered, "I know, Father. But I'm making this plate for *you*, when you grow old like Grandfather. And when your hands begin to shake, why then I'll have this wooden plate *ready* to give you in your little room."

When the father heard this, he ran to *his* father and fell to his knees. "Forgive me, my father. Forgive me for not showing you the respect and honor due you." And he wept.

Yes, the father forgave his son. And that evening the family sat together at the big round table.

As for the old man, he sat at the place of honor.

An Offspring's Answer

The Fifth Commandment states: "Honor thy father and thy mother that thy days may be long upon the land which the Lord thy God giveth thee."

How does a child honor a parent? Through respect, obedience, and love. Even beyond the grave, a child has an obligation to revere the memory of a parent in act and feeling. That is the Jewish way.

While a child has an obligation to respect his parents, the parents must be worthy of that reverence. These are fundamental moral laws. When one honors one's parents, one honors oneself.

This story, "An Offspring's Answer," is about honoring a parent. It raises some important questions about the things we often expect from our children, and it suggests that our children frequently help us understand or even reinterpret our expectations.

"An Offspring's Answer" is rarely found in European folktales, but is typed as A-T 244*** "Raven Carries Young across a Lake." There are several versions of this tale in the Israel Folktale Archives (IFA 6823, from Buczacz, Poland, can be found in Shenhar (1969)). There are also Rumanian (IFA 7015) and Russian (IFA 7895) versions. Several people have told me this tale in versions told to them by their mothers.

One of the eminent Jewish matriarchs of modern times, Glueckel of Hameln (1646–1724), wrote her memoirs primarily to help ease her sorrow after the death of her husband. But she addresses the memoirs to her children, so as to teach them, without seeming to preach, about life and about leading a moral Jewish life. One of her methods is to make a point through a story.

Glueckel begins her memoirs as if "talking" to her children, and she says, "We should, I say, put ourselves to great pains for our children, for on this the world is built. Yet we must understand that, if children did as much for their parents, the children would quickly tire of it." She then drives her point by telling the story of the father bird who is forced to carry his young in his strong claws over a windy sea—a variant of the story I am about to tell you.

Where did she get this story? A source is not given, but I would venture to say that she probably heard it from her mother. And as a mother, she told it to her children.

This is truly a tale that parents tell to their children from generation to generation.

here once was a mother bird who knew it was time to migrate to warmer lands. In order to get to the place where she went every year, she would have to cross a great sea. She began to get ready for the long journey. Knowing that her three fledglings were too young yet to fly, especially over such a great distance, she decided to take the three little birds on her back. She loved her children, and she was willing to do anything in the world for them.

And so the little birds got on their mother's back, and the mother bird began to fly. At first, the flight was easy enough. "Carrying my own young is never too burdensome," thought the mother bird. But as time went by, the little birds began to feel heavier and, after the first day, then the second and finally the third day, the mother bird was tired.

"My child, my birdling," asked the mother bird of the little bird sitting in front, "Tell me the truth. When I get old and will have no strength to fly across such an ocean, will you take me on your back and fly me across?"

"No mama," answered the fledgling.

"What? You disregard the *mitzva* of respect for your parent?" said the mother bird. And in anger she threw the little bird into the sea.

Then she turned to the second of her young and said, "Tell me the truth, my child, my birdling. When I get old and will have no strength to fly such a great distance, will you take me on your back and fly me across?"

"No mama," answered the second fledgling.

Again the mother bird became angry. "Indeed! You disregard the *mitzva* of respect for your parent." And the mother bird threw the young one into the sea.

With a hurt-filled heart, the mother bird turned to the third fledgling. Speaking in a guarded tone, she asked, "My child, my dear sweet fledgling, tell me the truth. When I get old and will have no strength to fly over such a big sea, will you take me on your back and fly me across?"

And the third fledgling answered, "My mother, I can't promise to do that. I may not be able to fly you across a sea because I may be busy flying my own children on *my* back just as *you* are doing for *me*."

When the mother bird heard this answer, she laughed with a joyful sound, and she and her fledgling continued on their flight.

The Golden Watch

The Jews are a people who remember their history, their customs, and, above all, their ancestors. The *Kaddish* prayer, with its mysterious origins (some believe angels brought it from heaven), possesses extraordinary power as it forms a bridge between the living and the dead. It serves as a strong reminder of those who came before us, without ever mentioning the word *death*, and it does so by affirming life. The focus of the *Kaddish* is on *continuation* of life. The question was once asked, "Can a people disappear and be annihilated so long as children remember their parents?"

This story is my way of answering the question. The idea for the story came from a Liberian folktale called "The Cowtail Switch." When I heard this African tale, it seemed to me to be Jewish in its message, namely, that a person is not really dead *until* he is forgotten. This is a strong message that Jews have guarded for centuries.

I have transposed the story— a cumulative story—to the immigrant experience of so many Jews, including those in my family. A golden watch, similar to the one mentioned in this tale, was actually treasured and passed down through several generations in my family. It represents for me the transmission of cycles of time and life, cycles of time that all Jews share—the holidays, *Shabbat*, *Rosh Hodesh*, a time to say *Kaddish* and *Yizkor*, and more.

It is my way of remembering my mother and my father, their parents, and all who came before them: all those who shaped the destiny of our Jewish family through their decisions, their treasured beliefs, their stories, and their remembrances.

The lullaby I have chosen to include in this story is "Shlof Main Kind, Main Treist, Main Sheiner" from Rubin (1965). One of the most popular songs of the mass migration years of East European Jews to America, this lullaby was sung among the people even before it was published by Sholem Aleichem in 1892. Perhaps your mother or grandmother also sang this lullaby.

veryone was going off to America—or so it seemed. The *balagolas* were kept busy driving their horses and wagons to the railroad stations from all the small towns and villages in Russia. On one such wagon rode Berl, carrying with him a large suitcase filled with his clothes and prayer books, and a basket filled with food for the journey across the continent on a train and across the ocean by steamship. In his pockets, he carried his papers—passport, visa, steamship ticket—and in secret pockets in his lining, sewn by his wife Rivke, he had the money he had saved so he could survive in America until he got a job.

Berl also carried with him the golden pocket watch given to him long ago by his father. Just before his father died, he had called Berl over to him and said, "Take this watch and keep it always, no matter what. My father gave it to me, and it has always brought me good luck." As a child, Berl had always imagined walking in his father's footsteps, even to the point of actually walking behind him as they would return home from the synagogue on Shabbos mornings. In the winter he loved to walk in his father's footprints in the snow. After all, he had always been told, "A child should walk in his father's footsteps." And he wondered, "Will my feet ever grow to fit my father's shoeprints?" And always in his imaginings, he wore his father's golden pocket watch, even on Shabbos.

Like so many others in his village, Berl had decided to leave Lepl and go to America, in the hope that he would find the "streets paved with gold" and would be able to live freely as a Jew. He planned to bring over his wife and children at a later time, when he had established himself and could earn a good living.

Berl and Rivke had three children, all sons. At the time Berl left Lepl, Rivke knew that she was going to have another child, but she told her husband nothing. She did not want anything to delay the realization of his dream.

At first, letters from Berl came frequently. In one of the early letters, he wrote: "My dear Rivke, How are you and the children? I am fine. I look for work but find nothing. I keep up my hopes that tomorrow will be better. I am a boarder in the home of Mrs. Markman. I eat meals here too. She is a real *balabuste*, but not like *you*. You should not work too hard. Remember me to the children and I hope we will be together soon. Berl."

As the months passed, Rivke received fewer and fewer letters. And after a while, the letters Rivke sent to Berl were returned to her unopened and marked, "Name unknown" or "Not at this address." Every few weeks Rivke wrote again, but each time she received back only her own letters.

When the time came, Rivke gave birth to a healthy, beautiful little girl. She named her daughter Dvora, for the sweetness of honey, and everyone called her by the Yiddish diminutive Dvorele.

Life, however, was anything but sweet for Rivke. All day long she worked in her little grocery store, took care of the children, carried pails of water from the well, washed the laundry on the banks of the local stream, cooked and baked. Even on Shabbos there was little rest for her.

In the evenings, when she put the baby to sleep, Rivke often sang her a lullaby:

Bai dain vigel zitst dain mame,
Zingt a lied un veint.
Vest amol farshtein, mistame,
Vos zi hot gemeint.

In Amerike iz der tate,
Dainer Dvoirenyu,
Du bist nokh a kind, le'eis ata
Shlof-zhe, lyu-lyu-lyu.

Mother sits beside your cradle
Crooning tearfully.
Some day, you will understand
What these tears mean to me.

Your daddy's in America
A thousand miles away,
You are still a tiny baby,
What more can I say?

Rivke's tears would fall on the sleeping child, and in this way she was able to talk out her bitterness and loneliness, for to whom else could she tell what she was feeling inside.

As the boys grew older, they helped their mother more and more with the work. While the silent yearning for her husband grew, her sons seemed to have forgotten about their father. They never mentioned him. They never talked about him. No more letters came from America.

One day, Dvorele began to form words, and her first words were, "*Tate. Vu iz der tate?*" ("Where is my Papa?").

When Rivke and the boys heard this, there was a moment of stunned silence. "Papa!" they cried out, "Papa! Papa! We must find Papa!"

"He is dead!" shouted the oldest son angrily.

"But maybe he's not!" answered the others.

"Then why hasn't he written us and sent for us as he promised to do!" replied the first harshly.

"Because he's busy in America," said the second son. "Why don't we go look for him?"

"Why waste our time and money," the oldest son said as he returned to his work. "To me he is dead. We might as well say *kaddish* for him."

The idea of finding their father took hold of the two younger sons, and they began to plan the journey to America. They worked and saved, and with the help of their mother, they started on their long trip. The mother gave them a bag filled with food to eat on the way, a paper with all the information about their father, and a letter to their father when they found him. They hugged their mother and sister, but their oldest brother did not even come to see them off. The *balagola* shouted "*Hayta!*" to the horses and they were off to the train station.

Arriving in America, the two brothers began to search for their father. They went to every address their mother had written down from his old letters. They could find no one who knew where Berl Hovshovitch was. "No, he doesn't live here anymore," and "I don't know where he moved."

Then the youngest son had an idea: "Let's put a notice in *Der Forvertz, The Jewish Daily Forward*, the Yiddish newspaper, with our names and the address where we are staying." They had found a room to share in a crowded apartment close to their father's last address.

One day, a man appeared and asked for the boys by name. He had a copy of *The Jewish Daily Forward* under his arm. The boys looked at this stooped, beardless man and asked, "Who are you?" He looked young and old at the same

time, and he was shabbily dressed. They were sure that they
had never seen him before, and yet he looked familiar; there
was something about his eyes, the cleft in his chin, his
voice.

"My name is Bernard Hoffman," the man answered
hesitantly, "but I am your father Berl Hovshovitch."

The three men stood there with open mouths for what
seemed a long time. Then they hugged each other and cried,
each son trying to answer the father's questions between
their tears and their laughter and, at the same time, to ask
as many questions of their father.

Then they suddenly remembered their mother's letter.
As Berl read the letter telling about the birth of his daughter
years before, about the rest of the family, and also what was
happening in their town, he sat down, held his head in his
hands, and wept. A long time passed. When Berl finally
stood up, he announced, "My sons, we must bring your
mama and the other children to America."

Berl immediately sent a letter to Rivke begging her
forgiveness and asking her to make plans to come to America. By borrowing some money, Berl scraped together
enough to send for Rivke and their two other children.

The answer came soon afterwards. "We are coming to
America," wrote Rivke, and she noted the date and the name
of the boat. Berl and the two boys were waiting for them at
Castle Garden when the ship arrived in New York. Tears of
joy were shed when Berl and Rivke saw each other again.
Berl could not recognize his oldest boy, for he had grown so
tall, and he met his young daughter for the first time. He
gathered up their bundles, and they made their way to
Berl's flat.

At first, they were all shy with one another—this was a
strange land, a strange language, even a strange papa. But
soon every one was talking, exchanging stories about their
adventures. Mama suddenly said, "My husband, my children, thank God we are all alive and together again. We
must say a prayer and be grateful for what we have." So they
stood together as a family and said a prayer of thanksgiving
for having been reunited.

Then Berl spoke to them about his life in America. "These years in America were hard times for me," he said, "but I was too ashamed to write you and tell you how I was failing in this golden land. Nothing I touched turned to gold, only to sawdust. *So* I became bitter and stayed alone, working at odd jobs and losing all faith in myself. I was like a dead person.

"But I always kept the golden watch given to me by my father, maybe because I never really lost all my hope and faith in God. I never sold it, even when I had no money to pay for food. I now want to give it to the child who did the most to bring me back to my family."

Berl looked at his oldest son, but the boy looked at the ground, shifting his weight, and said, "Papa I was angry about your leaving us. I was sure you were dead."

"I understand, my son," said Berl. "I see now that I was wrong to leave you all for so long a time."

Each of the other sons began to argue. The second son said, "*I* came to America to find you, Papa."

"I knew you were alive and came to look for you, too," said the third son. "*I* put the advertisement in the Yiddish newspaper."

"Yes, my sons, you were courageous and brave to come across the ocean to look for your papa," said Berl. "Thank you from the bottom of my heart. It was an excellent idea to put that notice in the newspaper. I thank you for that also."

Then Berl turned to his daughter. "And Dvorele," he asked, "what did *you* do to help bring me back to all of you?"

And Rivke answered for her. "She asked for you. She asked, '*Vu iz der tate?*' Those were her *first* words."

Berl looked at his little daughter and said, "To you, my Dvorele, I owe the most, because your first words were, 'Where is my Papa?' I was not dead as long as someone remembered me. Those words made everyone else remember they had a papa. I give the watch to you, my child."

And the other children knew that their father was right.

The Cycle

When we tell stories and when we listen to them, a sense of our humanity reaches us in hidden ways. That is why stories with animals, often mistaken as being only for children, can help create understanding far beyond their words alone.

One of the most influential books of wisdom in the Middle Ages was *Kalila and Dimna*, known as the "lawbook" of India's rulers and filled with fables and parables. The Arabic translation was extremely popular among Arabs and Jews, and the first Hebrew translation appeared during the thirteenth century. John of Capua, a baptized Jew, used a Hebrew translation to produce his Latin version, entitled *Directorium Vitae Humanae*, which circulated in Europe and was translated into many other languages. (See introduction to "The Leopard and the Fox.")

As we see from other stories in this book, and from other collections, *Kalila and Dimna* served as the springboard for a great number of European folktales, many of which Jews adapted and retold as Jewish folktales. This is the way of folklore.

This story, "The Cycle," was inspired by a particular moral lesson in a story in *Kalila and Dimna*. Bialik (1938) created a "chain" story called "Whose Was the Blame?" which may have been similarly inspired by *Kalila and Dimna*, a text he would have known well since he was the editor of the 1922 Hebrew edition.

In any case, the idea and practice of peace has been promised to us by God, as His covenant with the beasts of the field and the fowls of heaven, and with the creeping things of the ground:

> And I will break the bow and the sword and the battle
>   out of the land,
> And will make them to lie down safely. (Hosea 2:20)

How wonderful, indeed, to have an assurance of peace awaiting both land and people, protecting the world from hostile elements in nature and from hostile people whose weapons of warfare would be broken forever.

Peace, according to the rabbis, is one of the pillars of the world. We pray for peace when we say, "Nation shall not lift up sword against nation, nor learn war any more"; or when we pray "Spread over us Thy canopy of peace"; or when we hope that we will one day be able to beat our swords into ploughshares. We pray for universal peace and harmony among people and the animal world when we recite Isaiah (9:6-8):

> And the wolf shall dwell with the lamb,
> And the leopard shall lie down with the kid;
> And the calf and the young lion and the fatling together;
> And a little child shall lead them.
> And the cow and the bear shall feed;
> Their young ones shall lie down together;
> And the lion shall eat straw like the ox.
> And the suckling child shall play on the hole of the asp,
> And the weaned child shall put his hand on the basilisk's den.

A love for peace can be effectively transmitted through stories. Through stories we can understand each other better and listen to each other's dreams, values, and hopes. Although they may differ somewhat from our own, we can listen and understand, relate our own stories, and exchange feelings and ideas. Most important, we will then be listening, as well as talking, and thus creating the atmosphere of peace we all pray for and hope to share in our world, our only world.

This is my peace story.

ing Solomon was noted, not only for his great wisdom and his skill as a judge, but also for his ability to understand the languages of the birds and the beasts of the fields. Thus, he would sometimes listen to the complaints of animals against each other and against humanity.

Once, a grief-stricken lioness came before Solomon with a bitter complaint. "Say what is in your heart," said Solomon, "I will hear you out."

And the lioness spoke. "Why must there be war? Why must we attack one another? Can there be no peace in the world? Is it right that the hunter comes to my den and robs me of my babies and then, before my own eyes, strips off their skin? Does he have no *pity* for the *mother*? No *pity* for the *babies*? *That hunter must be punished*, Your Honor, and be shown no mercy, for he is guilty of killing my babies."

And the lioness began to cry with great anguish.

When King Solomon heard this, he said, "Listen to my story and tell me *who* is to blame?"

And Solomon told this story.

One day, the mongoose and the weasel were talking, and the weasel was complaining, "That snake has eaten up so many of my babies. He comes and attacks them when I run out for a few moments to get them some food." And the weasel moaned with grief.

"Well then," suggested the mongoose, "why not devise a scheme to get the snake out of his cave and then *attack him*? Let's see. The snake loves fish, so we'll put a trail of fish leading away from his cave right to where we can kill him."

"Good," replied the weasel. "That will be a just dessert for him, and a good dinner for you, my friend."

So the mongoose and the weasel caught some fish and dropped them in a row on the path to the snake's cave. When the snake smelled the fish, he left his cave and ate each of the fish. As he slithered past a scorpion, the scorpion sharpened its stinger to attack the snake and accidentaly struck the hen nearby.

The hen ran to the rooster and alerted him that the scorpion was ready to make war.

The rooster called out "cock-a-doodle-doo," which sounded the alarm and the wolf ran out of his den.

As he ran by the weasel's home, the wolf saw that the weasel's babies had been left unguarded, so he ate them.

When the weasel returned home after having helped the mongoose kill the snake, she found her babies gone, and she knew that they had been killed.

Weasel ran to the Judge and cried, "The wolf has killed my children. Punish him, punish him!"

Then the Judge asked her just one question: "What did *you* bring for food for your children, Mother weasel?"

And when the weasel answered, "Birds, Your Honor," the Judge said, "*You*, yourself, are to blame for your children's death—and no one else."

Then Solomon looked at the lioness and waited. The lioness lowered her eyes and head in shame. And the lioness understood. Yes, the lioness *understood*.

The Talmud says: "What you do not want to have happen to you, do not do to another."

The Lullaby

I began this book with a story that I first heard from my father ("Elijah and the Three Wishes"). Here is another story of remembrance—this time of a lullaby I learned from my father. Lullabies are very special songs. They stay with us throughout our lives and bring back to us warmth, good feelings, our childhood homes, and parents' voices.

Elie Wiesel wrote a beautiful essay called "Echoes of Yesterday" for the Yeshiva University Centennial, in which he recalls a lullaby, "*Oifn pripitchik*," and he writes:

> "*Oifn pripitchik brennt a feierl.*" I remember the lullaby, so beautiful and moving. It accompanies me and haunts me. Thanks to it, words start singing on my lips and on my pen.
>
> "I recall my teacher and his pupils. I recall their shadows on the wall. Their melancholy and fervent voices reach me from far, very far away, from the other side of a vanished world. I look there for my own voice with an inexpressible anguish."

In the nineteenth century Yiddish lullabies were numerous and expressed the dreams and aspirations of the Jewish mother in the Czarist Pale of the Settlement. Ruth Rubin (1979) elaborates on this number and variety of lullabies by stating that they were "spontaneous expressions in the simplest structure, created at the cradleside, and . . . poetic creations of more literary origin, current among the folk" (p. 29). There are lullabies describing the coming of the matchmaker; recounting the importance of becoming a Torah scholar, who would bring economic security and prestige to the family; reflecting the personal hardships of the mother or the religious, political, and social atmosphere of the times. Whatever the mother sang, though, the child hopefully went to sleep peacefully.

The lullaby that my father's mother sang to him in Lithuania was called "*Az ikh volt gehat dem Keiser's oitzres*" ("If I could have had all the king's treasure"), which was written by the folk poet Mikhl Gordon (1823–1890), who was born in Vilna. Gordon sometimes combined his own melodies with his poetry; at other times he set the written text to music. Whichever may be the case, the lullaby appeared as a folk song in his first anonymous collection in 1868 and was sung throughout Russia during the later part of the nineteenth century.

This is my family lullaby story.

y father, Cantor Samuel E. Manchester, came to America at the turn of the century. He was born about 1878 in Sapieshok, a village near Kovno, in Lithuania, and later studied with his father, who was a *hazen-shohet-mohel*. At 16, my father married, had children soon after, and came to America, where he served as *hazen-shohet-mohel* in several cities. In 1929, he became a widower. The following year he met and married Dora Markman, an immigrant from Lepl in White Russia. When they married, they moved to New London, Connecticut, where I was born four years later.

When I was about 8 years old, I began to take piano lessons. The first piece of music my father put on the piano for me to learn was Beethoven's *Moonlight Sonata*. I did learn to play it, but not for another few years.

Then one day, I remember, my father returned from a trip to New York City, where he had gone to buy some music at the Metro Music Company on Second Avenue and to bring them more copies of his book of cantorial compositions, *Kol Rinah Utfilah*. With great excitement, he took a book out of his suitcase, *Jewish Folk Songs*, opened it to page 29, and announced, "This is the lullaby my mama sang to me when I was a child. It's a lullaby that's almost a hundred years old." And he sang the lullaby in Yiddish:

אַז איך וואָלט געהאט דעם קיסרי'ס אוצרות
מיט זיין גאנצע מלוכה,
וואָלט דאָס ביי מיר ניט געווען אַזוי ניחא,
ווי דו ביסט ביי מיר ניחא, מיין קינד, מיין שיין!
אַז איך דערזעה דיך, דוכט זיך מיר,
די גאנצע וועלט איז מיין.

שלאָף, מיין קינד, שלאָף, מיין קינד,
זאָלסט לאנג לעבען און זיין געזונד.

Az ikh volt gehat dem keiser's oitzres,
Mit zain ganze melikhe,
Volt dos bai mir nit geven azoi nikhe,
Vi du bist bai mir nikhe, main kind, main shain.
Az ikh derzei dikh, dukht zikh mir,
Di ganze velt iz main.

Shlof main kind, shlof main kind,
Zolst lang leben un zain gezunt.

If I could have had all the king's treasure
And all of his dominions,
It would never bring me as much pleasure
As you now bring me pleasure, my child, my light!
When I see your face, then I feel
The whole wide world is bright.

Sleep, my child, sleep, my child;
May life be long and fortune ever smile.

He sang it with his eyes closed, as if he were back in his childhood once again, with his mama singing it. When he had finished, he opened his eyes, reoriented himself, and with smile, said to me, "Peninnah (my name is his mama's name), bring this to your piano teacher; she should teach you to play it on the piano."

I brought the piece to my teacher, and I soon learned to play it and to sing it. I would often play it for my father on our mahogany Marshall and Mendel upright piano, which stood majestically in our living room, so he would sing it for me, over and over. I loved the words and the tune—the lullaby of a grandmother I never met.

Years later, after I had finished college and married, I had my two children, Rebecca and Michael. I sang this lullaby to them as I tucked them in and kissed them goodnight. Even when they had grown beyond early childhood, they still wanted to hear the lullaby, especially when they didn't feel well or needed some extra attention. I would then sit on the edge of their beds to talk. And then they would say, "Sing *der zade*'s lullaby to me—sing Grandpa's lullaby." And I would sing it to them.

Years later, when my son had come home from college, he came to my bedroom one morning. Seeing that I was asleep, he tiptoed into the room. I sensed someone was there, but I kept my eyes closed and pretended to sleep. Michael sat on the edge of my bed, he pulled the blanket up closer under my chin, and he sang:

Shlof main kind, shlof main kind,
Zolst lang leben, un zain gezunt.

That lullaby is now his, and it's my daughter's, too. And someday, God willing, it will belong to their children, and to their children's children, and it will live for another hundred years—and hopefully for hundreds of years and even longer.

And so must our stories!

Interweaving Stories

here was once a king who had an only
daughter. And when it became time for her to
marry, he announced to the entire kingdom
that everyone was to be invited to her wedding. But no one was to bring a gift—they
were only to bring a bottle of wine from their own vineyards. . . .

You are about to embark on another journey that may
never end. Safe within the arms of your easy chair, the
warm colors of the classroom where you teach, or the bright
pillows of your bedroom, you may continue to travel from
the pages you have just read to a world as ancient as the
Jewish heritage. This book is a beginning, a threshold. But,
while you will find only some mention of the future of storytelling here in this book, *that,* my friend, is now left to you.

Jewish storytelling is a double heritage. Tales and
heroic sagas taught, entertained, and passed on the lessons
of each generation in pre-literate cultures. How these tales
were enriched by the succeeding years is measured in the
layers of meaning and detail, in the primal themes underly-
ing more culturally specific plots and characters. In every
country, certain basic stories are told and retold; only the
setting changes. Storytelling existed before video games and
surfboards and television and will exist long after, because

it grows and changes as society changes. It will not be left behind.

The Jewish storytelling heritage spans three thousand years of sameness and change. The messages are the same: hope, belief in God, love of Israel (the holy place) and Israel (the holy nation). A mixed past has added the oppression and the joy, the enlightenment from within, the darkness constantly threatening from without. Stories of the past tell us, "We have felt all this before. You are not alone in your sorrow; we share your joy as well."

Who else lives so close to the past, while changing and growing *now*? Only a people whose Torah is copied, word for word, by scribes who dare not lose one letter in all the generations since the Torah existed—and who are, nevertheless, taught, *Torah lo bashamayim hi: The Torah is not in Heaven.* It is now up to all of us to bring our own interpretation, our own wisdom to understanding the text.

They were only to bring a bottle of wine from their own vineyards. And everybody would line up and empty their bottles of wine into a huge vat in the royal gardens. At an appropriate time, the King would step forward and draw the wine from the communal wine vat to make a lehayim, *to toast the bride and groom. So early on the morning of the wedding . . .*

I was told a lot of stories as a child. Around the Shabbat table, my father used to enthrall me with stories of Elijah the Prophet, stories of Joseph and other biblical characters, and tales of his own life in Eastern Europe. My mother spiced her conversation with a running commentary of proverbs and folk wisdom. To my children I tell the stories of my parents, and of our teachers, and I hope the tradition will continue in their own families. Stories have given us more than a repertoire of tales, a set of plots to fit various teaching occasions. After hearing and loving a story, what remains, if the story remains, is a single point of contact in our minds, a complex emotion, or a texture; a piece of mental shorthand that recalls the feel of the story and the lesson it taught, where it was told, who did the telling. At a moment of crisis what comes to my aid is not an intellectual lesson learned, but an image that represents the story and the benefit I can take from it at that moment.

What does this mean to me, and to my children—to all the children who have ever been told stories at any time, anywhere? It means that the sense of ritual that accompanies stories preserves the Jewish ritual. It means that stories of our heritage preserve the heritage itself.

Stories can be cathartic in a way that other lessons or entertainments do not approach. Storytelling is a *personal* experience for both teller and listener: An audience, even an audience of one, is there before the storyteller, unobscured by distance, cameras, light shining in one's eyes. How can I *not* live a story when I am so closely bound to my audience— and they are living it? To hear a story read or told live is to receive a gift from a friend—an earnest friend.

Fantasy is neither harmful nor a waste of time: everything, even some violence in stories, serves its purpose in stretching the imagination, in cleansing the mind of hurts and conflicts that would seethe and disturb.

Early on the morning of the wedding, everyone in the kingdom lined up, ready, holding their bottles of wine and then emptying them into the enormous vat. At the appointed moment, the King turned on the spigot and drew the first glass of wine from the combined wine of the entire kingdom. But what came out was a clear liquid. . . .

As an adult, as a parent or a teacher, as a rabbi or a counselor, and always as a storyteller, you can learn from these stories and be inspired to bring more stories into your life and the lives around you. It is better to be told two stories in one day than to be told none at all. The rich history of oral tradition is behind you and before you: In these pages, acquaint yourself with storytelling's heritage and the heritage of stories among the Jews.

What came out was a clear liquid: water. Well, it seemed that someone in the kingdom thought to himself: "Why should I bring my good, precious wine that I've worked so hard to produce? I'll bring a bottle of water. No one will know the difference in the thousands of bottles of wine: this won't dilute it at all. But it seems that everyone had the same thought, and everyone brought a bottle of water!

If you are reading this book, then you care, you feel the responsibility to tell stories, you are choosing to pass along the riches of an ancient people. You are someone we cannot do without: fighting against the diluted vintage of modern society, you as a storyteller can help restore pure wine to the communal wine vat.

Glossary

Unless otherwise noted, the following expressions are Hebrew, with one or two in English. Nearly all of them are used in Yiddish as well as Hebrew. Ashkenazic pronunciation is indicated by (A), Sefardic pronunciation by (S). Vowel combinations: ei = long a; ai = long i.

Aggada—Those sections of Talmud and Midrash containing homiletic expositions of Bible, stories, legends, folklore, anecdotes, maxims. Aggada is found throughout the Talmud, intermingling with *halakha* (law), and deals with the spirit, rather than the letter, of the law.

Aguna—A woman who cannot remarry under Jewish law because her husband has deserted her or because his death cannot be verified.

Alef—The first letter of the Hebrew alphabet. The alphabet is referred to as *alef-beis*.

Aliya—Ascent; being called up to read a portion of the Torah.

Apocrypha (Greek)—Moralistic and historical books, dating from the Second Temple period. Not included in the canon of the Bible, they include Tobit, Judith, Ben Sira, Maccabees, Additions to Daniel, and others.

Arabot—The seventh heaven.

Baal Korei—The one who reads Torah in the synagogue.

Badhan—A merrymaker or jester who entertained through song and rhyme at weddings in Eastern Europe.

Balabuste—A housewife, or head of a household; by extension, a super-homemaker.

Balagola—Wagon driver in Eastern Europe.

Bamidbar (Numbers)—The fourth book of the Five Books of Moses.

Bamme Avarekhekha—"How shall I bless you?"

Bar or Bat Mitzva—Son or daughter of the Commandment at 13 years of age.

Bashert—Destined, preordained, fated.

Basherte—Destined wife.

Basherter—Destined husband.

Beis—Ashkenazic pronunciation of the second letter of the Hebrew alphabet, *beit.*

Beis Medrash (A); Beit Midrash (S)—House of Study; a part of every synagogue.

Beit Din (S); Bez Din (A)—A rabbinical court.

Bereshis (A); Bereshit (S)—"In the beginning." The book of Genesis.

Bima—An elevated place or platform in the synagogue where the rabbi and cantor stand and where the Torah is read.

Brit Mila—Covenant of the circumcision, performed on every male Jewish child when he becomes eight days old. Brit (S); Bris (A).

Cherubim (plural)—Winged celestial beings who were at the entrance of the Garden of Eden. Two cherubim faced each other in the First Temple in Jerusalem.

Daven (Yiddish)—To pray.

Der Roiter (Yiddish)—The red head.

Devarim (Deuteronomy)—The fifth book of the Five Books of Moses.

Elan—A tree.

Eliahu Hanovi—Elijah the Prophet.

Esrog (A); Etrog (S)—A citron, a fruit over which a benediction is said during Sukkot.

Gam zu Letova (S)—This, too, is to the good. It's all for the best.

Gehenna—Hell, the place where the souls of the wicked are punished and purified.

Gemara—Relevant discussions and elaborations on Mishna in the Talmud.

Goldene Kepele (Yiddish)—Little golden head. An affectionate term.

Gut Shabbos (Yiddish)—"Good Sabbath." A greeting used on the Sabbath.

Haftorah—A portion from the Prophets read in synagogue following the Torah reading on Sabbaths, festivals, and fast days.

Haggada—A recounting of the Exodus from Egypt and freedom from bondage. It includes poems, songs, psalms, and stories and is recited at the Passover seders in the home.

Halla—A braided white bread baked especially for the Sabbath and festivals.

Hameaggel—The circle maker. Refers to Honi, a teacher of the first century B.C.E.

Hanukka—"Dedication." An eight-day festival, beginning Kislev 25, which commemorates the Maccabean victory over the Greek rulers of Syria and the rededication of the Temple in Jerusalem.

Hasid—"A pious one." A follower of Hasidism.

Hasidism—The Jewish religious sect founded by Israel ben Eliezer, also known as the Baal Shem Tov (the Master of the Good Name), in the eighteenth century. The emphasis is on faith and joy in prayer through song, story, and dance.

Havdala—"Distinction." The ceremony at the end of Sabbaths and festivals to separate the holy day from the weekday.

Hazen (A), Hazan (S)—Cantor; liturgical singer in the synagogue.

Hakham (A)—A wise man.

Hokhme (A)—Wisdom, cleverness.

Hakhama (A)—A wise woman.

Holy Hayyot—A class of angels who encircle God's Throne and are the mediators between Israel and the Holy One.

Huppa—A Jewish wedding canopy.

Ish—Man.

Isha—Woman.

Kaddish—Aramaic prayer recited by mourners.

Kalle Moid—A young woman who has reached the age of marriage.

Kiddush—"Sanctification." The prayer recited over wine. Recited prior to Sabbath and holiday meals.

Kohelet (Ecclesiastes)—One of the Five Scrolls (megillot). This scroll of wisdom literature has been attributed to King Solomon and is read on the harvest festival of Sukkot.

Krasavitza (Russian)—A beautiful woman.

Lamentations Rabba—Midrash on the Book of Lamentations, the first of the Five Scrolls in the Hagiographa section of the Bible.

Latte (Yiddish)—A patch.

Lehayim—"To life." A toast.

Leviathan—King of all the fish, who was created on the fifth day.

Loshen Hore (A)—Evil speech, slander. There is a commandment against slander or evil gossip.

Lulav and Esrog (A)—Lulav is a bundle of branches and leaves of three species: willow, myrtle, and palm. It is used with the esrog during Sukkot to symbolize the fruit and trees—the natural beauty of the Holy Land.

Maariv—Daily evening prayer service.

Maggid (Maggidim, plural)—A traveling preacher who teaches Torah through inspirational sermons and stories.

Mazel Tov—"Good luck" or "Congratulations." The traditional way to express joy at a birth, bar/bat mitzva, wedding, or other happy occasion.

Mieskait (Yiddish)—An ugly thing.

Megilla—Hebrew Scroll. There are five scrolls (megillot) of biblical Hagiographa: Ruth, Song of Songs, Lamentations, Ecclesiastes, and Esther. The Megilla of Esther is read on Purim and relates the story of Esther and Mordecai, who saved the Jews of the Persian Empire. The Megilla usually refers to The Book of Esther.

Mentsh (Yiddish)—A "whole" person, one who displays a sense of humanity and sensitivity.

Midrash (Midrashim, plural)—A method of interpreting Scripture to bring out lessons through stories or homilies. A particular genre of rabbinic literature. A midrash, sometimes in the form of a story or folktale, explains or "fills in the spaces between the words."

Minha—Daily afternoon prayer service.

Mishna—The code of basic Jewish law (Halakha) redacted and arranged into six orders and subdivided into tractates by

Rabbi Yehuda Hanasi c. 200 C.E. Contains the Oral Law transmitted for generations.

Mitzva (Mitzvot, plural)—A good deed; a commandment or precept.

Mohel—The person who performs the ritual circumcision.

Moshol (A), Mashal (S)—A parable used to explain a moral concept or value.

Neshome (A)—Soul.

Nigun (Nigunim, plural)—A melody without words.

Nimshal—The moral or meaning derived from a moshol.

Ofanim (Ofan, singular)—A kind of angel.

Olam Haba—The world to come. Paradise.

Peshat—The literal level. The first level of a four-part system of mystical interpretation called PARDES (peshat, remez, drosh, sod).

Pirkei Avot—"The Ethics of the Fathers." A tractate of the Talmud.

Pitgam—Moral (of a story or fable).

Rashi—Rabbi Solomon ben Isaac (1040–1105), the leading Jewish commentator on Bible and Talmud.

Reb (Yiddish)—A respectful form of address. Mister.

Rebbe (Yiddish)—A rabbi, a teacher, or a learned man.

Ribono Shel Olam (S), Riboine Shel Oilem (A)—Lord of the Universe.

Rosh Hodesh—First day of each Hebrew month.

Ruah—Spirit.

Ruble (Russian)—The monetary unit used in Russia.

Ruth—One of the five biblical scrolls (megillot). It is a story of love and trust between Ruth and Naomi. Read on the festival of Shavuot, the time of the giving of the Law.

Seder—Order. The order of service, including dinner, at the home on the first two nights of Passover. The religious home service, when the Haggada is read.

Sedra—The portion of the Torah that is being read in the synagogue.

Sefer—A book, usually one on a religious subject.

Seuda Shelishit—The third meal eaten on Sabbath afternoon after Minha services.

Shabbos (A); Shabbat (S)—Sabbath.

Sheindl (Yiddish)—A name meaning "pretty."

Shekel—A coin mentioned in the Bible, and the monetary unit used in the State of Israel today.

Shema Yisroel—"Hear, O Israel." The Jewish credo.

Shemot (Exodus)—The second book of the Five Books of Moses.

Shiddukh—An arranged match or betrothal.

Shir Hashirim, Song of Songs—One of the five biblical scrolls (megillot). Composed by King Solomon, it is considered the greatest Hebrew love poem, an allegory of the love between God and Israel.

Shohet—A ritual slaughterer of animals.

Sholom Aleikhem—A greeting that means "Peace be unto you." The response is "Aleikhem sholom." It is also the nom de plume of Shalom Rabinovitch, the writer of Yiddish literature.

Shtetl (Yiddish)—A town or village in Eastern Europe where Jews lived and frequently made up the majority of the population.

Shul (Yiddish)—Synagogue.

Shuvu Banai—Return, my children.

Simha—A joyful celebration, such as a wedding or bar/bat mitzva.

Sod—Secret. The fourth and highest level of the four-part mystical system of interpretation known as PARDES (peshat, remez, drosh, sod).

Sukkot—Booths. The harvest festival that begins on Tishri 15 and is known also as the Festival of Tabernacles.

Tal—Dew.

Tallis (A); Tallit (S)—A four-cornered prayer shawl with fringes worn in synagogue during morning services.

Talmid Hokhem (A) (Talmidei Hakhomim, plural)—Someone who is wise in the learning of Talmud.

Talmud—The commentaries on the Torah and the Oral Law that were transmitted through the generations. There are two Talmuds: the Jerusalem Talmud and the Babylonian Talmud. The Babylonian Talmud has had the greatest influence on Jewish thought, study, and practice. It is a storehouse of Jewish history and customs and is two-thirds aggada along with one-third law (halakha). The Talmud is the most sacred

Jewish text after the Bible and is comprised of the Mishna and the Gemara.

Talmud Torah—Study of the Law. Now used mainly to refer to afternoon religious schools.

Tav—Last letter of the Hebrew alphabet.

Tefillin—Phylacteries. They consist of two black leather boxes containing parchment inscribed with Bible verses and connected to leather straps. One is worn on the left arm and the other on the forehead during morning prayers, except on Sabbath and festivals.

Tikkun—The book used to learn the trope for reading the Torah. Also means "repair."

Torah—The first five books of the Old Testament, the Pentateuch. The Torah is read aloud in the synagogue on Mondays, Thursdays, Sabbaths, and festivals, as long as a quorum is present.

Torah Shebe'al Peh—The Oral Law given to Moses at the same time as the Written Law (the Torah). Later written down in the Talmud.

Treger (Yiddish)—A porter.

Trope—Musical notations for reading Torah and Haftora.

Tzedaka—Justice; charity.

Vayikra (Leviticus)—The third book of the Five Books of Moses.

Yahrzeit—Anniversary of a person's death.

Yiddish—The language spoken by Ashkenazic Jews over the past thousand years. Its origin is Medieval German but it is written in Hebrew letters and has a large Hebrew component. Slavic languages have also had a marked influence on Yiddish.

Yizkor—The prayer recited at memorial services in the synagogue four times each year.

Yomtovdik—In the holiday spirit. A Yiddishized use of the Hebrew Yom Tov.

Zemirot—Sabbath songs for the home.

Ziz—The gigantic bird created on the fifth day to rule over all the birds. Its ankles rest on the fins of Leviathan and its head reaches to the Holy Throne. The Ziz appears in a number of folktales.

Zloty—A Polish monetary unit.

Bibliography

Many of the stories in this volume, or variants of these tales, along with their motifs and types, have been classified according to the Aarne-Thompson (A-T) system, found in The Types of the Folktale (1964) and Thompson's Motif-Index of Folk Literature (1966) (TMI). Heda Jason added specific Jewish types to her index in Fabula (1965) and in Types of Oral Tales in Israel: Part 2 (1975). These references to tale types and motifs can be especially useful to folklorists, educators, and storytellers who wish to find and compare both Jewish and non-Jewish variants of a tale. The Israel Folktale Archives (IFA), founded in 1956 by Dov Noy, has collected over 17,000 folktales in Israel from storytellers in Israel. These tales are published in the IFA Publication Series, with over thirty-five volumes published by the Haifa Municipality Ethnological Museum and Folklore Archives. Each tale is assigned an IFA number and is kept in the archives.

Aarne, A., and Thompson, S. (1964). *The Types of the Folktale: A Classification and Bibliography*. 2nd rev. ed. Helsinki: Academia Scientarum Fennica.

Arabian Nights' Entertainments. Trans. by E. W. Lane. London: C. Kings, 1839–1841. (Rev. ed. *Tales from the Thousand and One Nights*. Trans. by N. J. Dawood. Great Britain: Penguin Books, 1955).

Ashkenazi, S., ed. (1687). *Yalkut Shimoni*. (Hebrew). Frankfurt.

Asseret Hadibberot (Midrash of the Ten Commandments). (Hebrew). Printed in *Beit Hamidrash*.

Attias, M. (1976). *The Golden Feather*. (Hebrew). Haifa: IFA Publication Society.

Aunt Naomi. (1921). *Jewish Fairy Tales and Legends*. New York: Bloch.

Ausubel, N. (1948). *A Treasury of Jewish Folklore.* New York: Crown.

Baharav, Z. (1964). *Sixty Folktales.* (Hebrew). Haifa: IFA Publication Society.

Barkton, S. R. (1937). The dukhifas. *The Menorah Journal,* Spring issue.

Ben Hamelekh Vehanatzir (1557). Mantova.

Ben Haviv, Y. (1883–1884). *En Yaakov.* 3 vols. Vilna.

Benfey, T., ed. (1859). *Panchatantra.* 2 vols. Leipzig.

Ben-Yehezkel, M. (1946). The simpleton's prayer. *La-Moed* 2:112–139.

——— (1957). *The Book of Tales.* (Hebrew). 2nd ed. Tel Aviv.

Bialik, H. N. (1938). *And It Came to Pass.* New York: Hebrew Publishing Co.

——— ed. (1922). *Abraham Al-Maliah.* Jerusalem: Devir.

Bialik, H. N., and Ravnitsky, J. H. (1935). *Sefer Haagada.* (Hebrew). Tel Aviv.

Bin Gorion, M. J. (1916–1921). *Der Born Judas.* 2 vols. Leipzig (*Also* Frankfort, 1966–1973).

——— (1976). *Mimekor Yisrael.* 3 vols. Bloomington, IN: Indiana University Press.

Black, D. W. (1984). Laughter. *The Journal of the American Medical Association* 252:2995–2997, 3014.

Borkhi, N. (1985). *Ruach.* LP recording.

Brayer, M. M. (1986). *The Jewish Woman in Rabbinic Literature.* Hoboken, NJ: Ktav.

Bronner, L. (1968). *The Stories of Elija and Elisha.* Leiden.

Bronstein, H. H., and Friedlander, A. H., eds. (1984). *The Five Scrolls.* New York: Central Conference of American Rabbis.

Cahan, J. L., ed. (1931). *Yiddishe Folksmaises.* (Yiddish). New York, Vilna: Yiddishe Folklor Biblyotek.

——— (1938). *Yiddisher Folklor.* (Yiddish). Vilna: YIVO Institute for Jewish Research.

Campbell, M. (1960). The three teachings of the bird. In *Studies in Biblical and Jewish Folklore,* ed. R. Patai et al., pp. 97–107. Bloomington, IN: Indiana University Press.

Carnes, P. (1985). *Fable Scholarship: An Annotated Bibliography.* New York: Garland.

Cheichel, E. (1968). *A Tale for Each Month 1967.* (Hebrew). Haifa: IFA Publication Society.

—— (1970). *A Tale for Each Month 1968–1969.* (Hebrew). Haifa: IFA Publication Society.

—— (1973). *A Tale for Each Month 1972.* (Hebrew). Haifa: IFA Publication Society.

Cohen, E. (1721). *Me'il Tzedaka.* Smyrna. (Also Lemberg, 1856).

Cousins, N. (1979). *An Anatomy of an Illness.* New York: Norton.

Cowell, E. B. Masnavi by Rumi. *Journal of Philology* 6:189–195.

de France, M. (1978). *Lais of Marie de France.* Trans. by R. Hanning and J. Ferrante. New York: Dutton.

de la Pryme, A. (1699). *Diary of Abraham de la Pryme.* Entry of Nov. 10.

Derenbourgue, J., ed. (1881). *Kalila VeDimna.* (Deux Versions hebraiques du livre Kalilah et Dimnah). Paris.

Dov Baer of Linitz, ed. (1811). *Shivhei Habesht.* Kopys, Poland.

Eisenstein, J. D., ed. (1915). *Otzar Midrashim (Treasury of Midrashim).* (Hebrew). 2 vols. New York.

Faerber, R. (1902). *König Salomon in der Tradition.* Vienna.

Farhi, Y. S. (1870). *Ose Pele.* (Hebrew). 3 vols. Livorno. (Also Leghorn, 1902).

Feldman, A. (1924). *The Parables and Similes of the Rabbis.* Cambridge, UK: Cambridge University Press.

Friedmann, M., ed. (1904). *Seder Eliyahu Zutta (The Scroll of Creation).* Vienna.

Friend, A. C. (1970). The tale of the captive bird and the traveler. *Medievalia and Humanistica* N.S. 1:57–65.

Gamliele, N. B. (1978). *The Chambers of Yemen.* (Hebrew). Tel Aviv: Afikim.

Gaster, M. (1924). *The Exempla of the Rabbis.* Leipzig. (Also New York: Ktav, 1968).

—— (1934). *The Maaseh Book of Jewish Tales and Legends.* 2 vols. Philadelphia: Jewish Publication Society.

Ginzberg, L. (1909–1938). *The Legends of the Jews.* 7 vols. Philadelphia: Jewish Publication Society.

—— ed. (1923). *Haggadot Ketu'ot. Hagoren* 9:31–68. Berlin.

Ginzberg, L., and Horodezkey, S. A. (1912–1922). *Hagoren.* Berdishev and Berlin.

Glueckel of Hameln. (1977). *The Memoirs of Glueckel of Hameln.* Trans. by M. Lowenthal. New York: Schocken.

Goldschmidt, L., ed. (1923). *Sefer Hayashar (Book of the Straight).* Berlin.

Gorovets, E. (1977). *I Am A Jew: Emil Gorovets Sings in Yiddish.* LP recording. New York: Workmen's Circle.

Gressmann, H. (1907). Das Salomonische Urteil. *Deutsche Rundschau* 130:212–228.

Haimovits, Z. M. (1976). *Faithful Guardians.* (Hebrew). Haifa: IFA Publication Society.

Hanakdan, B. (1921). *Mishlei Shualim (Fox Fables).* (Hebrew). Ed. by L. Goldschmidt. Berlin: Erich Reiss. (Also Jerusalem: A. M. Habermann, 1946).

—— (1966). *Fables of the Jewish Aesop: From the Fox Fables of Hanakdan.* Trans. by M. Hadas. New York.

Heller, B. (1930). Das Hebräische Märchen. In *Anmerkungen zu den Kinder- und Hausmärchen der Brüder Grimm,* ed. by Bolte/Polivka, vol. 4, pp. 315–364. Leipzig.

Hertz, J. H. (1981). *Commentaries: The Pentateuch and Haftorahs.* London: Soncino.

Hibbur Maasiyot. (1647). Verona.

Ibn Attar, H. (1799). *Or HaHayim.* Zolkiew, Poland: G. Madfis.

Ibn Shahin, N. (1577). *Hibbur Yafe Mihayeshua.* Ferrara. *(Also Amsterdam, 1745; Trans. by H. Z. Hirschberg, Jerusalem, 1953; (1977). An Elegant Composition Concerning Relief After Adversity.* Trans. by W. M. Brinner. New Haven: Yale University Press).

Ibn Zabara, J. (1912). *The Book of Delight (Sefer Hashaashuim).* Trans. by I. Abrahams. Philadelphia: Jewish Publication Society.

Idelsohn, A. Z. (1932). *Songs of the Chassidim.* Vol. 10. Leipzig: Friedrich Hofmeister.

Itakhimzade, O. (1967). *A Tale for Each Month 1966.* (Hebrew). Haifa: IFA Publication Society.

Jacobs, J. (1922). *More English Fairy Tales.* New York, London: G. Putnam's Sons.

—— (1966). *Fables of Aesop.* New York: Schocken.

Jason, H. (1965). Types of Jewish-Oriental oral tales. *Fabula* 7:115–224.

—— (1975). *Types of Oral Tales in Israel: Part 2.* Jerusalem: Israel Ethnographic Society.

Jellinek, A., ed. (1853–1877). *Beit Hamidrash.* (Hebrew). 6 vols. Leipzig and Vienna. (2nd ed. Jerusalem: Bamberger and Wahrmann, 1938).

John of Capua (1262–1279). *Directorium Vitae Humanae.* Trans. by J. Derenbourgue, 1887.

Kaidanover, Z. H. (1705). *Kav Hayashar (The Moral Code).* Frankfort. (*Also* 1903; Constantinople, 1932).

Kohut, H. Y., ed. (1892). *Mantzur al-Dhamari.* New York.

Lefkowitz, H. (1935). *Jewish Folk Songs.* New York: Metro Music Co.

Lévi, I. (1880–1897). *Revues des Etudes Juives* 34:67ff.

Likkutei Hamaasim. (1648). Verona.

Marcus, E. (1966). *From the Fountainhead.* (Hebrew). Haifa: IFA Publication Society.

Mayer, F. H. (1986). *Ancient Tales in Modern Japan.* Bloomington, IN: Indiana University Press.

Meshalim Shel Shlomo (Parables of King Solomon). (Hebrew). In *Beit Hamidrash* 4:145–152.

Mizrahi, H. (1967). *With Elders is Wisdom.* (Hebrew). Haifa: IFA Publication Society.

Nachman, A., ed. (1896). *Maasiyot Umeshalim.* In *Kokhevei Or* (Hebrew). Jerusalem.

Neuman (Noy), D. (1954). *Motif-Index of Talmudic-Midrashic Literature.* Dissertation. Bloomington, IN: Indiana University Press.

Noy, D. (1961). The first thousand folktales in the Israel folklore archives. *Fabula* 4:99–110.

—— (1963a). *Folktales of Israel.* Chicago: University of Chicago Press.

—— (1963b). *A Tale for Each Month 1962.* (Hebrew). Collected by A. Elbaz and S. Elbaz. Haifa: IFA Publication Society.

—— (1965). *The Beautiful Girl and the Princes.* (Hebrew). Tel Aviv: Am Oved.

—— (1966). The folktales of the communities of Israel. *Mahanayim* 104:44–53.

—— (1967). *Jewish Folktales from Libya.* Jerusalem: IFA Publication Society.

—— (1972). *A Tale for Each Month 1971.* (Hebrew). Haifa: IFA Publication Society.

—— (1976). *The Jewish Animal Tale of Oral Tradition.* (Hebrew). Haifa: IFA Publication Society.

—— (1979). *A Tale for Each Month 1976–1977.* (Hebrew). Haifa: IFA Publication Society.

Noy, M. (1968). *East European Jewish Cante Fables.* (Hebrew). Haifa: IFA Publication Society.

Patai, R., Utley, F. L., and Noy, D., eds. (1973). *Studies in Biblical and Jewish Folklore.* New York: Haskell House.

Perry, B. E. (1952). *Aesopica.* Urbana, IL: University of Chicago Press.

Pipe, S. Z. (1967). *Twelve Folktales from Sanok.* (Hebrew). Haifa: IFA Publication Society.

Rivlin, J. J. (1959). *Shirat Yehudei HaTargum* (*Poetry of the Aramaic Speaking Jews*). Jerusalem: Mosad Bialik.

Rosen, G. (1858). *Tuti Nameh: Das Papegeienbuch.* (German). Leipzig.

Rubin, R. (1965). *Jewish Folk Songs.* New York: Oak.

—— (1979). *Voices of a People: The Story of Yiddish Folksong.* Philadelphia: Jewish Publication Society.

Sandrow, N. (1977). *Vagabond Stars: A World History of Yiddish Theater.* New York: Harper & Row.

Sawyer, R. (1962). *The Way of the Storyteller.* New York: Viking.

Schwartz, H. (1983). *Elijah's Violin & Other Jewish Fairy Tales.* New York: Harper & Row.

Shah, I. (1979). *World Tales.* New York: Harcourt Brace Jovanovich.

Shahn, B. (1954). *The Alphabet of Creation.* New York: Schocken.

Shenhar, A. (1969). *Honor Your Mother.* (Hebrew). Haifa: IFA Publication Society.

—— (1974). *A Tale for Each Month 1973.* (Hebrew). Haifa: IFA Publication Society.

Singer, I. B. (1967). *Mazel and Schlimazel, or the Milk of a Lioness.* New York: Farrar Strauss & Giroux.

—— (1970). *Elijah the Slave.* New York: Farrar Strauss & Giroux.

Steinschneider, M., ed. (1858). *Alphabet of Ben Sira*. Berlin.

Thompson, S. (1966). *Motif-Index of Folk Literature*. 6 vols. Rev. ed. Bloomington, IN and London: Indiana University Press.

Waxman, M. (1960). *A History of Jewish Literature*. 5 vols. South Brunswick, NY, and London: Thomas Yoseloff.

Wiesel, E. (1966). *The Gates of the Forest*. New York: Holt, Rinehart & Winston.

—— (1972). *Souls on Fire: Portraits and Legends of Hasidic Masters*. New York: Random House.

Wistinetski, Y. H., ed. (1538). *Sefer Hasidism*. (Hebrew). Bologna.

Wright, W. (1977). *The Chicken Prince and Other Old Tales of Cabala*. El Cerrito, CA: Rhinoceros Press.

Yalkut Sippurim Umidrashim. (Hebrew). (1923). Warsaw.

Zinberg, I. (1972). *A History of Jewish Literature*. 12 vols. Trans. and ed. by B. Martin. Cleveland and London: The Press of Case Western University.

Pronunciation Guide

The spellings of Yiddish or Hebrew words and names are written phonetically so that *each* letter is sounded (including a final e).

Letter	IPA	Examples
e	[e]	Similar to e in bet; Eliahu, esrog, Gemara, mazel tov, balabuste, shtetl
a	[a]	Similar to a of father; Akiva, aggada, aguna, alef, aliya, bima
o	[o]	Similar to tall or raw; hokhem, moshol, zemirot
ai (long I)	[ai]	Similar to aisle or high; Mieskait, vais
ei (long A)	[ei]	Similar to grey; Sheindl, beis, Pirkei (exception: yahrzeit, which has long I sound)
h	[h]	Similar to h in happy (when Hebrew letter is hei); Haftorah, Haggada, Havdala, mohel
H		Similar to ch in German ach (when Hebrew letter is het); Hayim, huppa, hazen, halla

498

kh   Similar to <u>ch</u> in German ach (when Hebrew letter is <u>khaf</u>); ho<u>kh</u>em, Sholom
Alei<u>kh</u>em, i<u>kh</u>

i   Somewhere between the <u>i</u> of mitt and the
long <u>e</u> of meet; bereshi<u>t</u>, <u>Yi</u>ddish, b<u>i</u>ma,
bri<u>t</u> m<u>i</u>la, n<u>i</u>gun

Index